MENTAL HEALTH:
the public health challenge

MENTAL HEALTH:
the public health challenge

E. James Lieberman, M.D.
Editor

apha

Interdisciplinary Books, Pamphlets & Periodicals
For the Professional and the Layman

Publisher:
American Public Health Association
1015 Eighteenth Street NW
Washington, DC 20036

Printed in the United States of America

Library of Congress Catalog Number: 74-34564
International Standard Book Number: 0-87553-075-3

April, 1975

Library of Congress Cataloging in Publication Data
Main entry under title:
Mental Health, the public health challenge

    Includes index.
        1. Community mental health services--United States.
    2. Mental hygiene--United States. I. Lieberman,
    E. James, I934-   [DNLM: 1. Community mental
    health services--U.S. WM30 M5534]
    RA790.6.M46   362.2'0973   74-34564
    ISBN 0-87553-075-3

Project Steering Committee

Ruth V. Lewis, R.N., *Chairwoman*
Bertram J. Black, M.S.W.
J. Wilbert Edgerton, Ph.D.
Archie R. Foley, M.D.
Leonard J. Ganser, M.D.
James G. Kelly, Ph.D.
Ruth I. Knee, M.A.
H.G. Whittington, M.D.

E. James Lieberman, M.D., *Editor*

TABLE OF CONTENTS

PREFACE

In September, 1972 a project was launched at the American Public Health Association to produce a monograph which would "document and reflect the many changes in the concepts of mental health problems and approaches to mental health service delivery that have occurred during the past decade." The contract, which provided for two years support from the National Institute of Mental Health, the Ittleson Family Foundation, and the Nathan Hofheimer Foundation, is gratefully acknowledged, as is the work of some 60 colleagues, most of whom responded to a letter sent to all members of the APHA Mental Health Section shortly after the project began.

"The monograph will be a guide expressing a consensus of expert opinion for a public health approach to meeting community mental health needs, including the prevention and control of mental disorders. The monograph shall take into account, but not duplicate *Mental Disorders: A Guide to Control Methods* (APHA, Program Committee on Mental Health, 1962)." Our attempt to honor this imposing commitment consists of a series of brief papers by leaders and future leaders in their fields, designed to be understood by students of public health and by mental health specialists. It is therefore written in rather plain English, and may be useful to social planners, legislators, and other citizens interested in a concise, authoritative introduction to a broad, important subject.

The Mental Health Section is just 20 years old—APHA is 103 this year. The Section, about 1000 members strong, is a truly interdisciplinary group with no axe to grind for a particular profession. We can expect the Association to be an effective voice in support of equitable, sound, and well-integrated mental health programs, and we hope this book contributes toward that goal.

In addition to the Steering Committee and the Associate Editors who are credited within, I wish to thank Margaret Miner, who painstakingly reviewed the first draft, and Barry Levin, Carol Mitchell, Elliot Liebow, Harold Hunter, Warren Vaughn, and Herzl Spiro who offered many valuable suggestions along the way. Arthur Cosing of NIMH and William Beaty of the Ittleson Foundation made their interest felt in a genuine, nonbureaucratic way. James R. Kimmey, Marion L. Henry, and William H. McBeath were consistently helpful during times of transition within APHA, Ruth Knee, an initiator and prime mover of the project, chaired the Mental Health Section in 1971-72 and gave editorial, administrative and emotional support throughout. The project could not have been completed without the administrative support of Carol Pewanick, whose intuitive grasp of what needs to be done is matched by her devotion to the task and her ability to do it. Allen Seeber and Deborah Watkins put the book securely to bed under the cover designed by Leo Swain.

The work has been challenging and satisfying for the participants; may the reader find the results a source of stimulation if not contentment! Of course the editor is soley responsible for errors of commission or omission. At the current pace of change, another overview will be needed before another decade goes by. In the meantime, it can be said that the project forged another strong link between mental health and other disciplines within APHA. I thank my colleagues in the Association office for their cooperation and encouragement, and look forward to further collaboration in the service of the nation's health.

E. James Lieberman, M.D., M.P.H.
Editor

INTRODUCTION

The changing panorama of mental health services training and research in relation to public health and individual well-being is a national challenge. It is a challenge not only of need, but of new opportunities. The complexities of this scene result from an increase of scientific knowledge and operational insights and of the resources for putting them into action. There now exists a real opportunity to make important changes in how services are delivered and resources used.

This monograph provides a discussion of these changes and their implementation. But it is also a kind of atlas, presenting a broad view of issues in mental health and services to people with mental illnesses, mental retardation, problems of addiction, substance abuse and in human services generally. It attempts to put these issues into a perspective of their importance for the community and the individual for prevention, treatment, program design and a health environment.

Historically, a unique feature of efforts to cope with mental illness and mental retardation has been the public responsibility for them. The reason for public concern is apparent. These problems are expressed not only in a compelling need for care, but also in problems of behavior and competence. Public attention reflects a mixture of repugnance and humanitarian concern for the individual. The emotion aroused by an epidemic of a contagious disease is a similar mixture of fear of the afflicted and the affliction, concern for their care and for one's own well-being.

Thus, a major factor in the early development of public measures for handling persons with mental illness and mental retardation was protection of the community from unacceptable or irrational behavior. As a result, in most of our states a substantial institutional system developed as a repository for these persons extruded from the community. Such custodial arrangements had little reason to become part of any public health system that might be developing. For many years, prior to new knowledge of treatment for the mentally ill and of training methods for the mentally retarded, these institutional systems constituted an "all or none" resource. Either the individual stayed home with no service or care, or he was put in an institution where total maintenance was provided. Once there, he was likely to remain; whatever skills he once possessed for coping with society withered in isolation.

After World War II, and the experience of providing mental

health services for the military, considerable new knowledge became available. At the same time disturbing descriptions of the nation's mental health problems created an impetus for change. The passage of the National Mental Health Act in 1946 was an indication that Congress recognized mental illness as a major public health problem. That Act, along with the establishment of the National Institute of Mental Health in 1948, was the first substantial entry of the federal government into the mental health arena.

Starting in 1954, at about the same time the use of new drugs was initiated for the relief of symptoms of mental illness, and alternatives to institutional care became better understood, some states began passage of progressive community mental health program statutes, and provided for local-state combined funding.

As a result of state experience in these community-based programs, as well as of some federally funded research, training and demonstration efforts and the impact of the 1960 report by the Joint Commission on Mental Illness and Health, a federal statute was passed to implement these progressive ideas in mental health services. This act, The Federal Comprehensive Community Mental Health Center and Mental Retardation Facilities Construction Act of 1963, stimulated other states to move in the direction of community-based programs. The key concepts were comprehensive services, continuity of care, and close association with other care-giving agencies—including school systems and health facilities—through consultation and the provision of education services.

Every state now has a public mental health system, usually with a very large budget and roster of personnel. These systems vary in their progressiveness, ranging all the way from those that still depend heavily on state institutions to others, as of this writing, such as Kentucky, Wisconsin, Minnesota and California, in which each area has a local community-based program with cost sharing between the state and the community. During the last decade there has been a large increase in the private resources available, especially for treatment of emotional disorders and alcoholism. This has varied from state to state, but some state systems have productively incorporated these private resources into the public system of community-based services, along with increased services supported by health insurance and federal programs—Medicare and Medicaid. This beginning partnership between public programs and private facilities denotes progress toward a major goal of all health delivery—a single standard of service.

Much of the future of mental health and mental retardation planning and administration, and quality assurance, will lie in the hands of the states. It is they, rather than the federal government, who have the responsibility of carrying out the service programs. Their health systems—some of them massive—are complex enterprises, and clearly need much greater administrative and management skills than have been available in the past.

In order to achieve such skills, and to cope with the present period of drastic transition, the states need to continue their innovative planning. An area in which the need for intelligent planning is urgent, and which promises particularly high pay-off, is the linking or fusing of the delivery of mental health services with that of other, health-related and social service systems. The advantage would be mutual; in many cases the mental health service delivery system is considerably more advanced than that of other health and social service systems. Some interdependence already exists, of course, among human services agencies. State executives and legislatures, motivated by many forces, but perhaps most of all by consumer dissatisfaction, are actively seeking ways of joining mental health functions with public health and social services. Innovative designs for collaboration, in the direction of human resources departments, are no longer rare. But the real operational combinations and fusions have yet to be made. They are imperative if mental health skills and knowledge are to become an accessible, lifelong influence for members of a community.

It is important that new programs, and new legislation provide increased flexibility in community-based services, rather than creating yet another institutionalized, isolated system of care. This volume underlines the importance of setting standards and of utilization review, peer review, and inclusion of mental health services in health insurance plans. These are issues which cannot be over-emphasized if we are to build systems of care, using both public and private resources, that can avoid depositing long-term patients or residents into inadequate programs. In the past, this silting-up process has taken place in mental hospitals, but there will be similar hazards in community programs, especially in nursing homes and day programs, unless safeguards are built in.

In order to support a flexible range and variety of services, special attention must be directed toward multiple source funding. It will be especially important to bring the "hard money" intended for payment of patient care from all third party sources, including future National Health Insurance, into the financing of these direct services. As that happens, some of the extensive state investments in mental health care might be redeployed into preventive, consultative, and other activities which could not be included under any system of mental health coverage for patients.

The trend in the general health care field for more and more services to be paid for through health insurance or employer-financed health programs with concomitant quality, cost and utilization controls, has also reached into mental health services. The first national standards for psychiatric facilities were those developed for certification of providers in the Medicare and Medicaid programs. Both public and private mental health agencies have had to learn how to justify diagnoses and treatment approaches in order to receive reimbursement from fiscal intermediaries. The review of mental health services by Professional Service Review Organizations (PSRO)—mandated by the Social Security Amendments of 1972 as a means of controlling quality and costs of services paid for by the federal programs—will give additional impetus to specificity in definitions of both problems and therapeutic approaches, and to a better understanding of the multi-faceted and multi-disciplinary nature of mental health.

The aim of this volume is to provide stimulus and guidelines for improving the nation's burgeoning mental health systems and to bring increased awareness to workers in health, education and social service who are concerned with mental health values. In addition, we hope it will spark new exploration of ways that mental health skills can be brought to bear on other areas obviously important to personal and family growth, and on significant social issues. Mental health personnel must move with special caution in these tangential areas, to make a solid contribution without raising the image of implied omnipotence—assumption of an ability to solve by ourselves problems that require many resources beyond those of mental health.

The talented professionals who have contributed their skills to this book have provided unusual stimulation for our future activities, and the American Public Health Association is the logical base from which to launch this challenge. Through our diverse material we have tried to state it clearly, and with all due respect for the complexity of the issues and the times in which we live.

Leonard J. Ganser, M.D.
Mental Health Section Chairman
APHA, 1972-73

LIST OF CONTRIBUTORS

Mildred B. Arrill, M.A., M.S.W.
Consumer Liaison Officer
Office for HMOs
Bureau of Community Health Services
Health Services Administration, PHS-DHEW

Irving N. Berlin, M.D.
Professor of Psychiatry & Pediatrics
Head, Division of Child Psychiatry
School of Medicine
University of Washington
Seattle, WA

Irving Blumberg, Executive Vice President
International Committee Against Mental
    Illness
New York, NY

Nona Boren, M.S.W.
Coordinator in Education
Department of Psychiatry and Behavioral
    Sciences
The George Washington University Medical
    Center
Washington, DC

M. Frances Bradley
Information Services
National Association for Mental Health
Arlington, VA

Edith G. Calhoun
Technical Information Specialist
National Library of Medicine
Bethesda, MD

Robert L. Chapman, Ph.D.
Systems Consultant and Lecturer
School of Business Administration and
    Economics
California State University
Fullerton, CA

Jules V. Coleman, M.D.
Chief, Mental Health & Psychiatry
Community Health Care Center Plan, Inc.
New Haven, CT

Karen Davis, Ph.D.
Visiting Lecturer on Economics
Harvard University
Cambridge, MA
(On leave from the Brookings Institution
    as Senior Fellow)

J. Richard Elpers, M.D.
Program Chief
Orange County, Department of Mental
    Health
Santa Ana, CA

Donald Vincent Fandetti, M.S., D.S.W.
Assistant Professor,
School of Social Work and Community
    Planning
University of Maryland at Baltimore
Baltimore, MD

Armando R. Favazza, M.D., M.P.H.
Associate Professor of Psychiatry
School of Medicine
University of Missouri
Columbia, MO

Joseph J. Friedman, M.D.
Commissioner, Mental Health Services
Broome County
Binghamton, NY

Martin Gittelman, Ph.D.
Associate Professor, Department of
    Psychiatry
New Jersey College of Medicine and
    Dentistry
Newark, NJ

Evelyn L. Goldberg, Sc.D.
Research Associate
Department of Epidemiology
School of Hygiene and Public Health
The Johns Hopkins University
Baltimore, MD

Stephen E. Goldston, Ed.D., M.S.P.H.
Coordinator for Primary Prevention Programs
Center for Studies of Child and Family
   Mental Health
National Institute of Mental Health
Rockville, MD

Brenda D. Gurel, Ph.D.
Associate Administrative Officer
Office of Social and Ethical Responsibility
American Psychological Association
Washington, DC

Lee Gurel, Ph.D., Director,
Division of Manpower, Research and
   Development
American Psychological Association
Washington, DC

Paul W. Haberman, M.B.A.
Senior Research Associate
Division of Sociomedical Sciences
Columbia University School of Public Health
New York, NY

Robert N. Harris, Jr., Ph.D.
Chief, Research and Evaluation, Alcoholism
   Services
Orange County Department of Mental
   Health
Santa Ana, CA

Ferdinand R. Hassler, M.D., M.P.H.
Associate Director for International
   Programs
Office of Mental Health Education and Staff
   Development
National Institute of Mental Health
Rockville, MD

Loretta Hervey
Division of Sociomedical Sciences
Columbia University School of Public Health
New York, NY

Hans Rosenstock Huessy, M.D.
Professor, Department of Psychiatry
College of Medicine
The University of Vermont
Burlington, VT

Gertrude Isaacs, D.N.Sc.
Frontier Nursing Service
Hyden Hospital
Hyden, KY

Robert I. Jaslow, M.D.
Health Services Module Director
Woodhaven Center
Philadelphia, PA

James G. Kelly, Ph.D.
Dean, School of Community Service and
   Public Affairs
University of Oregon
Eugene, OR

Morton Kramer, Sc.D.
Director, Division of Biometry
National Institute of Mental Health
Rockville, MD

Gare LeCompte, Ph.D.
Dean and Professor of Behavioral Sciences
Ohio College of Podiatric Medicine
Cleveland, OH

Paul V. Lemkau, M.D.
Professor of Mental Hygiene
School of Hygiene & Public Health
The Johns Hopkins University
Baltimore, MD

Robert L. Leopold, M.D.
Professor and Chairman
Department of Community Medicine and
   Professor of Community Psychiatry
School of Medicine
University of Pennsylvania
Philadelphia, PA

Ruth V. Lewis, R.N., M.A.
Program Coordinator
Division of Psychiatric and Mental Health
   Nursing Practice
American Nurses' Association, Inc.
Kansas City, MO

E. James Lieberman, M.D., M.P.H.
Director, Mental Health Project
American Public Health Association
Washington, DC

Craig Messersmith, D.Ed.
Counselor and Associate Professor of
    Education
University Counseling Center
The American University
Washington, DC

Richard G. Morrill, M.D.
Associate Professor
Departments of Psychiatry and Community
    Medicine
Boston University Medical School
Boston, MA

B. James Naberhuis, Jr.
College Park, MD

Ronald H. Nelson, Ph.D.
Director, Program Analysis and Evaluation
Herman M. Adler Center
Champaign, IL

Scott H. Nelson, M.D., M.P.H.
Director, Office of Program Planning and
    Evaluation, ADAMHA
Alcohol, Drug Abuse, and Mental Health
    Administration, DHEW
Rockville, MD

Ralph H. Ojemann, Ph.D.
Director, Child-Educational Psychology and
    Preventive Psychiatry Dept.
The Educational Research Council of
    America
Cleveland, OH

Lucy D. Ozarin, M.D., M.P.H.
Program Development Officer
Division of Mental Health Service Programs
National Institute of Mental Health
Rockville, MD

Daniel Y. Patterson, M.D., M.P.H.
Chief of Psychiatry
Group Health Association, Inc.
Washington, DC

E. Mansell Pattison, M.D.
Associate Professor and Vice-Chairman
Department of Psychiatry and Human
    Behavior
University of California, Irvine
Irvine, CA

Barbara P. Penn, M.A.
Counseling Psychologist
University of California, San Diego
LaJolla, CA

Nolan E. Penn, Ph.D.
Professor, Department of Psychiatry
School of Medicine
University of California, San Diego
La Jolla, CA

Carol A. Pewanick
Administrative Assistant
Mental Health Project
American Public Health Association
Washington, DC

Martin Reiser, Ed.D.
Department Psychologist
Los Angeles Police Department
Los Angeles, CA

Alix H. Sanders, J.D.
Lawyers' Committee for Civil Rights Under
    Law
Jackson, MS

Irwin G. Sarason, Ph.D.
Professor, Department of Psychology
University of Washington
Seattle, WA

Andrew L. Selig, M.S.W., M.S.Hyg., Sc.D.
Assistant Professor of Psychiatry and Social
    Work
The University of British Columbia
Vancouver, B.C. Canada

Steven S. Sharfstein, M.D.
Chief, Evaluation Branch
Office of Program Development and
    Analysis
National Institute of Mental Health
Rockville, MD

Nathan Sloate, M.S.
Special Assistant for Aging to the Director
National Institute of Mental Health
Rockville, MD

Herzl R. Spiro, M.D.
Professor of Psychiatry
Rutgers Medical School
College of Medicine and Dentistry of New
  Jersey
Piscataway, NJ

E. Fuller Torrey, M.D.
Special Assistant to the Director
National Institute of Mental Health
Rockville, MD

Edward R. Turner, M.S.W.
Department of Psychiatry
School of Medicine
Howard University
Washington, DC

Morton O. Wagenfeld, M.A., Ph.D.
Professor, Department of Sociology
Western Michigan University
Kalamazoo, MI

Joseph Westermeyer, M.D., M.P.H., Ph.D.
Department of Psychiatry, Medical School
University of Minnesota
Minneapolis, MN

H. G. Whittington, M.D.
2754 South Paris Place
Denver, CO

Barbara S. Williams, R.N., M.D., M.P.H.
Resident in Psychiatry
Howard University
Washington, DC

Melvin W. Williams, M.D., M.P.H.
Associate Director
Office of Mental Health Education and Staff
  Development
National Institute of Mental Health
Rockville, MD

Milton Wittman, D.S.W.
Chief, Social Work Education Branch
Division of Manpower & Training Programs
National Institute of Mental Health
Rockville, MD

Jane Divita Woody, Ph.D., M.S.W.
Coordinator and Counselor
Parent Education and Counseling Service
The Ohio University
Athens, Ohio

Robert Henley Woody, Ph.D.,
Professor of Education and Psychology
College of Education
The Ohio University
Athens, OH

Isaiah M. Zimmerman, M.S.W., Ph.D.
Clinical Psychologist
Washington, DC

MENTAL HEALTH:
the public health challenge

I. Historical and Cultural Perspective

1. General Functions of Public Health

Public health's persistent (and one might properly say, shortsighted) preoccupation with mortality resulted in many distortions of perspective. One of the most marked distortions has been its underestimation of the importance of mental disorders. Mortality statistics do not reveal the effects of mental disorders. Indeed more than one benevolent witness of the ravages of mental disorders has asked, "Why don't they die?"

—Ernest M. Gruenberg, M.D., Dr. P.H.
The Definition and Measurement of
Mental Health, 1968

The promotion, protection and restoration of a state of physical, social and mental well-being are the broad responsibilities of public health. The global character of this responsibility is obvious and echoes Virchow's conclusion, in 1840, that "Medicine is a social science and politics are nothing else than medicine on a large scale."

The reduction of such a massive goal to a succession of means for working toward it is the aim of public health planning and administration. At this still very broad conceptual level, public health goals become the art of applying knowledge gained in the laboratory and consulting room to the promotion, protection and restoration of health. The "consulting room" or clinical knowledge represents the individuality, the uniqueness of each person, be it in type of reaction to stress or quality of leadership in a group. It implies what Pasteur had in mind when he concluded "the bacterium is nothing, the host is everything." Such knowledge of individual variations has to be combined with more easily measurable characteristics of populations and of individuals gained through the biochemical, radiological, epidemiological and other types of laboratories. Dr. A. W. Freeman said that anything intended to affect the health of populations has to be within the intellectual grasp and technical competency of thousands, not hundreds of people. The attainment of public health goals requires that they be reduced to multiple jobs that can be done by many.

This partitioning of the overall goals into functioning programs presents many difficult decisions, and continuing controversies, such as whether categorical programs against specific diseases are "better" than efforts to improve the overall quality of life, which might make many kinds of illnesses less threatening and all kinds more tolerable. In the field of mental health, the prophylatic and treatment successes have been mostly in specific disease areas, such as the control and treatment of syphilis (which has greatly reduced the scourge of general paresis) and immunization against rubella (to protect the fetus against birth defects including mental retardation).

For the control of diseases such as syphilis, rubella, pellagra, phenylketonuria, Down's Syndrome and Friedreich's ataxia, categorical programs are necessary, if not sufficient—i.e., the cure of syphilis does little to prevent the disease. Prevention involves much more complicated functions, functions of the person, not merely of his cells. In the case of syphilis it involves refraining from hazardous sexual activity—a much more complex prophylactic problem than placing a barrier between a treponema and a host organism, or injecting penicillin in a known victim of the disease.

The issue is even more complex in Down's syndrome and Friedreich's ataxia since the definition of prophylaxis becomes confused; after diagnosis by amniocentesis, it has become possible to prevent the birth of children who suffer from these illnesses. Although this is far from a satisfactory prophylaxis against these and other diseases of similar mechanism, it does protect against the social costs incident upon the presence of victims of these diseases in the population.

The conundrums presented by these problems reach their most difficult form in conceptualizing the prevention of illnesses in which no single or obligatory factor in etiology is known. In many illnesses of this group factors of motivation, attitude, and life style appear to be important though the evidence is often contradictory. Expected associations between presumed social stresses and certain kinds of ill health turn out to be equivocal and lacking clear direction. Presumably psychosomatic diseases such as ulcer and coronary occlusion may prove unassociated with stressful antecedents and often unassociated with personality type as well. Alcoholics and women with post-partum psychoses prove to be little if at all different from others who did not become ill under apparently similar circumstances. Aside from certain very general statements of statistical risk on the basis of kinship, prediction of schizophrenia has no guidelines established.

As already noted, mental illnesses are not the only ones involved in this category of vaguely sensed rather than clearly known etiology. Arteriosclerosis, many types of neoplasms, the timing of the onset of senility, and diabetes in middle and old age are in somewhat the same category as schizophrenia, neurosis and affective disorders from this point of view.

4

In summary, the public health responsibility of promoting, preserving and restorin well-being in populations becomes more difficult as one moves from diseases of well-understood etiology and pathological mechanisms to those of which less is known and/or what is known points to highly complex, multifactorial etiology. Mental illnesses of the first group are easily controlled as the somatic illnesses of the group. But arteriosclerosis, cancer and senility have proved about as recalcitrant as schizophrenia, affective psychoses, behavior disorders and neuroses, from the latter group.

Public health programs in the latter instance begin to shift from more established concepts of primary prevention and usually consist of more general efforts to promote and protect health. We assume that to protect the young child from under-or over-stimulation will decrease the risk of functional mental illness. The education of parents for the protection of the child has been the mainstay of such mental health preventive efforts. Desirable as mental health promotion programs may be, we must not abandon the search for more precise primary preventive intervention.

The next step is identification and treatment of early cases (secondary prevention). This involves systems of mass screening of populations on the assumption that early treatment will arrest the progress of at least some diseases and that successful control of symptoms will prevent both somatic and social complications which might lead to greater disability. Mental health programs were, until the last 15 or 20 years, not very well prepared to carry out such tasks, mainly because the control of symptoms required interpersonal relationships of helper and patient that were expensive and not clearly effective. Group and milieu therapies and the symptom-controlling drugs have more recently reduced the costs of motivational types of therapy.

The third goal in management is, of course, rehabilitation, (tertiary prevention, i.e. of chronicity or disablement). The goals and techniques involve vocational retraining and education, job placement, arranging living quarters with or without supervision, sheltered workshops, child care, homemaker support, etc.

Traditionally, public health agencies, like school systems have aimed at building organizational structures which could reach the total population. This has been done through local or regional health centers or services providing prophylactic and very limited therapeutic services, the latter mostly in the areas of tuberculosis, venereal diseases and some major crippling conditions in childhood. Occasionally, chronic conditions such as epilepsy are included. Mental health programs have in a large number of instances been associated with other public health disease control programs, both in Europe and in the United States, but not until the 1960's, with the development of the Community Mental Health Center program, did

5

U.S. mental health leaders accept responsibility for whole populations, i.e., defined catchment areas. However, as Ralph Nader's study pointed out in *The Madness Establishment* (Chu, 1974), little attention was given to correlating the new CMHC areas with existing service areas in the community. Often enough, not even psychiatric services were integrated, and few CMHCs used the knowledge accumulated by public health nursing on motivating people toward health promoting activities.

Mental illnesses are found in probably every gradation of etiological complexity. Acceptance of responsibility for the health of population groups exists now in the mental health field, which must apply knowledge built up by public health, social and educational research and experience in order to reduce the load of mental ill health borne by a population.

Responsibility for populations involves service to the mildly and severely ill, and primary preventive efforts as well. These are relatively direct and simple for some mental illnesses, involving such matters as nutrition, immunization or use of antibiotics. The etiological complexities of other mental illnesses are, however, so great that preventive efforts remain very general, such as the promotion of general health and social well-being, mental health educational efforts and, particularly, the promotion and protection of the mental health of children.

Paul V. Lemkau, M.D.

References

Chu, Franklin D., and Trotter, Sharland. 1974. The Madness Establishment: Ralph Nader's Study Group Report On the National Institute of Mental Health, New York: Grossman Publishers. 222 pp.

2. Human Services: Evolution of New Principles and Policies

> In the course of their development, hygiene, social work, education, industrial management, medical practice, and criminal law have departed from the standardized measures they used to rely upon and are now doing more and more individualized work. But what is individualized work if it is not the study of and the action on a personality, which leads us straight to individual psychology and mental hygiene? .... It seems to me, therefore, more important for the mental hygiene movement than for any other phase of health work to recognize these connections and to build up a system by which all these efforts can be brought to cooperate harmoniously. They are not only parallel; they are all part of what we may call the same service.
>
> —Rene Sand, M.D.
> First International Congress on
> Mental Hygiene, 1930

Change is the order of the day in medicine, in psychiatry, and in public health. In medicine, technological advances have led to the crowding out of general practice by specialization, to the development of a vast medical research establishment, and to a lessening of interest in the ancient and honorable tradition of comprehensive patient care. Psychiatry has followed in the footsteps of medicine with increasing subspecialization, but in addition, since the end of World War II, there has been a five-fold increase in the number of psychiatrists, a significant expansion in the private practice of psychiatry and in psychiatric wards in general hospitals, major changes in admission and discharge policies in public mental hospitals, and the rise of the community mental health movement. Public health as a discipline is no longer faced with the control of epidemic death from infectious disease but is more urgently concerned today with the challenges of chronic illness and such bio-psycho-social disorders as alcoholism, drug abuse, venereal disease, illegitimacy, poverty, and racism. These raise problems of prevention and control which the field of public health shares with psychiatry, medicine in general, educational and social service organizations in the community, and state and federal legislatures.

7

The heady momentum of growth, change and power has drawn the mental health field increasingly into an orbit of its own, to the relative neglect of its ties to medicine and established community service institutions, particularly those involved in education and welfare. Psychiatry has been preoccupied with new concepts of mental illness, with new modalities for the care of the disturbed, and with efforts to define the problem and to develop methods for the prevention of mental disorder. Now we face a time of stocktaking, an assessment of the direction from which we have come, and serious consideration of what the future should bring.

The extraordinary increase in size of the psychiatric enterprise, the great diversity of its program, and its claims of expertise in many fields hitherto not associated with psychiatry (at least not on any important scale) have created problems of definitions, boundaries, competence, and training. In addition there have been serious counter-reactions from critics in and outside the field, e.g. Thomas Szasz, certain social scientists and clinical psychologists, and the Ralph Nader organization, to the territorial claims of the mental health field.

Psychiatry's major concern is still the care of the severely disturbed: patients with psychoses, serious character disorders, disabling neuroses, and the behaviorally unstable with organic brain disease. With regard to other human problems, such as the socially more stable neuroses and character disorders, the psychophysiological illnesses, the less severe behavior problems of childhood, alcoholism and drug dependency, certain forms of social maladaptation (sometimes pejoratively called inadequate personality) and to problems of living, psychiatrists could make more effective contributions if they worked closely with other professional disciplines as consultants and collaborators, rather than as independent agents.

In general, changes in patterns of psychiatric care have developed along with major changes in the goals of medical care. With the rise in living standards and in the general welfare, life expectancy has been prolonged, and an aged population makes increasing demands on medical, social, and psychiatric services. Moreover, the concept of the right to health, and to medical services, will undoubtedly be reflected in national health legislation and the gradual or even rapid emergence of a national health plan.

Medical care of the chronically ill and maintenance of health in the general population, require new and sophisticated concepts of the delivery of health services. Our current notions of good medical care are based upon a high level of specialized services. Specialists are more or less independent of each other, and there is little insistence on establishing patterns of coordination, as might be expected from a primary-care physician or nurse. There is evidence that our present system of medical care does not serve the interests

8

of the general population (Duff and Hollingshead, 1968). Not only do the poor fare badly but even those who can afford expert services may find themselves suffering from gaps and deficiencies in coordination of care. Coordination of health care, e.g. by a primary physician, promises fundamental improvements in the quality of services, and eventually, with the passage of a national health program, in their more effective distribution.

The guiding principle of health care should be health maintenance, defining health broadly to include physical, emotional, and social well-being. Health in this sense is not only the concern of the physician but also of the host of care-taking persons in the social environment, including the family. Chronic illness becomes a way of life, and adaptation is stretched to encompass its special handicaps, constrictions, sufferings, and demands. People can learn to live with great handicaps and burdens, but continuity and coordination of humane health care is essential to enhance lives in addition to simply prolonging life. Dr. O. W. Holmes gave this formula for longevity: "Have a chronic disease and take care of it."

Public health today has set itself the goal of a broadly-based philosophy of preventive medicine with a deep concern for the person in his biological, cultural, social, and environmental engagements. Its practitioners are particularly concerned with the social and institutional organization of health care and the ways in which support may be mobilized through the educational, health and welfare services of the community to exploit most fully the preventive possibilities in current medical knowledge. The institutional interests of public health, i.e. its view of health care as a system of services, allow it to develop a perspective toward health services which place them appropriately within the broad network of the community's comprehensive human services (MacMahon and Coleman, 1969).

The treatment of well-defined, discretely organic illnesses lies properly in the hands of the highly skilled medical specialists; but, particularly in the chronic illnesses, the level of the patient's adaptation depends markedly upon social experience, individual predispositions, and vulnerabilities (Hinkle and Wolff, 1957). The care of illness is the province of the physician and his associates. The care of the ailing person as a member of a family, a social circle, and a work group, is a broader responsibility, and may in time become the professional obligation of human services centers, or organizations working with families and with the institutions which are engaged in maintaining and protecting health and welfare, and in helping with the adverse life experiences of individuals and families.

The public health and the public welfare are in principle indistinguishable concepts. However, our current human services are fragmented in institutional compartments with vested interests in

9

"health and welfare" interfering with cross-communication and coordination of effort. Once services have become fragmented, as they are now, efforts to bring them together, e.g. interagency teams to work with multi-problem families, have proved difficult. As a result, there continues to be both overlap and gaps in services, work at cross purposes, administrative inefficiency—in other words, wasted time, effort, and money (CRA, 1973).

Separate systems of professional education and practice in the health/welfare field create complicated, possibly insoluble, problems of inter-professional collaboration. Each discipline, with its own professional definition of competence and status needs, works toward the goal of autonomy in its defined areas of education and practice, and the result is somewhat similar to the problems created by over-specialization in medicine. Nurses, social workers, physical therapists, nutritionists, psychologists, and so on, are striving in their training and practice to move away from what they interpret as subordination and status discrimination in a hierarchic system in which the physician is the final authority, complicating the problem of coordination of health services. With the development of a new discipline of physician's associate, there may be some easing of the problem for the physician, but the history of the doctor-nurse relationship forebodes similar difficulties further ahead.

It is conceivable that the health/welfare field in attempting to meet the challenge of care of the chronically ill, may yet develop a new kind of professional, a *human services generalist*, highly trained across disciplines, able to assess problems and provide basic services in areas including physical and mental health, family and marital difficulties, childrearing and child development problems, welfare, housing, employment, industrial safety, retirement and aging. While the list may seem long, these are problems which occur and recur in the lives of most individuals and families, and have a special impact in illness. Many of these problems can either be resolved by a good generalist or referred to an appropriate specialist for service or consultation. Knowledge of consultation and referral resources, and indications for their utilization, is indispensable for the human services generalist.

What is envisioned, then, is a pyramidal structure of health/welfare services, resting on a broad base of generalist practitioners, with a lesser number of increasingly specialized professionals on the narrower levels of the pyramid. Demonstration programs of such a health/welfare system would provide insights into problems of administration, professional practice, and funding (CRA, 1973).

Our rampant technology has run a course out of phase with biological, psychological and social pulse and rhythm, creating a new world for man to inhabit. Individual adaptability is very great and is

10

equal to most demands of social change, often at a terribly high cost in pain and inner dislocation. A task of mental health is to identify the new problems of individuals in a changing social scene, and to explore new ways to help people in their coping efforts.

Jules V. Coleman, M.D.

References

Community Research Associates. 1973. Solving Community Problems. CRA, 124 East 40th St., NY, NY 10016.

Duff, R.S. and Hollingshead, A.B. 1968. Sickness and Society. Harper & Row. New York.

Hinkle, L.E. and Wolff, H.G. 1957. Health and the Social Environment: Experimental Investigations. In Explorations in Social Psychiatry. Eds. Leighton, A.H., Clausen, T.A., Wilson, R.N. Basic Books.

MacMahon, B. and Coleman, J.V. 1969. Chronic Diseases and Mental Health. In Mental Health Considerations in Public Health, Ed. Goldston, S.E. National Institute of Mental Health.

Other Sources

Journal of the History of Behavioral Sciences
Journal of the History of Medicine and Allied Sciences
Journal of the History of Ideas
History of Childhood Quarterly: The Journal of Psychohistory

3. Health and Illness, Physical and Mental

> Health is a state of complete physical, mental and social well-being and not merely the absence of disease or infirmity.
>
> —*World Health Organization Constitution, 1946*

Health and illness are complex ideas, not easily defined terms. In some preliterate societies the concepts are mutually exclusive (Fabrega, 1974), but it is accepted today that health and illness may co-exist within an individual. A pragmatic way to evaluate health and illness is to define a range of normality for biological and psychological functioning in a particular sociocultural setting. In addition to this normative, observable spectrum there is the clinical concept of covert or latent disease, e.g. latent schizophrenia. The term is sometimes applied to an individual who, while not sick enough to warrant a formal diagnosis, is undergoing a shift towards illness which is evident, if at all, only with specialized investigative methods. A third concept to be considered is that of the person or group not ill, overtly or covertly, but at increased risk of illness.

Insurance companies utilize statistical norms to define risk, e.g., a person with mild hypertension, high blood cholesterol and a family history of heart disease would be at high risk for early disability or death. Insurance premiums more or less reflect the expectations of health and disease. A current example is that of sickle cell anemia, an inherited blood condition found principally among blacks. Medical science has not concluded whether sickle cell trait (asymptomatic) is a disease although some insurance companies arbitrarily may have done so. Thus ambiguity exists in defining genetic disorders, especially when genes are recessive or have only partial penetrance.

Norms for biological functioning may be objectively clear, especially if they can be quantified by laboratory tests. Thus, a person experiencing tremulousness, heat intolerance, and palpitations may have a thyroid gland abnormality, confirmed by a specific laboratory finding. At times, however, a laboratory test result may be abnormal while the individual feels well; the chemical test may presage clinical illness, or it may be a "false positive." With few exceptions biological tests are not yet very helpful in determining psychiatric illness. Much promising work, however, is being done in neurochemistry and psychophysiology.

12

Norms for psychological functioning are difficult to determine. Mental health is hard to define, much less measure. Sigmund Freud (1856-1939) once defined mental health as the ability to work and to love; but it is then a problem to evaluate working and loving! English and Pearson (1963) describe a mature, mentally healthy adult as one who can (1) work usefully without undue fatigue or strain, (2) like and accept many lasting friendships and love and be affectionate with close friends, (3) conquer guilt, doubt or indecision and oppose impositions on himself and his family, (4) treat all persons with appropriate respect, (5) give and receive love with joy in a conventional heterosexual way, (6) extend his interests and seek to contribute to the general welfare, (7) advance his own welfare without exploitation of his fellow man, (8) alternate work with play, (9) be dependable, truthful, openminded and imbued with a philosophy that includes a willingness to grow, improve and achieve wisdom; and (10) be interested in passing on his knowledge to the young. Today many would object to the conventionalism of point (5); the American Psychiatric Association in 1973 struck homosexuality out of the disease classification, substituting "sexual orientation disturbance."

Erikson (1963) has outlined an age-related sequence of psychosocial development. In this scheme a mentally healthy person is one who successfully develops through eight basic psychological stages in a socio-cultural context. The first stage (infancy), poses alternatives of basic trust versus mistrust, and the quality of the mother-child relationship is understandably crucial in achieving trust. The failure to do so impinges on subsequent stages; in childhood it may be reflected in feeding problems, later on in paranoid thinking and behavior. Erikson's other stages postulate: autonomy versus shame and doubt (toddler); initiative versus guilt (preschool or "genital" stage); industry versus inferiority (school age); identity versus role confusion (adolescence); intimacy versus isolation (young adult); generativity versus stagnation (adult); and ego-integrity versus despair (aging). Ego-integrity implies an understanding of one's place in the universe, the continuity and betterment of the human condition, and an acceptance of death. The mentally healthy individual, therefore, develops throughout the entire life cycle.

Psychological tests (such as the WAIS, MMPI and Rorschach) are an attempt to determine objectively a range of normal functioning. None of them, however, has the specificity of most biochemical tests, and there is frequently a wide variation in the interpretation of test results. Furthermore, the tests themselves, used en masse and uncritically, can reify concepts, impose labels and pigeonhole people, as in the case of intelligence (I.Q.) tests which may be biased against some individuals or cultural subgroups.

Psychoanalytic theory developed by Freud and others conceptualizes groups of mental functions as "structures" (ego, super-ego, id) which operate at conscious and unconscious levels. Mental illness is seen as the result of repressed (i.e. hidden-from-self) intrapsychic conflict. The theory emphasizes early upbringing, i.e. environmental factors in psychosis and neurosis.

The psychoanalytic system holds that therapy, the process of arriving at self-understanding, increases health through mastery of primitive mental processes by more mature mental processes (i.e., ego masters id). Bandura (1969), a critic of psychoanalysis, says of it: ". . . attention is generally focused, not on the problem behavior itself, but on the presumably influential internal agents that must be exorcised by catharsis, abreaction, and acquisition of insight through an extended interpretive process."

Behaviorism attempts to bridge the psychological and social sciences by emphasis on observable behavior and predictive laws of learning (conditioning). Behavior can be called pro-or anti-social, adaptive or unadaptive. Symptoms are called response patterns, and the distinction between normal and abnormal behavior depends upon the tolerance of those who are judging the behavior—a clinician, a court, or a social group: mental health and illness become scientifically meaningless terms although important social labels. Wolpe defines neurotic behavior as persistent habit of learned (conditioned) unadaptive behavior acquired in anxiety generating situations. Notwithstanding their disparities, behaviorism and psychoanalysis deal with many of the same events and as a result there are efforts to synthesize the two systems.

Some social scientists hold that mental illness is a construct which does not exist in reality. Such an argument provokes thought but provides little guidance when one is confronted by an individual shaking with anxiety or frightened by hallucinations and bizarre behavior. While much remains to be learned about the nature and scope of mental illness, it is unwarranted to reduce the whole subject to a set of problems in living, or iatrogenic myths.

A burgeoning area of interest to sociologists is the study of deviance (Smith, R. and Douglas, J. 1972). Primary deviance refers to an individual's disturbed mental functioning and behavior. Secondary deviance refers to a process in which a label or set of expectations are conferred upon the individual by others. A deviant identity may result from illness or the labeling of illness, and an individual may progress through various positions within the social system (a career). Others will react to him, in part, according to whether or not they regard his behavior as rational (controlled, understandable) or irrational (uncontrolled, inexplicable).

The report, *Crisis in Child Mental Health*, states that poverty and racism are the number one mental health problems in America (Joint Commission, 1969). Most epidemiological studies demonstrate that a high prevalence of mental disorders occurs in individuals in the lowest socio-economic status (Dohrenwend and Dohrenwend 1969). Thus, lower socioeconomic patients have a longer duration of mental illness than high social economic patients, and this finding is related to decreased access to mental health facilities as well as to less desirable treatment (Hollingshead and Redlich, 1958). The finding of a high incidence of severe mental disorders in the lowest socioeconomic class is, in part, related to social drifting down of mentally ill individuals from higher classes.

Cultural factors influence mental disorders in various ways (Leighton and Hughes, 1961). Culture may determine the pattern of specific mental disorders, e.g. syndromes such as koro in China or amok in Indonesia. While the literature has stressed the noxious influences of some childrearing patterns it is important to recognize that different cultural practices may also influence mental health and psychopathology in adolescence, maturity and senescence. Some cultures may reward certain forms of mental illness, e.g. a person who has epileptic seizures or hears voices may be regarded as a healer or holy man. Cultural change, such as through industrialization, immigration, and war, may affect mental health and illness at the individual and community level. The distribution of mental illness in a population may be affected by cultural patterns such as breeding and poor physical hygiene, e.g. preferential deficient diets or deficient diets which result from even more deficient welfare programs. One of the clearest examples of the influence of culture is in the case of alcoholism. In Italy, for example, where the alcoholism rate is low, the cultural preference is for wine to be drunk in moderation at meals. In the United States and U.S.S.R., where the alcoholism rates are high, the cultural preference is for high-alcohol content drinks, before, during and after meals.

Conclusion: A balanced consideration of an individual's state of health demands attention to the whole (bio-psycho-social) person. A person, for example, may be depressed as a result of the interplay among chemical imbalances in his nervous system, a punitive superego, economic failure and intolerant peers. All these factors must be considered in theory and practice. The determination of the relative importance of these factors and the nature of their interaction is the major challenge for mental health in the foreseeable future.

Armando R. Favazza, M.D., M.P.H.

References

Bandura, A. 1969. Principles of Behavior Modification. New York: Holt, Rinehart and Winston.

Dohrenwend, B.P. and Barbara S. 1969. Social Status and Psychological Disorders. New York: Wiley Interscience.

English, O. and Pearson, G. 1963. Emotional Problems of Living. New York: W. W. Norton.

Erikson, E. 1963. Childhood and Society (2nd edition). New York: W. W. Norton.

Fabrega, H. 1974. Disease and Social Behavior. Cambridge: M.I.T. Press.

Hollingshead, A. and Redlich, F. 1958. Social Class and Mental Illness. New York: J. Wiley and Sons.

Jahoda, Marie, 1958. Current Concepts of Positive Mental Health. New York: Basic Books.

Joint Commission on Mental Health of Children. 1969. Crisis in Child Mental Health. New York: Harper and Row.

Kittrie, N. 1971. The Right to Be Different. Baltimore: Johns Hopkins Press.

Leighton, A.H. and Hughes, J.M. 1961. Culture as a causative of mental disorder. Milbank Memorial Fund Quarterly, 39:446-88.

Smith, R. and Douglas, J. 1972. Theoretical Perspectives on Deviance. New York: Basic Books.

Wolpe, J. 1958. Psychotherapy by Reciprocal Inhibition. Stanford: Stanford University Press.

16

4. Ethics: Biomedical and Social

> There is an inescapable need for . . . moral sensi-
> bility, or the exercise of good judgment, morally
> speaking. We must have some way of applying gen-
> eral principles to particular cases, and we cannot
> do that by rule. For if we had rules for the applica-
> tion of the general to the particular, we would still
> need sensibility and judgment to decide which rules
> to apply where.
>
> —*Abraham Kaplan*
> *in Shils et al., 1968, p. 163*

The consumer movement has been gaining new supporters
rapidly in the last decade, nowhere more significantly than in the
area of health. Human rights violations in research and treatment,
hazards of drugs, and the fallibility of science and human judgment
are widely broadcast. Physicians, psychologists, social workers,
and other health care professionals are no longer held in awe, as
possessors of mystical knowledge beyond the ken of the average citizen; nor are they considered the sole or even best-qualified, judges
of ethical decisions affecting their patients, their research, and the
public health.

Recent issues that have raised ethical debate include: surgical
sterilization without informed consent; experimentation on subjects
without their full knowledge or in a coercive situation, as in prison;
psychosurgery; aversive conditioning (e.g., painful shocks) in the
treatment of autistic children, certain prisoners, and sex offenders;
the definition of death; the right to refuse treatment, life-saving or
otherwise; euthanasia; confidentiality of records and of client-ther-
apist relationships; the use of surrogate partners in sex therapy;
genetic counseling and the right to reproduce; abortion; and sexual
interaction between therapist and patient.

What are some of the factors that perpetrate ethical affronts?
One, of course, is ordinary human fallibility. Even the most scientifically sound and humanistic training program cannot render the
fledgling professional morally perfect. Nor can it inculcate ethical
precepts in students who are blithely amoral. Additionally, as yet
there are no predictive tests or other means for selecting candidates
for professional training who meet particular moral standards.

A second factor identified by some authors may be the lessened

17

societal impact of traditional religion with its special stress on moral values. (e.g. Torrey, 1968) Adding this to our tumultuous, frenetic, technologically sophisticated and products-oriented world—a world that seems to offer few opportunities for self-reflection and examination—one might expect to find many people lacking direction in ethical matters.

Although it does not excuse the professional's later misconduct, it is helpful to examine the typical student's more mundane career goals, and to consider how these may interact with the stress and tensions of training programs. Basically, students tend to endure these pre-professional growing pains and to even retain high motivational levels through the years of hard work and financial deprivation by looking forward to the many rewards attendant upon becoming a professional. Among these are intellectual and emotional satisfaction in one's work, income, and status, be it prestige in the community, subordinates to do one's bidding, or a position of authority among colleagues. Professional certification also presumably entitles the person to function with a high degree of autonomy and freedom from supervision, especially in the private practice situation.

Stresses of training include the need for money to pay off debts, to live again as an adult, and to gain status in recompense for the years of feeling inferior as a student. Moral values may be eroded by the notion that, upon graduation, the world "owes" the individual something. Training programs are not renowned for educating students to the rights of patients, clients, and subjects, as many professionals can attest from their training days. Ethical concerns are frequently given short shrift in courses, and the new professional's subsequent behavior in research, teaching, treatment or administration, may reflect failings of both preaching and practice in academe.

Some of the values at stake in relation to health and illness do, indeed, change over the years along with changing social and world conditions. It would be ideal if ". . . there were a definite set of rules in accord with which we could apply to these vexed questions the moral consensus of society" (Kaplan, op. cit., p. 163), but such is not the case. Professionals at times look to philosophy or law for answers, but this approach, while necessary, is not sufficient. The dialogue on values must include not only the professional's peers, but clients, students, and the public whose interests are involved.

The standard practice of professional associations in confronting these problems has been to codify general principles describing the relevant moral standards for practitioners of the discipline concerned. These may be obtained from the relevant associations. Summaries of codes pertinent to research with humans are also given in Beecher (1970). Upon joining such associations, the member agrees to uphold, practice, and work in accord with these standards.

Failure to do so violates the terms of the membership contract and may subject the member to a series of actions by the association including, at worst, loss of membership. Implementing and interpreting the code typically falls within the purview of an ethics committee, which examines the evidence of misconduct and which also makes recommendations regarding suitable education, supervision, or penalty for ethical violations.

But it has become increasingly clear to concerned professionals and laymen that codes of ethics do not solve all the dilemmas, or protect the consumer as one might wish. Although state licensing regulations also aim to protect the public against incompetence and fraud, many of the laws are neither as well nor as fairly enforced as would be desirable. Further, while various examples of unprofessional behavior can be found, examples of ethical dilemmas and conflicts are more plentiful. These, moreover, are not always amenable to simple description and conceptualization.

For instance, often the more significant research and treatment procedures are also those involving problems of informed consent. Yet in order to conduct a study and obey the tenets of good science, the investigator may be constrained from obtaining such consent because subjects' knowledge of the study's design would render the results invalid or unreliable. Worse still, as Beecher (1970) has commented, if informed consent is possible and this requires describing the risks to the subject, the investigator may find that such a prediction of possible outcomes is not possible, given the state of knowledge in the particular field.

If informed consent poses operational problems, so does the notion of coercion, although it might appear that this concept could be readily defined. The following illustrates:

> We were studying the use of a new psychological test
> with psychiatric inpatients, and tried to get as complete a
> sample as possible by urging the patients to participate
> while not insisting on it. Part way through the brief test-
> ing, an occasional patient expressed a wish to leave the
> situation. In these cases, they were strongly reassured
> and encouraged to persist. Where was the line between
> reasoning and coercion under these circumstances?
> (American Psychological Association,
> 1973, p. 41)

While this example concerns the research scientist, dilemmas for practitioners and teachers are no less common, although they have had less prominence in the recent literature.

To better protect the public's rights, the law has increasingly been used. Recently, a Michigan court ruled that state funds might not be used to finance experiments on mental patients in circumstances where the patients' informed consent could not possibly be obtained. Such decisions will, of course, prevent specific types of ethical violations from recurring. But what of the others? How can they be guarded against?

It appears that professionals and their respective associations must be called upon to shoulder a greater portion of the task. Rhoades (1968) has suggested that state boards of examiners be empowered to discipline the incompetent or unethical professional. Today, few such laws having "teeth" exist at all. Nor are there laws giving state boards appropriate investigatory powers and resources to carry them out. Further, good laws which protect the right of professionals, to which they are also entitled, must be enacted. The informed consumer's advice should be elicited, as should the advice and experience of allied health professionals with similar ethical dilemmas.

Professionals and their respective associations must also encourage state boards and their own ethics committees to be more aggressive in publicizing their availability to consider grievances involving abuse of public trust. Boards and committees should similarly be prepared to instruct and educate the public regarding their rules and procedures, describe how cases are handled, and to be ready to apply the appropriate rules to complaints as fairly and expeditiously as possible.

A final suggestion: Individually and collectively through their respective associations, professionals should encourage educators to incorporate more ethics guidance into curricula and clinical practice. This training, of course, will continue to be neglected if educators maintain their ivory tower stance toward public service, because many have been simply ignorant of or indifferent to ethical failings in their professions. Better use of adjunct teaching appointments, special symposia utilizing community practitioners, members of ethics committees, state boards, and the like, could provide a practical solution for the problem of how academicians can locate the right people to fill this training gap.

Overall, however, professionals should become much more active in teaching the public how to judge the moral and ethical issues affecting personal and community health, since "Science can tell us what we *can* do but not what we *should* do" (Torrey, 1968, p. 414).

It is in the historical tradition of psychology, to move into areas formerly considered philosophical, Piaget, Kohlberg (1969) and others have taken moral development as a major issue for scientific study. Earlier, psychoanalysis had a profound effect on social mores. The values of professionals overtly and covertly affect clients and society. The Socratic "know thyself" is a lasting imperative, for mental health practice and moral well-being.

Brenda D. Gurel, Ph.D.

References

Adams, Margaret. 1973. Science, technology, and some dilemmas of advocacy. Science, 180, 840-42.

American Psychiatric Association, 1973. The Principles of Medical Ethics with Annotations Especially Applicable to Psychiatry. APA, Washington, D.C. 8pp.

American Psychological Association. 1967. Casebook on Ethical Standards of Psychologists. APA, Washington, D.C.

American Psychological Association. 1973. Ethical Principles in the Conduct of Research with Human Participants. APA, Washington, D.C.

American Psychological Association. Rev. ed. 1972. Ethical Standards of Psychologists. APA, Washington, D.C.

American Psychological Association. December 1972. Proposed Procedural Guidelines for State Psychological Association Ethics Committees. APA, Washington, D.C.

Beecher, Henry K. 1970. Research and the Individual: Human Studies. Boston: Little, Brown, & Co.

Ethical aspects of experimentation with human subjects. 1969. Daedalus, 98 (2).

Etzioni, Amitai. 1973. Regulation of human experimentation. Science, 182.

Glass, Bentley. 1965 Science and Ethical Values. Chapel Hill, N.C.: University of North Carolina Press.

Kelman, Herbert C. 1968. A Time to Speak: On Human Values and Social Research. San Francisco, California: Jossey-Bass, Inc.

Kohlberg, L. and Kramer, R. 1969. Continuities and discontinuities in childhood and adult moral development. Human Development, 12, 93-120.

Mann, Kenneth W. 1970. Deadline for Survival: A Survey of Moral Issues in Science and Medicine. New York, N.Y.: Seabury Press (published with the Academy of Religion and Mental Health.

Medical Malpractice. 1969. A Study Submitted by the Subcommittee on Executive Reorganization to the Committee on Government Operations, U.S. Senate. U.S. Government Printing Office, Washington, D.C.

Merlis, Sidney (Ed.) 1972. Non-Scientific Constraints on Medical Research, New York, N.Y.: Raven Press.

Rhoades, Paul S. 1968. Medical ethics and morals in a new age. Journal of the American Medical Association, 205(7), 517-522.

Rules and Procedures: Committee on Scientific and Professional Ethics and Conduct. 1974. American Psychologist, (September) 703-710.

Shils, Edward; St. John-Stevas, Norman; Ramsey, Paul; Medawar, P.B.; Beecher, Henry I.; and Kaplan, Abraham. 1968. Life or Death: Ethics and Options. Portland, Oregon; Reed College, and Seattle: University of Washington Press.

Shore, Milton F. and Golann, Stuart E. (Eds.) 1973. Current Ethical Issues in Mental Health, N.I.M.H., National Clearinghouse for Mental Health Information, U.S. Government Printing Office, DHEW Publ. No. (HSM) 73-9029.

Sullivan, David S. and Deiker, Thomas E. July 1973. Subject-experimenter perceptions of ethical issues in human research. American Psychologist, 587-591.

Torrey, E. Fuller (Ed.) Ethical Issues in Medicine: The Role of the Physician in Today's Society. Boston: Little, Brown, & Co. 1968.

Other Sources

Hastings Center Report. Institute of Society, Ethics, and The Life Sciences, 623 Warburton Ave., Hastings-on-Hudson, New York 10706.

II. Determining Mental Health Needs

1. Statistics and Epidemiology

No human investigation can be called true science
without passing through mathematical tests.

—*Leonardo da Vinci (1452-1519)*
Treatise on Painting

During the past decade, state, national and international health
authorities have placed much emphasis on the use of rational and
scientific methods in planning health services and evaluating their
effectiveness (WHO, 1967; 1970; 1971). Such activities require considerable amounts of demographic, morbidity, mortality, health services, social, economic, manpower and related types of statistics
(Kramer and Taube, 1973; Kramer, 1967, 1975).

Ideally, every administrator of a mental health program should
have a statistical and epidemiological research unit as an integral
part of his organization. (WHO, 1960; APHA, 1962). A unit of this
kind would be responsible for demographic studies of the population
served, patterns of utilization of mental health services, evaluations
of program activities, and periodic assessments of the prevalence
and incidence of specific disorders in various segments of the population. At present, however, because of the complex nature of the
mental health problem and the acute shortage of trained psychiatric
epidemiologists, biostatisticians and social scientists to design and
implement surveys and evaluation studies, extensive programs can
be developed only in relatively few places.

It is possible, however, for every mental health program to use
data derived from records of patients admitted to psychiatric facilities as the basis for a program of statistical research on the mentally
ill.

Despite their limitations for estimating the total incidence and
prevalence of mental disorders (e.g., Kramer et al, 1972), operational data obtained from records of psychiatric patients can provide a firm starting point. These data may be used to demonstrate
the volume of the services available to a community, patterns of use
and the characteristics of users, and also some indicators of the
success or failure of the programs.

The following are some guidelines for the development of a
basic statistical program for mental health services. Although the
discussion is directed towards the production of data at the state
level, the ideas may be adapted for use at the local level (county,

city, catchment area), and individual facility level. (See also Cooper, 1973; and Kramer, 1969).

A state government desiring to develop systematic statistics on the number and characteristics of its psychiatric facilities, and of patients using them, should adopt the following minimum requirements: 1) designate a central agency with the authority to collect, process and analyze basic data from all psychiatric facilities; 2) develop and maintain a current inventory of the individual psychiatric facilities of the state from which the data are to be collected; 3) develop a record system within each facility from which pertinent data concerning the characteristics of the services provided, of the patients admitted to them, and of the patterns of patient flow can be abstracted and transmitted to the central agency; and 4) provide feedback to the staff of the reporting facilities on the uses made of the data collected, and develop other activities (meetings, seminars, technical assistance) to ensure their continued cooperation.

The mental health statistician should coordinate his activities with those of the governmental units responsible for the collection and analysis of basic census, morbidity, vital and social statistics of the state or locality so as to insure the integration of mental health with these other essential types of statistics.

Before making decisions on the extent to which computer technology should be utilized in a given statistical unit, its director should familiarize himself with studies on the use of computer techniques for automating records of patients in psychiatric facilities, facilitating care of patients, producing statistical tabulations and data analysis (e.g. Pollack et al, 1974). In addition, he should explore carefully the personnel and financial requirements of a computer system that would meet his needs.

The administrator of the mental health program, the director of the statistical unit, and other appropriate personnel must protect the rights of the individuals whose records they compile. There is a need for standard safeguards to protect against violations of confidentiality and for due process (U.S. DHEW, 1973).

Various types of vital, morbidity and social statistics are frequently needed in planning, monitoring and evaluating mental health programs and should be used to supplement statistics on patterns of use on mental health facilities. The following are some examples:

MORTALITY STATISTICS. A variety of studies have demonstrated that the age-specific mortality rates among the mentally ill, the hospitalized, as well as those under care of outpatient clinics, private psychiatrists, and psychiatric units of general hospitals are considerably in excess of those in the corresponding age groups of the general population (Yolles and Kramer, 1969; Babigian and Odoroff, 1969; Keehn, et al., 1974).

26

The excess mortality is the resultant of a variety of factors. These include: (a) the high fatality rates for many of the conditons (infective diseases, metabolic disorders, neoplasms, cerebrovascular diseases, skull fractures, intracranial injuries, poisonings, etc.) that cause or are associated with organic brain syndromes); (b) patterns of behavior and attitudes of persons with mental disorders which, in turn, affect their lifestyle, living arrangements, general health status, and the extent to which they seek and obtain psychiatric and medical care and related human services; (c) the extent to which psychiatrists are able to predict suicidal and violent behavior in patients and are successful in preventing such acts; (d) possible effects of somatic, pharmacologic and other treatment procedures for mental disorders on essential life processes; (e) problems specific to the hospital, nursing home or other facility in which the patient receives treatment (e.g., lack of adherence to sanitary, safety and other standards for hospitals, clinics, etc.; inadequate and substandard psychiatric, medical care and related health maintenance services; inadequate staff, etc.), and (f) problems associated with longterm institutionalization that affect the physical and mental health and the social well being of patients. Knowledge of conditions associated with the death of patients with mental disorders may provide practical information that can be used to develop psychiatric, medical care, social and related human services that can possibly prevent deaths.

Death certificates provide some information on diseases and events which can damage the central nervous system, e.g., deaths from certain communicable diseases (meningitis, encephalitis, syphilis), nutritional diseases (pellagra, beriberi, and other nutritional deficiency states), vascular lesions affecting the central nervous system (cerebral hemorrhage, embolism and thrombosis), birth injuries, accidents and poisonings. Deaths from cirrhosis of the liver subdivided by those with and without mention of alcoholism may also be of use in studies of alcoholism.

Of particular importance are the deaths from suicide. The death certificate provides information on the various demographic characteristics of the patient and the method of self-destruction. These data can be used to determine areas with high or low rates of suicide and can serve as a starting point for studies that may be undertaken to define more clearly the factors associated with suicide in a specific locality. Although suicide per se is not a mental disorder, it is an act that, at least in Western cultures, is considered to be carried out by persons who, while alive, manifested a variety of underlying types of personality problems and psychopathology (Shneidman and Farberow, 1957; Kessel and Grossman, 1961). Thus, high suicide rates also indicate population groups with high rates of psychopathology and a variety of social problems (e.g. Brooke and

Glatt, 1964; Dublin, 1963; Kramer et al., 1972).

Data on attempted suicides can also provide useful information for control programs and in some countries, reporting programs have been started (Prokupek, 1965). Additional sources of information are records of patients admitted to emergency wards for treatment of self-inflicted poisoning (Kessel, 1965), poison control centers, police departments, coroners, and psychiatric inpatient and outpatient departments. Careful follow-up studies of individuals who attempt suicide will provide valuable data for the operation of control programs.

STATISTICS OF PREGNANCY, NATALITY AND PERINATAL MORTALITY. A number of factors operating during pregnancy are known to be capable of causing fetal injury, particularly injury to the central nervous system (Pasamanick and Knobloch, 1961). The sources of data related to pregnancy, natality and perinatal mortality are quite well known to health officers. Thus, birth certificates contain data that can be studied in relation to prematurity (birth weight and length of gestation), previous reproductive losses and legitimacy. In some areas, complications of pregnancy and delivery, congenital malformations, and certain concurrent disease present in the mother during pregnancy are also reported on birth certificates. Infants born prematurely, as well as those born to mothers who experienced complications of pregnancy and delivery, constitute a vulnerable group. Rate analyses of such factors by age of mother, order of birth, socioeconomic variables, etc. can be used to define groups with high rates of prematurity and complications, leading to intervention which might reduce these rates. In addition, lists of children and mothers in the vulnerable groups can be obtained from health departments to provide necessary services, to investigate various phenomena including short and long range outcomes and to evaluate the results of programs of care for these individuals and their families. Similarly, data on perinatal deaths, on illegitimate births and on abortions can be used to identify susceptible groups for service and study.

POPULATION DATA AND NEEDS ASSESSMENT. Data from the decennial census of population are essential in the planning of community mental health services. These data provide the denominators for the various morbidity, mortality and facility usage rates described in the previous sections. In addition, they provide basic information on the size and demographic characteristics of the residents of target populations, such as a region, state, county, city, health district, census tract, or some other subdivision of an urban or rural geographic area. Occasionally, universities, survey groups and community agencies have carried out special population surveys which provide additional data of value to mental health planners.

Redick, Goldsmith and Unger (1971) have provided a useful

summarization of the way in which data from the 1970 census of population may be analyzed by various demographic factors (such as age, sex, race, ethnic composition, marital status, household composition, social and economic status, etc.) to obtain indicators which identify areas with high risk populations.

The NIMH has made available to each State Mental Health Authority the computer tapes which provide the basic data for analyses of the populations of each catchment area within each state. (See Rosen, 1974).

In the planning of mental health services, it is important to take into account the expected changes in the size and demographic composition of the population. Of particular importance are the expected numbers in the different age groups. Large increases or decreases in the various age, sex, or race groups will have considerable effects on the need for professional qualified staff in the mental health field, the need for beds in mental hospitals and other inpatient services, and for other types of psychiatric services (Kramer, 1969; Kramer, et al., 1973; U.S. Bureau of the Census, 1972).

HOUSEHOLD COMPOSITION, LIVING ARRANGEMENTS AND FAMILY STATUS. Community mental health programs place much emphasis on providing diagnosis, treatment and rehabilitation services at the local level to protect the patients' links with their families and communities and to maintain them in their home and community environments. The planning and implementation of such programs require data on characteristics of persons according to the composition and social, economic and housing characteristics of the families of which they are members.

Since 1960, the Bureau of the Census has prepared tabulations of individuals by family characteristics, i.e., of individuals in the various age-sex-marital categories according to whether they live in households with related or with nonrelated persons, live alone or in group quarters. Persons living in a family were further classified by their relationship to the head of the household (U.S. Bureau of the Census, 1964; 1973).

Several recent publications present analyses of the population by living arrangements and discuss their relevance to mental health planning e.g., Kramer, Taube and Redick, 1973; Redick, Goldsmith and Unger, 1971; Rosen, 1974. Studies have also been published which provide information on the relationship of household composition and the role the person occupies in the household to admission to psychiatric facilities (Pollack, et al., 1968) and the uses of such data in planning (Pollack, 1968).

DATA FROM RECORDS OF OTHER HEALTH, SOCIAL, EDUCATIONAL AND RELATED AGENCIES. In addition to birth and death records, marriage certificates and records from a large variety of health, social and welfare agencies can be used to supplement records of patients admitted to psychiatric facilities as starting points for studies of mental disorders, the problems they create and the effectiveness of efforts made to prevent and control such disorders. A partial list of these agencies includes: health departments, including poison-control and accident-prevention centers; businesses and industries with health and safety programs; public and private schools; special hospitals for tuberculosis, crippled children, chronically ill, alcoholism; nursing homes; boarding homes; police courts and legal institutions; counseling agencies; adoption agencies; health insurance plans; workmen's compensation; and records of private psychiatrists and general practitioners.

Epidemiology is playing an increasingly important role in basic, clinical and applied research on the mental disorders (Reid, 1960). Epidemiology has been defined in a variety of ways, but a definition quite relevant to the purposes of this chapter is "a science concerned with the study of factors that influence the occurrence and distribution of disease, defect, disability or death in aggregations of individuals" (Clark, 1953). In effect, "Epidemiology relates observed distributions of disorders to environments in which people live—the physical, biological and social environments" (Gruenberg, 1968).

A basic task facing the epidemiologist is to determine the incidence and prevalence of the condition being studied in a defined population and the variations in these rates among the various strata of the population and over time. These basic statistical indices are defined as follows: Incidence is the number of new cases of mental disorders occurring per year per 100,000 population exposed to risk. The prevalence rate is defined in several different ways: One is the number of cases of mental disorder present in a population as of a given day per 100,000 population (point prevalence); another is the number of cases present in a population during a year per 100,000 population (interval prevalence). (For more detailed discussion of these indices see Cooper and Morgan, 1973; Fleiss, 1973; Gruenberg, 1968, Kramer, 1957; MacMahon, et al., 1960.)

Although it is possible to develop systematic annual statistics on rates of use of mental health facilities by age, sex, diagnosis, race, marital status, place of residence and other demographic variables for a state and its catchment areas, it is not possible to develop corresponding systematic statistics on the incidence and prevalence of mental disorders in the noninstitutionalized population. The major impediments to their development are the continued absence of standardized case-finding techniques capable of uniform application from time to time and place to place for detecting persons in the noninstitutionalized population with mental disorders; reliable differential diagnostic techniques for assigning each case to a specific diagnostic group; and methods for determining dates of

30

onset and termination of the disorder. A considerable number of prevalence surveys of mental disorders have been done. However, none has yielded case-finding techniques which have been adapted for general use. (See reviews and critiques of these surveys by Dohrenwend, 1970; Dohrenwend and Dohrenwend, 1969; Goldberg, 1972; Lapouse, 1967; Lin and Standley, 1962; Shepherd, et al., 1966).

If it is necessary to carry out a prevalence survey of mental disorders or related types of special surveys within an area to supplement facility-use data, the investigator(s) should become thoroughly familiar with the survey techniques that have been used for these purposes and should keep in mind the following basic principles (WHO, 1966): 1) the purpose of the survey should be stated clearly at the outset; 2) the target populations should be clearly specified; 3) case-finding procedures should be developed for use in the survey, relevant to the purposes of the survey and tested in pilot studies; 4) the members of the survey team must be trained in the use of the case-finding techniques so as to ensure that all members of the team apply procedures uniformly in areas where surveys are to be carried out; 5) standard data-collection forms must be developed together with instructions that will ensure uniformity in recording observations; 6) decisions must be made concerning the size of population sample to be surveyed, taking into account available funds, personnel, time factors and degrees of accuracy required in final results (APHA, 1954; WHO, 1966); 7) plans for coding, processing and analyzing the data should be developed before starting the field work; 8) appropriate steps must be taken to gain the cooperation of the various governmental and nongovernmental health, social and related agencies.

Epidemiologic techniques have been applied not only to research on morbidity rates of mental disorders but also to investigations of many problems relevant to the prevention and control of these disorders. Studies have been reported in the mental health literature that illustrate the uses of epidemiology enumerated by Morris (1964), namely: historical study of the health of populations and the rise and fall of diseases; community diagnosis; the working of the health services; individual risks and chances; completing the clinical picture; identification of syndromes; and search for causes. The following references provide relevant examples of these uses in research on the mental disorders: Angrist, et al, 1968; Cooper and Morgan, 1973; Davis, et al, 1974; Gruenberg, 1964, 1968; Gruenberg and Huxley, eds., 1961; Kramer, 1967; Pasamanick, et al, 1967; Robins, 1966; Shepherd, Oppenheim and Mitchell, 1971; Shepherd and Cooper, 1964; Shepherd, et al, 1966; Susser, 1968; Wing and Haley, eds., 1972; Wing and Haffner, eds., 1973; Zussman et al, 1970.

Morton Kramer, Sc.D.

31

References

American Public Health Association. 1954. On the use of sampling in the field of public health. Am J Public Health, 44:719-740.

American Public Health Association Program Area Committee on Mental Health. 1962. Mental Disorder: A Guide to Control Methods. New York: American Public Health Association.

Angrist, S.S., Lefton, M., Dinitz, S., and Pasamanick, B. 1968. Women After Treatment. New York: Appleton-Century-Crofts.

Babigian, H.M., and Odoroff, C.L. 1969. The mortality experience of a population with psychiatric illness. Am J Psychiatry, 126:470-480.

Brooke, E.M., and Glatt, M.M. 1964. More and more barbiturates. Med Sci Law, 4:277.

Clark, E.G. 1953. An Epidemiologic Approach to Preventive Medicine. In: Leavell, H.R. and Clark, E.G., eds. Textbook of Preventive Medicine, Chapter 3, pp. 28-64. New York: McGraw Hill.

Cooper, B., and Morgan, H.G. 1973. Epidemiological Psychiatry. Springfield, Ill.: Charles C. Thomas.

Cooper, E.M. 1973. Guidelines for a Minimum Statistical and Cost Accounting System for Community Mental Health Centers. National Institute of Mental Health, Mental Health Statistics Series C, No. 7. DHEW Publication No. (ADM) 74-14. Washington, D.C.: U.S. Government Printing Office.

Davis, A.F., Dinitz, S., Pasamanick, B. 1974. Schizophrenics in the New Custodial Community. Columbus, Ohio: Ohio State University Press.

Dohrenwend, B.P. 1970. Psychiatric disorder in general populations: Problem of the untreated "case." Am J Public Health, 60:1052-1064.

Dohrenwend, B.P. and Dohrenwend, B.S. 1969. Social Status and Psychological Disorder: A Causal Inquiry. New York: Wiley Interscience.

Dublin, L. 1963. Suicide: A Sociological and Statistical Study. New York: Ronald Press.

Fleiss, J.L. 1973. Statistical Methods for Rates and Proportions. New York: John Wiley and Sons.

Goldberg, D.P. 1972. The Detection of Psychiatric Illness by Questionnaire. Institute of Psychiatry, Maudsley Monographs 21. London: Oxford University Press.

Gruenberg, E.M. 1964. Epidemiology. In: Stevens, H.A. and Heber, R., eds. Mental Retardation: A Review of Research, pp. 259-306. Chicago and London: University of Chicago Press.

Gruenberg, E.M. 1968. Epidemiology and medical care statistics. In: Katz, M.M.; Cole, J.O.; and Barton, W.E., eds. The Role and Methodology of Classification in Psychiatry and Psychopathology. Public Health Service Publication No. 1584, pp. 76-99. Washington, D.C.: U.S. Government Printing Office.

Gruenberg, E.M. and Huxley, M., eds. 1961. Causes of Mental Disorders: A Review of Epidemiological Knowledge, 1959. New York: Milbank Memorial Fund.

Hare, E.H., and Wing, J.K., eds. 1970. Psychiatric Epidemiology. An International Symposium. London: Oxford University Press.

Keehn, R.J.; Goldberg, I.S.; and Beebe, G.W. 1974. Twenty-four year mortality follow-up of army veterans with disability separations for psychoneurosis in 1944 Psychosom Med, Vol 36, pp 27-46.

Kessel, N. 1965. Self-poisoning. Br Med J, 2:1265-1336.

Kessel, N. and Grossman, G. 1961. Suicide in alcoholics. Br Med J, 2:1671.

Kramer, M. 1957. A discussion of the concepts of incidence and prevalence as related to epidemiologic studies of mental disorders. Am J Public Health, 47:826-840.

Kramer, M. 1967. Epidemiology, biostatistics and mental health planning. In: Monroe, R.M.; Klee, G.D.; and Brody, E.B., eds. Psychiatric Epidemiology and Mental Health Planning. Psychiatric Research Report No. 22. Washington, D.C.; American Psychiatric Association.

Kramer, M. 1969. Applications of Mental Health Statistics. Geneva: World Health Organization.

Kramer, M. (in press) Diagnosis and Classification. Their purposes and uses in epidemiological and health services research, Chapter III. In: Hobbs, N., ed. Issues in the Classification of Children. San Francisco: Jossey-Bass.

Kramer, M.; Pollack, E.S.; Redick, R.W.; and Locke, B.Z. 1972. Mental Disorders/Suicide. Vital and Health Statistics Monographs, American Public Health Association. Cambridge: Harvard University Press.

Kramer, M. and Taube, C.A. 1973. The role of a national statistics program in the planning of community psychiatric services in the United States, Chapter 4. In: Wing, J.K., and Hafner, H., eds. Roots of Evaluation: The Epidemiological Basis for Planning Psychiatric Services. London: Oxford University Press.

Kramer, M.; Taube, C.S.; and Redick, R.W. 1973. Patterns of use of psychiatric facilities by the aged: past, present and future. In: Eisdorfer, C. and Lawton, M.P., eds. The Psychology of Adult Development and Aging. Washington, D.C.: American Psychological Association.

Lapouse, R. 1967. Problems in studying the prevalence of psychiatric disorder. Am J Public Health, 57:947.

Lin, T., and Standley, C.C. 1962. The Scope of Epidemiology in Psychiatry. WHO Public Health Paper No. 16. Geneva: World Health Organization.

MacMahon, B.; Pugh, T.; and Ipsen, J. 1960. Epidemiologic Methods. Boston: Little, Brown and Company.

Monroe, R.R.; Klee, G.D.; and Brody, E.B., eds. 1967. Psychiatric Epidemiology and Mental Health Planning. Psychiatric Res Rep No. 22. Washington, D.C.: American Psychiatric Association.

Morris, J.N. 1964. Uses of Epidemiology (Second Edition). Baltimore: The Williams and Wilkins Co.

Pasamanick, B.; Scarpitti, F.R.; and Dinitz, S. 1967. Schizophrenics in the Community: Experimental Study in the Prevention of Hospitalization. New York: Appleton-Century-Crofts.

Pasamanick, B., and Knobloch, H. 1961. Epidemiologic studies on the complications of pregnancy and the birth process. In: Caplan, G., ed. Prevention of Mental Disorders in Children. New York: Basic Books.

Pollack, E.S. 1968. Monitoring a Comprehensive mental health program: Methodology and data requirements. In: Roberts, L.; Greenfield, N.S.; and Miller, M.H., eds. Comprehensive Mental Health: The Challenge of Evaluation, pp. 137-167. Madison: University of Wisconsin Press.

Pollack, E.S.; Redick, R.W.; and Taube, C.A. 1968. The application of census socio-economic and familial data to the study of morbidity from mental disorders. Am J Public Health, 58:83-89.

Pollack, E.S., Windle, C.D.; and Wurster, C.R. 1974. Psychiatric information systems: An historical perspective, Chapter 15. In: Crawford, J.L.; Morgan, D.W.; and Gianturco, D.T., eds. Progress in Mental Health Information Systems: Computer Application. Cambridge: Ballinger.

Prokupek, J. 1965. K Problemum evidence sebevrazednosti v CSSR. Cs Zdrav, 13:550.

Redick, R.W.; Goldsmith H.F.; and Unger, E.L. 1971. 1970 Census Data Used to Indicate Areas with Different Potentials for Mental Health and Related Problems. National Institute of Mental Health, Mental Health Statistics Series C, No. 3, PHS Publication No. 2171. Washington, D.C.: U.S. Government Printing Office.

Reid, D.D. 1960. Epidemiological Methods in the Study of Mental Disorders. Public Health Papers No. 2. Geneva: World Health Organization.

Robins, L.N. 1966. Deviant Children Grown Up. Baltimore: Williams & Wilkins.

Rosen, B.M. 1974. A Model for Estimating Mental Health Needs Using 1970 Census Socioeconomic Data. National Institute of Mental Health, Mental Health Statistics Series C, No. 9, DHEW Publication No. (ADM) 74-63. Washington, D.C.: U.S. Government Printing Office.

Shepherd, M., and Cooper, B. 1964. Epidemiology and mental disorder—A review. J Neurol Neurosurg Psychiatry, 27:277-290.

Shepherd, M.; Oppenheim, A.N.; and Mitchell, S. 1966. Childhood behaviour disorders and the child-guidance clinic: An epidemiologic study. J. Child Psychol Psychiatry, 7:39-52.

Shepherd, M.; Oppenheim, A.N.; and Mitchell, S. 1971. Childhood Behavior and Mental Health. London: University of London Press Ltd.

Shneidman, E.S., and Farberow, N.L., eds. 1957. Clues to Suicide. New York: Blakiston Division, McGraw Hill.

Susser, M.W. 1968. Community Psychiatry: Epidemiologic and Social Themes, pp. 175-182. New York: Random House.

U.S. Bureau of the Census. 1964. U.S. Census of Population: 1960. Subject Reports. Persons by Family Characteristics. Final Report PC (2)-4B Washington, D.C.: U.S. Government Printing Office.

U.S. Bur. of Census. 1972. Projections of the Population of the United States by Age and Sex: 1972 to 2020. Series P-25, No. 493. Washington, D.C.: U.S. Government Printing Office.

U.S. Bur. of Census. 1973. Census of Population: 1970. Subject Reports. Final Report PC(2)-4B. Persons by Family Characteristics. Washington, D.C.: U.S. Government Printing Office.

U.S. Department of Health, Education, and Welfare. 1973. Records, Computers and the Rights of Citizens. Report of the Secretary's Advisory Committee on Automated Personal Data Systems. DHEW Publication No. (OS) 73-94. Washington, D.C.: U.S. Government Printing Office.

Wing, J.K., and Hafner, H., eds. 1973. Roots of Evaluation: The Epidemiological Basis for Planning Psychiatric Services. London: Oxford University Press.

Wing, J.K., and Hailey, A.M., eds. 1972. Evaluating a Community Psychiatric Service: The Camberwell Register 1964-71. London: Oxford University Press.

World Health Organization Expert Committee on Health Statistics 1966. Sampling methods in morbidity surveys and public health investigations, Tenth Report. WHO Tech Rep Ser, 336.

World Health Organization Expert Committee on Health Statistics. 1971. Statistical indicators for the planning and evaluation of public health programs. WHO Tech Rep Ser, 472.

World Health Organization Expert Committee on Mental Health 1960. Epidemiology of mental disorders. WHO Tech Rep Ser, 185.

World Health Organization Expert Committee on National Health Planning 1967. National health planning in developing countries. WHO Tech Rep Ser, 350.

World Health Organization Expert Committee on National Health Planning 1970. Training in National health planning. WHO Tech Rep Ser, 456.

Yolles, S.F., and Kramer, M. 1969 Vital Statistics. In: Bellack. L. and Loeb, L., eds. The Schizophrenic Syndrome. New York: Grune & Stratton, Inc.

Zusman, J.; Hannon, V.; Locke, B.Z.; and Goller, M. 1970 Bibliography: Epidemiology of Mental Disorders 1966-1968. National Institute of Mental Health, Washington, D.C.: U.S. Government Printing Office.

2. Ecology of Psychosocial Problems

> The assigned causes of insanity of those admitted last year, are, ill-health, 23; intemperance, 17; domestic affliction, 7; puerperal, 6; religious excitement, 5; loss of property, 5; masturbation, 5; disappointed affection, 5; spiritualism, 4; over-exertion, 4; epilepsy, 2; exposure to cold, 2; fright, 2; perplexity in business, 1; loss of friends, 1; old age, 1; blow on the head, 1; loss of sleep, 1; suppressed eruption, 1; unknown, 51.
> Seventy of these have insane relations, and are hereditarily predisposed to the disease. . . . There are but few insane persons whose disease can be traced to any one particular cause . . . we believe the foundation to the disease is mostly laid in early life.
>
> —*Dr. Henry M. Harlow*
> *Superintendent's Report,*
> *Maine Insane Hospital, in the Portland*
> *Advertiser, Jan. 26, 1858*

The purpose of this section is to examine personal problems from an ecological perspective with careful attention to research. Such a perspective has been seen as the province of such diverse fields as epidemiology, psychology, community psychiatry and sociology from which we borrow freely.

Rueul Stallones (1971) has defined *ecology* as "the study of the relation of a biological species to its environment . . . which includes the matrix of physical, biological and social circumstances within which complex interactions occur." Roger Barker (1968), an ecological psychologist, differentiates between the psychological and ecological environment. The former is "the world as a particular person perceives and is otherwise affected by it." The latter is the "objective, preperceptual context of behavior. The real-life settings within which people behave."

Matthew Dumont (1968), a community psychiatrist, defines *mental health* as freedom, "the widest conceivable range of choice in the face of internal and external constraints." That is, despite given constraints of the environmental influences mentioned above, freedom is achieved by the healthy individual. "Just as the neurotic is restricted by internal constraints of repetition-compulsion . . . the freedom of the slum dweller is limited by poverty, unemployment and segregation." Therefore, any ecological approach to mental illness must assume vital interaction between notably "high-risk" groups, such as, the poor (Hollingshead and Redlich, 1958), the unmarried and the very old (Silverman, 1968) and the chronically hospitalized schizophrenic (Fairweather, 1969), and their environments.

Problems of population control, pollution, energy, transportation, etc. have recently loomed large. But consideration of how man copes with environmental stresses has been overshadowed by consideration of man's effects on the environment. It is only recently that community mental health efforts have been addressed to such environmentally-related problems as alcoholism, poverty, delinquency and defects in the educational system in an attempt more adequately to meet environmental and psychological needs of the community.

The epidemiological approach to personal problems is intimately related to ecology and mental health. Cassel (in le Riche and Milner, 1971) says that "In the final analysis, epidemiology is certainly concerned with etiology and with the adaptation of the individual to a noxious environment." Identification and classification are important, leading to the work of epidemiology which contributes in turn to prevention treatment and further research. (Dohrenwend and Dohrenwend, 1969; Faris and Dunham, 1939; and Leighton, et al., 1963).

Although epidemiologists include prevention and treatment in their purview, the host-agent-environment analysis has too often slighted the environment. Gruenberg (1956) emphasized that, "One must be able to classify the conditions under which these disorders arise or fail to arise." Classification of environmental conditions is a new challenge for epidemiology, consistent with the principles of public health approaches to mental disorder.

The following are salient and often controversial issues which bear directly on the topic of ecology and personal problems: 1) Etiology or causation—what causes personal problems? 2) Multivariate approaches—the need to examine a whole host of variables involved in the development of personal problems. 3) Longitudinal studies—the need for studies in which subjects are followed for many years so that long term effects can be seen. 4) Environmental manipulation—the need to change environmental stimuli so that individuals are able to better cope with problems.

CAUSATION. Most professionals in public health have struggled with the question of the causes of illness and various personal problems. The major controversy seems to focus around a single vs. a multiple or system-oriented approach to the question. The "medical-reductionist" model has in some ways become the symbol for a single causation theory while the ecological approach symbolizes multiple causation. Stallones (1971) advocates the ecological approach to health and disease in which, for example, ". . . tubercle bacilli, malnutrition, overcrowding, broken hearts and people all exist and (are shown to) interact with each other. These interactions determine . . . how healthy and happy they (the people) will be . . ."

Dumont (1968) also takes issue with the "medical-reductionist" model which stresses individual patient care and clearly defined cause and effect: "(single) causation is a fiction, an absurd abstraction, superimposed on a panoply of events to give it a semblance of meaning, order and direction." Something as complex as "a collection of behavioral characteristics" cannot have a single cause, unless we broaden it to "being human in a complex environment": true, but not useful.

MULTIVARIATE APPROACHES. Numerous writers have emphasized the need for a multivariate approach to personal problems. For example, Plunkett and Gordon (1960) in the examination of causation have described two distinct steps: identify single causal factors; trace the interaction of multiple factors by multivariate statistical procedures. As an example of the application of these steps we can turn to alcoholism research. The single causal factors may include the following partial list: parental influence; socio-economic level; organic impairment; age of first drink; hormonal imbalance; psychological stresses; and educational level.

The second step would involve an examination of these and other factors in some multivariate technique such as correlations, factor analysis, and cluster analysis. In this way, single factors can be investigated not as individual causes, but as interrelated factors each of which plays an important role in the development of alcoholism.

LONGITUDINAL STUDIES. The need for longitudinal studies is implicit in any ecological approach to personal problems. An example from alcoholism is once again appropriate. Sobriety is the traditional outcome criterion for alcoholism programs. However, one week, one month or even several months of sobriety does not usually satisfy the researcher, the clinician or the client. Therefore, a longer follow-up period is needed such as 1-5 years. In this way long term results of programs can be examined.

Silverman (1968), however, cites a major obstacle to a longitudinal study of the natural history of depression: except in the cases of recurrences and deaths by suicide, there are no end points, and past attempts at longitudinal research in this area have been hampered by inadequate follow-up, analysis and periods of observation.

ENVIRONMENTAL MANIPULATION. Psychologists, especially in the behavioral therapies, have had extensive experience in the manipulation of individuals. This has only recently been translated into the manipulation of environments. For example, Fairweather (1967) has developed a research methodology, Experimental Social Innovation (E.S.I.) which includes the manipulation of environments. E.S.I. involves setting up models of social programs (e.g. residences for alcoholics, educational programs for population control, etc.) in the natural environment, evaluating those models and then implementing them in the wider community. He has shown that chronic schizophrenics can adapt to new environments as long as these environments are carefully adapted to their specific needs. (Fairweather, 1969). The Community Lodge was thus developed and has shown that with training, groups of patients can live in the community without resident staff, with self-government and a business of their own.

Robert N. Harris, Jr., Ph.D.

References

Barker, Roger. 1968. Ecological psychology, Stanford, California: Stanford University Press.

Dumont, Matthew. 1968. The absurd healer, New York: Science House.

Fairweather, G.W. 1967. Methods for experimental social innovation, New York: John Wiley and Sons, Inc.

Fairweather, G.W. 1972. Social change, the challenge to survival, New Jersey: General Learning Press.

Fairweather, G.W., Sanders, D., Cressler, D., and Maynard, H. 1969. Community life for the mentally ill, Chicago: Aldine Publishing Co.

LeRiche, W. and Milner, J. 1964. Epidemiology as Medical Ecology, Baltimore: The Williams and Wilkins Co.

Pasamanick, B. 1959. Epidemiology of Mental Disorder, AAAS publication No. 60, Washington, D.C.

Shepherd, M. and Cooper, B. 1964. "Epidemiology and Mental Disorder: A Review," in J. of Neurol. Neurosurg. Psychiatry (27), 277-290 pp.

Stallones, R. 1971. Environment, Ecology and Epidemiology, Pan American Health Organization, WHO.

Harshburger, D., Maley, R. 1974. Behavioral Analysis and Systems Analysis: An Integrative Approach to Mental Health Program, Behaviordelia.

Other Sources

American Journal of Public Health, APHA.

American Psychologist, APA

Evaluation, Program Evaluation Project, Minneapolis, Minn.

Journal of Social Issues, The Society for the Psychological Study of Social Issues (Division of APA).

3. Etiology: The Search for Causes

... we could be free of an infinitude of maladies both of body and mind, and even also possibilities of the infirmities of age, if we had sufficient knowledge of their causes, and of all the remedies with which nature has provided us.

—*Rene Descartes (1596-1650)*

The time-honored dictum of Morgagni (1682-1771) "no disease without a lesion" was meant to tie etiology and pathogenesis to structural lesions in specifiable organs or tissues of the body. As our understanding evolved, however, we learned that many lesions do not fit concepts of visually observable tissue pathology. Medicine extended its etiologic concepts to include lesions of molecules, distortions of enzyme balance, etc. One type of disorder particularly difficult to incorporate into the logic of disease causation is that of behavior pathology, i.e., those problems which may result from a mistiming, mis-integration or distortion of experience. Such "lesions of learning" are associated with undeveloped capacities (which may be subject to disuse atrophy) or maladaptive patterns of emotion and cognition—a potential consequence of distorted rewards and punishments.

THE SEARCH FOR CAUSES. A lesion or pathological mechanism can, under some circumstances, produce disturbances in behavior. Whether such disturbances are called diseases depends upon the quality and the quantity of behavior which takes place in a particular context. It appears that the human organism has a finite number of ways of acting and that certain patterned combinations of behaviors tend to recur. The disturbances are sometimes related to specific causes or conditions e.g., delirium resulting from intoxication; loss of memory caused by senility. In other situations, few connections or predictions can be made as to etiology from the pattern of signs and symptoms. The pathological mechanisms for the most important "functional" mental illnesses, affective disorder, schizophrenia, neuroses, and personality disorders remain conjectural or unknown.

In brief, there are many discomforts related to ways of thinking and feeling which are recognized as symptoms of psychiatric disorder. These tend to occur in recognizable patterns which have been given names, and a classification—a system of nosology—based

39

upon reasonable agreement among experienced persons. Generally, the more severe the behavioral changes, the higher the replicability of the diagnosis. Validity of diagnosis is more difficult to evaluate than reliability, since the untreated, natural course of different "illnesses" is often not known.

There is a school of thought which carries on the tradition that mental illness is a state determined entirely by the number of symptoms present and that there are few or no qualitative differences to be seen. There is reason to dispute this notion on the basis of the epidemiology of the various patterns of symptoms as will be detailed below.

The number of symptoms exhibited in a population may be correlated with the amount of stress upon that population, though the supporting data are not very plentiful. Populations of poorly organized communities and those undergoing rapid change, e.g., urbanization, exhibit more symptoms than populations in more stable, presumably less stressful, communities.

THE EVOLUTION OF NOSOLOGY. Mental illnesses of varying forms have been described since the beginning of recorded history. Depression, delusional states, behavior changes due to head wounds, senility, states of nutritional deficiency and intoxication are described in the most ancient writings we possess. The modern terms are of fairly recent origin. Some, like melancholia and hysteria, reveal their ancient humoral theories in their fanciful names.

Modern terminology was codified by Kraepelin (1856-1926) whose work still underlies psychiatric classification. Kraepelin distinguished the symptom pattern characterized by youthful onset of bizarre thinking and affective disorders, which he called dementia praecox, from disorder of affect (elations and depressions) and from disorders invariably accompanying brain damage of one sort or another. This tripartite division of psychopathology remains basic as regards the major groups of psychotic disorders. Dementia praecox has been supplanted by the name "schizophrenia," introduced by Bleuler (1857-1939). The group of neurotic illnesses has been redefined by many, most notably Freud and his followers.

Symptomatology predominantly of neurotic type (e.g. phobias, obsessions, anxiety, depression) has been shown to be extremely common in populations. In as many as 30 percent the symptoms are sufficient to give rise to some impairment of social function, and less than a fifth of the population reports never having had any neurotic symptoms.

Since the invention of the intelligence test, it has been possible to evaluate quantitatively an individual's intellectual functioning in relation to others with some precision. Measurement of intelligence has led to a more rational organization of services for the various types and degrees of mental retardation.

40

Modern systems of nosology are a complex mixture of etiological concepts, symptom patterns, test results, etc. Conditions related to organic (brain) lesions are separated from those in which organic factors are not implicated. The latter, "functional mental illnesses" are usually divided into "thinking disorders" (schizophrenia and allied states), affective disorders (manic-depressive illness), psychophysiologic disorders and neuroses, including anxiety states, obsessive-compulsive and phobic states, and sensory and motor distortions still referred to as hysterical.

Almost all mental disorders appear to occur more frequently and to be more severe in the socio-economically deprived segment of the population. The discrepancy between the rates for rich and poor is probably less in the affective disorders and in the most severe types of mental retardation, and is most marked in the milder types of mental retardation and in schizophrenia.

Age differences are also prominent. Mental retardation is more common in children than in adults. This is probably because children are all screened in one way or another by school systems, while adults are required to deal only with practical work and other problems which do not require as much or at least the same type of intelligence as school. In general, schizophrenia occurs earlier than affective psychoses, the former having onset before the middle 20's, the latter a little later. A special form of depression "involutional melancholia" or "agitated depression" is commonly seen in middle age; it is often accompanied by feelings of suspicion and delusions of persecution which seem to relate this illness to paranoid schizophrenia. Both sexes are equally attacked by senile and arteriosclerotic psychoses though males are hospitalized earlier on the average. This may be due to earlier onset but may also be related to behavioral problems which usually are more severe, or more socially threatening, in the male.

The sex distribution of the major groupings of mental illnesses shows considerable variation. Illnesses characterized by antisocial behavior, particularly aggression, are much more common among males. In sociopathic and criminal behavior males are strongly over-represented. Among alcoholics and other drug abusers the male/female ratio is about 5:1. Mild mental retardation is usually more prevalent in males, in a ratio of about 1.5:1. Schizophrenia appears to strike the two sexes approximately equally, but the affective disorders are twice as common among females.

Paul V. Lemkau, M.D.

Addendum

Some Specific Etiologic Factors   Estimates of childhood mental disorder range from 0.05 percent autistic, to 2-3 percent retarded, to

41

10-12 percent with behavior problems, neuroses, learning disorders, etc. The relation between childhood mental disorder and adult psychopathology is still poorly understood. While debates still rage about the relative importance of genetic, physical and psycho-social factors in causation, it is reasonable to invoke multiple determinants of phenomena as complex as those manifest in mental disorder that undermine, limit or distort personality, the essence of humanity.

Some causes of mental disorders are known, but the causes of most are still unknown, or at least unproven. Some of the known etiologic agents are:

Poison   This includes a vast number of substances and various routes into the body—skin, mouth, lung, and directly into the blood stream. Effect on the brain may be direct, as with lead poisoning, or indirect via anoxia, as with carbon monoxide. The lesion may be acute, chronic, or both; the poisoning may be accidental, intentional or mixed (as with drug abuse or alcoholism); the intoxication process may be obvious or imperceptible or somewhere in between. The results appear as toxic psychosis, inebriation, disorientation; personality change. It is estimated that for every poisoning death, there are three who survive with lasting brain damage.

Infection   Brain damage due to many different infectious agents has been recorded—bacteria, virus, parasite are all implicated. Encephalitis and meningitis are the general names for infection of the brain or its membranes, respectively. The third stage of syphilis is probably the most notorious disease in this category, causing the general paresis syndrome which accounted for half of the mental hospital inmates a few generations ago. A recent discovery is the rubella virus, which causes fetal (brain and other) anomalies when the pregnant woman contracts German Measles during the first trimester.

Genetics   Phenylketonuria and Tay-Sach's disease are examples of genetically recessive; Huntington's Chorea and tuberous sclerosis of dominant diseases. Down's syndrome (Mongolism) is detectable now in utero by means of amniocentesis (uterine tap), as are some other conditions where chromosomal abnormality can be sought in fetal cells. Some investigators believe that schizophrenia, manic depressive disease and perhaps other conditions are genetically linked; there appears to be a genetic factor, at least, which may predispose to certain conditions depending on post-natal environment.

Nutrition   Deficiencies of thiamine (beriberi), niacin (pellagra) and protein (kwashiorkor) are associated with mental changes, as are some other specific nutritional states. Early post-natal deficiencies probably contribute to impaired neurological development, including problems of learning and behavior. Recently, food additives (preservatives) have been linked with hyperactivity in children: this is an example of an issue involving toxins as much as foods—there is no escaping the overlap. Among the many controversies in the area of nutrition and health is the megavitamin approach (orthomolecular) in psychiatry, or the theory (unproven) that schizophrenia is a deficiency disease. The dominant viewpoint currently rejects megavitamin therapies.

Physical Trauma Head injury can lead to acute or chronic impairment of mental functioning. Trauma suggests an obvious injury, but subtle forms exist. For example, we know that certain stimuli are traumatic in effect to susceptible individuals (i.e. visual stimuli which lead to seizures; noise leading to auditory impairment; repeated physical trauma leading to the "punch drunk" chronic brain syndrome; radiation, especially to the fetus, producing cellular changes).

General Systemic Disease Hepatitis is often associated with depression as a specific rather than general consequence; diabetes, arteriosclerosis and many other conditions change the chemical or physical surroundings of the brain and may directly alter mental functioning in addition to the general stress of being sick. In many psychosomatic illnesses the causative factor is not known; it may be general stress or something which affects the nervous system along with other organs (thyroid, stomach, intestine, genito-urinary, cardiovascular, etc.)

To summarize, most mental disorders have not been associated with specific causes. Probably the causes are complex—as is human development. We are biological organisms with physical and chemical needs and limitations; we are also psychosocial creatures with specifiable and other quite intangible needs, measured in terms of relationships, mood, time allocation, stimulus and response . . . or not measurable at all. The right mix of protoplasm, environment and life experience produces "mental health" and imbalances or deficiencies singly or in combination produce the so-called "mental illnesses."

The Editor

4. Troubled Persons and Personal Problems: Some Sociological Considerations

> As the clergy exists beyond worldliness, so does schizophrenia exist beyond sanity. Poverty and chastity are ways of removing oneself from worldliness—we all know how we remove ourselves from sanity. What symbolism is to religion—delusion is to schizophrenia. . . . We should try to be tolerant of all, including of doctors—for they helped us with our health although they seriously damaged our dignity. They should be regarded as friends.
>
> —A former mental patient, 1974

Who in our society renders psychological help? Who goes for help? How satisfied are the help-seekers with what they receive?

Mental illness or disorder—however defined—is a major problem in society. Researchers in New York City and elsewhere found that some eighty per cent of those interviewed showed some symptoms of psychological distress. (Langner and Michael, 1963) Along with the high prevalence of psychological disorder, much of it is undetected, and it is unevenly distributed in society: the poor suffer inordinately (Hollingshead and Redlich, 1958; Myers et al, 1968), are labeled sicker (Haase, 1964) and are least likely to receive adequate care (Schofield, 1964).

Ryan (1969) found that of the 150 persons per thousand identified as emotionally disturbed in Boston, only one will find his way to a private psychiatrist. Eight will apply for outpatient care in some clinic, of whom four will be accepted for treatment, and only two will remain for more than one or two sessions. Five will be admitted to a mental hospital. In sum, less than 10% of those with an identifiable need even approached formal mental health services: the tip of the iceberg. The majority of the others receiving care do so through non-psychiatric physicians whose usual approach is psychotropic medication with support and reassurance. Besides the family physician, there are social agencies, settlement houses, and various church groups which offer mental health counsel. Ryan finds that about two-thirds of the identified emotionally disturbed receive some form of help—much of it inadequate by contemporary standards. For the other one-third, nothing is done by these formal agencies or sources, a distressing finding especially in light of the fact

44

that the figures refer only to the known impaired, and Boston enjoys a relative abundance of mental health facilities.

With such widespread prevalence of "mental illness" and lack of agreement on what constitutes a case, it is not surprising to find a great variety of persons and groups, formal and informal, offering psychological help or healing: 1) Mental health professionals, (e.g., psychiatrists, clinical psychologists, social workers, nurses, counselors) in private practice, public and private hospitals and clinics, community mental health centers, and social service agencies. 2) Other professionals, e.g., ministers, physicians, teachers, parole and probation officers. 3) Marginal healers, such as chiropractors, naturopaths, and practitioners of folk medicine. 4) Groups such as Recovery, Incorporated; Synanon; Alcoholics Anonymous, and, stemming from the sensitivity group movement are the various "growth centers." 5) Mass media advice columnists, such as Ann Landers or "Dear Abby," "call-in" radio shows, and more personal but still anonymous telephone "hotline" services. 6) "Self-Improvement" groups such as dance studios, friendship clubs, or personality development courses. 7) De facto helpers such as pharmacists, neighbors, beauticians, barbers, taxi drivers, and bartenders.

In *Persuasion and Healing*, Frank (1973) argues that all forms of psychological healing are an extension of the universal process of personal influence. Therapy can be characterized as a relationship between a sufferer who seeks relief and a socially sanctioned healer who tries to produce changes in the sufferer's emotional state, attitudes, and behavior; all parties concerned believe that these changes will be salutary.

In all societies, at one time or another, healing of the mind has been the province of the clergy. In our society, clergy are still the prime source of help for personal problems. Gurin et al. (1960:307) reported that forty-two percent of their sample consulted clergy for professional help with their problems. Problems seen and counsel given tended to cover a wide gamut, but many were defined in terms of "sinfulness" or "unworthiness." Ryan (1969:17-18) estimated that the average clergyman each year saw between twelve and fifteen persons who he would judge to be severely disturbed, or a total of 3500 in Boston. Approximately 60,000 were seen by non-psychiatric physicians, who greatly outnumber the clergy.

A recent popular phenomenon is the self-awareness group: sensitivity, Encounter, T-Groups. Their appeal seems directed to middle class, college-educated persons seeking some existential alteration of their relationship to the world, perhaps an outgrowth of increasing affluence, secularization, mobility, and alienation in our society (Back, 1972; London, 1974; Rogers, 1970). The groups are largely viewed as "educational," rather than "therapeutic" and they place a good deal of emphasis on immediate beedback.

45

How satisfied are persons with the help that they do get? Fourteen per cent of Gurin's sample sought help for personal problems; another 9 per cent could have used help but did not seek it, because of felt stigma or unawareness of resources. Surprisingly, source was not related to the type of problem: psychiatrists, physicians, and clergy were consulted for much the same reasons. The person's education, age, degree of religiosity, income, and place of residence all influenced the selection of help source. The greatest consumer satisfaction was expressed by those visiting clergy and non-psychiatric physicians: almost two-thirds reporting that they had been "helped a lot." Psychiatrists were reported as having helped somewhat less than half, while marriage counselors helped only 25 per cent. (Note: patients were not randomly assigned, and these findings do not evaluate the capacities of different helpers.) Those who sought help with a personal adjustment problem or who perceived the problem as arising from some defect in themselves were most likely to report that therapy had helped them.

Hollingshead and Redlich (1958) found that lower class neurotics are more likely to express their problems in somatic terms, while higher status neurotics are more likely to express them psychologically. Also, lower-class patients tended to see psychological help as more directive and medical: they wanted "pills," to be "told what to do," and they also tended to terminate therapy prematurely (Overall and Aronson, 1964). They may feel estranged from therapists who are generally of middleclass background and orientation; further, attending therapy may cause practical problems in terms of lost wages, baby sitting arrangements, and transportation problems. Once in therapy, though, lower-class patients respond about as well as those of higher socioeconomic strata (Frank et al., 1957).

To sum up: mental illness or disorder and its natural history or outcome cannot be understood independent of socioeconomic conditions, which influence the decision to seek help, the help source consulted, the nature of the presenting problem, the diagnosis assigned, the likelihood of being accepted for treatment, and the type of therapy received.

How does one mobilize resources for improving the delivery of mental health services to those who are currently not being served, or served inadequately? Also, how does one motivate those who are suffering from emotional problems but do not elect to seek help? The answer to the first question would appear to lie in the expansion of health delivery systems such as community mental health centers. Evidence suggests that they are creating an impact in formerly underserved areas (Kramer and Taube, 1972). Along with an expansion of services, therapeutic programs should be oriented toward the needs and lifestyles of the populations being served.

The answer to the second question lies partly with public information and attitude change to reduce the stigma associated with mental or emotional disorder, and acquaint people with available resources. Furthermore, professional mental health consultation with societal gatekeepers such as ministers, physicians, teachers, and lawyers would strengthen them as mental health resources.

Perhaps proper and judicious use of informal caregivers can lessen the gap between need and services. There are difficult problems in granting social sanction to a wide variety of de facto helpers, and also the danger of "psychiatrizing" a wide variety of social problems—to widen still more the definition of mental disorder. These are thorny issues which should be high on the mental health agenda in coming years.

Morton O. Wagenfeld, Ph.D.

References

Back, Kurt. 1972. Beyond Words. New York: Russell Sage Foundation.

Frank, Jerome D. 1973. Persuasion and Healing (Second Edition). Baltimore, Maryland: Johns Hopkins University Press.

Gurin, Gerald, Joseph Veroff, Sheila Feld. 1960. Americans View their Mental Health. New York: Basic Books.

Hollingshead, August, and Frederic Redlich. 1958. Social Class and Mental Illness. New York: John Wiley & Sons.

Langner, Thomas, and Stanley S. Michael. 1963. Life Stress and Mental Health. New York: Free Press.

Mechanic, David. 1969. Mental Health and Social Policy. Englewood Cliffs, New Jersey: Prentice-Hall.

Roman, Paul and Trice, Harrison. 1974. The Sociology of Psychotherapy. New York: Jason Aronson.

Ryan, William. 1969. Distress in the City. Cleveland: The Press of Case Western Reserve University.

Sagarin, Edward. 1972. Odd Man In. Chicago: Quadrangle Books.

Schofield, William. 1964. Psychotherapy: The Purchase of Friendship. Englewood Cliffs, New Jersey: Prentice-Hall.

Other Sources

Journals:
Journal of Health and Social Behavior
Community Mental Health Journal
Society
Psychology Today

III. | Prevention

1. Primary Prevention and Health Promotion

> ... highly important as is the influence of true
> religion upon the mental faculties, religious teaching
> fails to comprise the duties of men and women in
> relation to the care of their minds; its expounder
> does not profess to understand the delicate mech-
> anism of the brain, the laws upon which its healthy
> working is dependent, the signs that this mechanism
> is getting out of order, that a wheel is revolving too
> slowly or too quickly here, or that a screw is loose
> there; and therefore cannot pretend to tell us how
> best and soonest to ward off attacks of mental
> derangement . . . . it is but too evident that a man
> may follow all the precepts of the religious teacher
> and yet fail to secure an immunity from madness
> . . . . The best of men may, and do, become a prey to
> this disease. The worst of men may escape.
>
> —D. Hack Tuke
> *Insanity In Ancient And Modern Life*
> *(1878)*

Prevention activities have traditionally been delineated into three areas, the boundaries of which are fuzzy both in theory and practice.

Primary prevention refers to activities which remove causes, known or hypothesized, of disease or disorder. Such causes or conditions range from deficiencies in nutrition or endocrine func- tioning to patterns of mental stimulus at variance with what is re- quired for human development. Besides prevention of specific dis- order, efforts to promote positive physical and mental health are in- cluded here. *Secondary prevention* focuses on early detection and prompt treatment to prevent disorders from becoming more serious. *Tertiary prevention* focuses on rehabilitation of the individual dur- ing or following illness along pathways, e.g., jobs, housing, training, which lead to independent living and minimize permanent disability. In this monograph, treatment and rehabilitation (see Chapter IV) have been separated from primary prevention which requires spe- cial emphasis in the mental health context.

Disease causation in the public health model diagrammed on the following page is viewed as a dynamic interrelationship be- tween agent, host, and environment. Prevention then focuses on the

51

alteration of those factors contributing to the development of a disorder.

$$\text{host} \rightleftarrows \overset{\text{agent}}{\longleftrightarrow} \text{environment}$$

The "medical model" emphasizes physical (organic) aspects of host (human body) and agent (bacteria, poisons, malnutrition, etc.). A psychosocial (non-medical) model applies to mental health more generally than the medical model. In the psychosocial model, "host" is the person, and experience, e.g., love, stimulation, and life stress, may reflect both "agent" and "environment." A public health model must integrate both medical and non-medical approaches.

Primary prevention is probably the least understood and most neglected of all the public health concepts adopted by the mental health field. This situation prevails because, by and large, mental health workers are not very knowledgeable about public health approaches, and public health values tend to be perceived as subordinate to clinical values. Consequently, for most mental health workers the term prevention has become synonymous with, and restricted to, early diagnosis and treatment (secondary prevention). One result has been that primary prevention, when acknowledged at all, is viewed as being elusive, lacking a theoretical base, impractical, and difficult to evaluate.

The confused status of primary prevention appears to be a reflection of the so-called medical model which focuses on such questions as: "What are you preventing?" The inference one may draw from this query is that the prevention of mental illnesses is the sole objective of preventive work, and that prevention is impossible to achieve in the absence of known etiology. Yet, from a public health viewpoint, preoccupation with illness to the total exclusion of health is irrelevant, when one conceives of the levels of prevention as defined by Leavell and Clark (1965). In their conceptualization primary prevention has two distinct aspects—specific protection and health promotion.

Specific protection refers to those activities and measures, both proven and presumed, which aim to avoid the onset of mental illness, i.e., intercepting the causes of disease before they involve man. Examples of specific protection having medical-psychiatric validity include the prevention of sequelae of German measles by vaccination of women prior to pregnancy, the prevention of paresis by the cure of syphilis, and the prevention of some birth defects by adequate and timely prenatal care.

Too little emphasized in the mental health field is the concept of health promotion (or the promotion of mental health) which focuses on improving the quality of life and well-being, not merely averting pathology. Illustrative activities include premarital counseling, parent education, and effective use of leisure time. Health promo-

52

tion is based on a socio-psycho-cultural-educational rather than a medical model. The key concerns involve social competence, coping skills, and ego-strengthening measures rather than psychiatric symptomatology. A paramount issue becomes how well an individual or community may be rather than how sick.

Bower (1963, p. 837) has defined primary prevention of mental and emotional disorders as: ". . . any specific biological, social, or psychological intervention that promotes or enhances the mental and emotional robustness or reduces the incidence and prevalence of mental or emotional illnesses in the population at large. In this framework, primary preventive programs are aimed at persons not yet separated from the general population and, hopefully, at interventions specific enough to be operationally defined and measured."

In a somewhat similar way Caplan (1961, ix) views primary prevention as: ". . . the promotion of mental health, and the protection against the possibility of mental disorder by measures which interfere with the equilibrium of organism and environment prior to the onset of a pathological condition."

The phenomena of life crises provide a theoretical construct for primary prevention activities. Crisis theory maintains that intervention at critical life points can allay the onset of emotional disturbance. Such presumptions offer justification for the participation of mental health workers in activities such as mental health education, anticipatory guidance, a variety of forms of mental health consultation, and the training of vital community caregivers. Both crisis intervention and anticipatory guidance are based on the premise that optimal human development can be enhanced by actions which aim to provide increments of ego strength and coping activities for persons to handle successfully the normal life situations which often contain some element of stress (e.g., beginning school and the transitions from grade school to college, dating, engagement and marriage, pregnancy and childbirth, career decisions, death in the family, retirement, etc.) as well as those special calamities which though not universal do occur with significant frequency (e.g., divorce, premature birth, amputation, etc.).

EDUCATION IN HUMAN BEHAVIOR. A comprehensive primary prevention program requires a rationale for understanding how mental strains are produced and how mental energies can be released in satisfying and constructive activity. It appears that when an individual learns to appreciate the dynamics of behavior, chances for cooperative and mutually satisfying interaction are increased. Accordingly, primary prevention encompasses the development of educational programs for assisting people at all age levels to acquire an understanding of the basic dynamics of human behavior. The purpose of such educational programs is to enable people to begin to take an understanding approach to the behavior of others in contrast to the arbitrary and often arbitrarily punitive approach that presently characterizes much of human interaction. A background in behavior dynamics will, of course, enable an individual to take a more understanding approach to his or her own development—another important consideration in prevention. It is axiomatic in mental health training programs that understanding of self and others is indivisible, and the same principle applies in mental health education for the schools and community. The child, beginning at the primary level, can learn a more causal-understanding-considered approach in contrast to the very prevalent noncausal-arbitrary-judgmental approach. There are a number of learning programs operating at both the elementary and secondary levels. Some studies of the effectiveness of these programs have been published, (Muuss, 1960; Ojemann and Snider, 1964; Griggs and Bonney, 1970).

The development of such programs requires some extensive changes in the school, home, and community, and in the subject-matter areas usually found in the school curriculum that deal with human behavior. One aspect of the setting is the behavior of all teachers with whom the child comes in contact. In their daily interactions with pupils, the teacher can demonstrate a causal-understanding approach by recognizing that human behavior is a complex phenomenon, and that if one is to deal with it, one has to get some indication of how it developed, what it means to those involved in it, and what its effects tend to be. The pupil is subjected to a demonstration in human behavior every time any teacher of any subject area handles a behavior situation, whether it involves cooperation or conflict. Thus, for a program in behavioral science to achieve its full effect, all teachers require competence in dealing in an understanding way with daily behavior of students and colleagues. This in turn requires that teacher-training institutions have among their objectives that of assisting all teachers to acquire a background in the dynamics of human behavior and the emotional development needed to use that background. Requirements for teachers also apply to parents and community leaders; they are all demonstrators, and teachers in human relationships.

In summary, an effective program in primary prevention requires the development of programs and settings that will enable all children, as they advance in school, to acquire in an elementary way some awareness of and a sensitivity to the factors underlying or causing behavior, just as all of us acquired a beginning awareness of the factors operating in our physical environment. An elementary understanding and appreciation of factors operating in the physical environment enables us to interact with our physical environment in more satisfying ways. Evidence is accumulating that similarly an elementary awareness of the meaning of behavior helps us to develop more satisfying interactions with our social environment.

54

Mental health consultation, which may be considered under a broad definition of prevention is carried out in relation to the location where the individual is at risk, e.g., in the classroom or work situation. The consultant goes into the school and on the basis of observations and discussion, offers suggestions to modify the environment, or otherwise effect change. Interventions can take place at several levels in the institution, e.g., teacher, counselor, and administrator. The task of consultation is twofold: increasing the resources of other care givers, and modifying programs (organizations) to support better mental health (NIMH, 1970).

SCOPE OF PRIMARY PREVENTION. Bloom (1968) has identified three different types of primary prevention programs. In *community-wide programs* the target group is comprised of everyone residing in a specific area. Mental health education efforts via the mass media illustrate this approach. Second are *milestone programs* in which residents of a particular community file past the program at a specified time, thus acquiring "protection." An example would be a pre-kindergarten screening program which focuses on identification of children's strengths on behalf of optimizing the school entry experience. Third are the *high-risk-group programs* wherein groups especially vulnerable to specific stresses are identified and programs are designed to decrease or prevent the occurrence of that condition. The economically and socially disadvantaged, children of schizophrenic or alcoholic parents, and the isolated elderly are usually considered to be at higher risk than average for the development of certain emotional conditions, and some activities have been directed to these high-risk groups.

From a public health viewpoint, improvement in individual and interpersonal functioning is inextricably interwoven with the creation and maintenance of sound community institutions, e.g., home, school, social agencies, recreation, health, housing, welfare, etc. Thus, primary prevention is the concern of the entire community rather than an exclusive responsibility of mental health workers. In this connection it has been pointed out that: "Over the long term, the likelihood of psychological dysfunction is increased if specified basic resources are not adequately provided for the population; these resources may be classified as physical, psychological, and sociocultural." (Caplan and Grunebaum, 1967).

A developmental approach to programming in primary prevention should focus on (1) activities related to early child development and to increased parental competence, and (2) programs devoted to the mental health aspects of public school education and on adolescence. Such programs should be addressed to specific high-risk target groups such as the poor and the Black, on identified social agents such as parents and public school teachers and administrators, and within definitive social contexts where human development is accessible to social intervention such as the school, the development center and the mass media. Areas for action include the problems of high-risk pregnancy and the provision of adequate prenatal care, mental health promotion in optimal human development, socialization for competence and self-esteem, and new social policies for childrearing and child-care.

Although the community mental health movement is philosophically and practically based on public health considerations, skepticism prevails about the efficacy of primary prevention and its place in mental health work. This condition would appear to be less a function of the overall value of primary prevention than it is a result of the limited outlook of mental health workers due to their professional training. However, slowly but increasingly, mental health workers are embracing a belief that the amelioration of environmental factors is possible, practical, professionally rewarding, and within the scope of mental health work. Yet, beyond some training in mental health consultation, by and large, academic centers have not interpreted the needs of the field to include skills in primary prevention. Thus, most mental health workers remain captives of their limited orientations to mental health issues, and no major investment of mental health staff time goes into primary prevention. For example, a recent National Institute of Mental Health study indicated that only 4.7 percent of all expenditures and 6.6 percent of the total staff time in 205 federally funded community mental health centers were devoted to consultation and education services (NIMH, 1971 a,b).

For early case finding, it is necessary to 1) consider populations at risk and, 2) screen patients for mental health as they present themselves for general health care. It has been shown that recently bereaved widows have a higher rate of physical and psychiatric illness and mortality for eighteen months after the loss of their spouse. Their needs are met by non-specific therapy and such programs have been described by Caplan under "Widows for widows." In the problem-oriented family practice of Cross and Bjorn at Hampden, Maine, 70 percent of patients ended up with a psychiatric diagnosis, most often depression. Studies of family crisis intervention show that energetic home-based family treatment can reduce the need for hospitalization (Langsley, 1969).

Industry offers great opportunities for timely intervention, e.g., for alcoholism, marital problems, and depression, problems which manifest themselves in the workplace and too often are ignored until the trouble is far advanced. The family physician, the minister, and the lawyer can be allies in case finding along with the teacher in school. Questionnaires, e.g. on life stress, can be useful screening devices but they do not work when someone wants to get past the screen in order to obtain a job or avoid "stigma." Stress scores have

56

been developed for various common experiences, which enable people to identify themselves at risk, (Dohrenwend, 1974).

Careful history taking and examination of the newborn infant allows us to identify children at risk for behavioral problems and learning disabilities. Since these difficult children are stressful to a family, early identification, and intervention with parents, should reduce the level of disability in the child while strengthening the coping skills of the family.

A few principles should undergird secondary prevention: (1) ready accessibility, (2) prompt assessment of need for therapy, (3) continuity of care, and (4) minimization of institutional confinement. As with primary prevention these principles call for a comprehensive system of services sensitive to needs and problems of the community. The same complexities of service delivery discussed for primary prevention again obtain for secondary prevention.

The ferment surrounding the place of mental health in the total spectrum of human service programs suggests that a dichotomy of mental health functions, philosophies, and purposes is emerging represented on one hand by the essential need to continue to provide care, treatment, and rehabilitation for the mentally ill while on the other hand dealing effectively with the imperative for mental health workers to be actively involved in clarifying and strengthening the social system, promoting social competence, and fostering preventive programs. Within a decade, we may anticipate a realignment of mental health priorities and activities to create a balance between services for the emotionally disturbed and mentally ill and involvement in primary prevention practices.

Stephen E. Goldston, Ed.D., M.S.P.H.
Ralph H. Ojemann, Ph.D.
Ronald H. Nelson, Ph.D.

References

Bloom, B.L. 1968. "The Evaluation of Primary Prevention Programs," in Roberts, L.M., Greenfield, N.S., and Miller, M.H. (eds.), Comprehensive Mental Health, Madison: University of Wisconsin Press, pp. 118-119.

Bower, E.M., October 1963. "Primary prevention of mental and emotional disorders: a conceptual framework and action possibilities," American Journal of Orthopsychiatry, 33 (5), p. 837.

Caplan G., (ed). 1961. Prevention of Mental Disorders in Children, New York: Basic Books, Inc., p. ix.

Caplan, G. and Grunebaum, H. September 1967. "Perspectives on primary prevention: a review," Archives of General Psychiatry, 17:3., p. 332

Dohrenwend, B.S. and Dohrenwend, B.P. 1974. Stressful Life Events: Their Nature and Effects, New York: John Wiley & Sons. 340 pp.

Griggs, J. W. and Bonney, M.E. 1970. "Relationship between 'causal' orientation and acceptance of others, 'self-ideal' congruency and mental health changes for fourth and fifth grade children." Journal of Educational Research 63: 471-477.

Langsley, D. et al. 1969. The Treatment of Families in Crisis. New York: Grune & Stratton.

Leavell, H. R. and Clark, E. G. 1965. Preventive Medicine for the Doctor in His Community, New York: McGraw-Hill, Inc., 689 pp.

McClung, F.B. and Stunden, A.H. 1970, Mental Health Consultation to Programs for Children. PHS-2066. Bethesda: National Institute of Mental Health.

National Institure of Mental Health, Biometry Branch, "Statistical Note 42, Expenditures and Sources of Funds—Federally Funded Community Mental Health Centers 1969," 4 pp., February 1971, (a); "Statistical Note 43, Consultation and Education Services Community Mental Health Centers—January 1970, 7 pp., February 1971, (b).

Muuss, R. E. 1960. "The relationship between 'casual' orientation, anxiety, and insecurity in elementary school children." Journal of Educational Psychology 51 No. 3: 122-129.

Ojemann, R.H. and Snider, B.C.F. January 1964. The effect of a teaching program in behavioral science on changes in causal behavior scores." Journal of Educational Research 57, No. 5: 255-260.

Sprinthall, N. A. and Ojemann, R. H. "Psychological Education and Guidance: Counselors as Teachers and Curriculum Advisors." Unpublished paper. Minneapolis: University of Minnesota, Decmeber, 1972. (To be printed as chapter for Volume in Counseling, edited by Gary Walz and Robert Smith, to be published by ERIC.)

2. Family Formation and Development: The Primary Institution

> . . . while the family is the most dangerous of human institutions, it is also the only specifically human institution and may be revised or flouted at great peril; . . .
>
> —Reynolds Price
> The Washington Post, April 28, 1972

The family is the primary group in which most children in most societies are nurtured physically and emotionally, and made ready for entry into the larger social system of the community. The family not only provides food, shelter, clothing, and love, but also determines the major elements of health: genetic inheritance; primary physical and psychosocial environment; and skills to cope with the physical and social environment of the community.

Growing attention is being given to the importance of marital and family relations in health and mental health. Significant aspects of conjugal life correlate with health, health knowledge, and health-related behavior of husbands and wives (Pratt, 1972). For example, health is known to suffer after bereavement among younger as well as older married persons (Parkes & Brown, 1972) and—lest it be thought that remaining single is protective—the various states of non-marriage correlate with a number of increased statistical risks, notably hospitalization for mental illness; suicide; and violent injury or death.

In the context of health care, persons without families tend to overuse hospitals, partly because intermediate institutions are lacking. Similarly, where family conflict is unmanageable, overt mental illness in at least one member is a common result, and failure to deal with the whole family may lead to chronic institutionalization of the identified patient. In days past, the family doctor delivered health care at home; nowadays, although family medicine and family psychiatry are emerging as major trends, home care is still the province mainly of the public health nurse, although it, happily, is being rediscovered by others.

Family, from the latin *familia*, "household," is both easy and difficult to define; almost everyone is in one, but the forms are varied (ultimately no two are alike) and increasingly the variations are becoming both visible and respectable. The one-parent family, the

59

one-child family, the inter-racial marriage or adoption, the commune, the assembled family (multiple adoptions) and the child-free couple are among the new variations in family forms which were rare, disparaged, or both, not long ago. *Nuclear family* is the term used for the modern standard form in industrialized societies: husband, wife, and their children as the unit forming a household—in our society, representing over 80 percent of households. The *extended family* includes in the household other kin (grandparents, parents, children, aunts, uncles and cousins), and was the dominant form in the U.S. until the early 20th century when urbanization and high social and geographic mobility led to break-up of larger units. The problems emanating from this change have been widely if not conclusively studied and discussed.

Family formation refers to the process of marriage and childbearing. Until the 1970's it could be predicted that over 95 percent of Americans would marry; that all but one percent of couples wanted children and all but six percent would have them. To be non-married or a non-parent by choice was statistically atypical and psychosocially aberrant; such aberration, not surprisingly, correlates with higher risk for health and mental health problems, (especially for single men, who tend to be at the bottom of the heap psychosocially, while women who are single are often near the top). Now, patterns and trends of family formation are less predictable. Rather than a cause for alarm, these changes can be seen as the basis for a stronger family institution.

In view of the importance of the family for child development and adult well-being, it is striking to consider the haphazard way in which family formation has taken place until now, even after educational levels and medical/contraceptive technology become rather advanced. Through the late 1960's, most marriages took place with brides under 21; most first births happened to women under 22, the majority of which were unplanned, although not necessarily unwanted. Some of the results of premature marriage and parenthood are evident in our high divorce rate, unmatched in the world; perhaps 25 percent of marriages end in divorce, and the rate is twice that high for teen-age marriages (most of which involve a premarital pregnancy). The interval between marriage and first birth is short—18 months—even when premarital conceptions are excluded. The American family plan has been essentially to get married and have children early, and start contraception after desired family size was reached or exceeded. Accidents do happen and excess fertility—having babies not wanted by either or both parents—characterized many if not most families. Timing failures were even more common, as indicated with the first births, and birth interval planning was mediocre.

All this is changing at a rapid rate with the pill, the IUD, and abortion services, coinciding with a dramatic, steady fall in overall birth rate, out-of-wedlock births, and maternal mortality. This occurred around 1970, as the number of women remaining single over 21 dramatically increased; the marriage rate fell, although remarriages increased.

Some 300,000 out-of-wedlock births occurred annually in the U.S. in the late 1960's, each affecting not only mother and child, but grandparents and siblings, too. The implications for prevention are clear—primary prevention of unwanted pregnancy; abortion, prenatal care, and child-care support for young mothers.

Divorces increased to over 700,000 annually in the early 1970's, most of these affecting children (1.1 per divorce). Later marriage and parenthood can be expected to reduce this toll, although changes in divorce law and in the status of women may produce a temporary upsurge of divorce first. Since family difficulties lead to or are associated with many mental health problems—suicide, alcoholism, child psychiatric problems—attention to the family promises to help in all respects.

Important trends affecting the family include a high percentage of women in the work force, including mothers of young children. With this, a rather high unemployment rate affects some sectors of the population, especially the young, the poorly educated, and minorities. Welfare programs in the past contributed to family break-up with "man-in-the-house" rules; although these are now out-lawed, their effects linger on in many cases. High mobility affects families, with one in five moving to a new community each year. Long distance commuting, and suburban development which isolates children and schools from workplaces and cultural centers are also important factors. New town development and rapid transit construction offers a small counterpoise.

New horizons for family mental health include areas defined by Clark Vincent (1973) and others as marital and sexual health. Marriage is a durable and important social institution which has little real societal support. With smaller families, the quality of the marriage becomes even more important in that wife and husband have more time together before and after child rearing. Although the concept of lifelong marriage has been challenged, no alternative seems attractive to most people.

A rational approach to lifelong marriage include pre-marital and periodic post-marital counseling; attention to age differences to reduce the bereavement differential (9 million widows; 2 million widowers in the U.S.); and marital and sexual health care as a practical reality. (Abse, et al., 1974) Need is clear; ramifications abound for prevention of family breakdown, delinquency, psychosomatic illness and other problems.

Family psychiatry has emerged as a major new force in the past

20 years, partly in reaction to over specialization which obstructed the therapist's view of patient in his natural setting. An important adjunct in practically all other treatment approaches—inpatient, shock, medication, psychotherapy—family interviewing is more practiced by pediatricians and home economists than by older mental health professionals. It can be argued that any treatment is incomplete without attention to the family—in person, by the responsible therapist. This departs significantly from the traditional medical model, in which only the identified patient is treated, and a family is not regarded as a patient. But a public health model is easily applicable. In other words, it appears that a systems orientation characterizes both the public health worker and the family therapist more than the conventionally trained clinician.

Langsley, et al. (1971), demonstrated that a family approach can prevent hospitalization in about 80 percent of cases, with an ultimate cost of 1/6 that of hospitalization.

Utilization of these findings is rather slow to take place; cost-conscious programs, including third party health insurers, should pursue such leads, insisting that home-based family-oriented programs be part of insured mental health services. Closed panel health programs of the HMO type can explore family-oriented approaches in conjunction with other health services, including obstetrics, pediatrics, and emergency medicine. The *Peckham Experiment* in England is a relevant early model of health maintenance on a family basis in a neighborhood center (Pearse & Crocker, 1943).

E. James Lieberman, M.D., M.P.H.

References

Abse, W., Nash E. and Loudon, L. 1974. Marital and Sexual Counseling in Medical Practice, Harper & Row.

American Families: Trends and Pressures, 1973. 1974. Hearings, Comm. on Labor & Public Welfare, U.S. Senate. Washington, D.C.: USGPO 22 949-0.

Bernard, Jessie. 1972. The Future of Marriage. New York: World.

Langsley, D.G., Machotka, P. and Flomenhaft; K. 1971. Avoiding mental hospital admission: A follow-up study. Am. Journal of Psychiatry. 127: 1391-94.

Parkes, C. Murray and Brown, R.J. 1972. Health After Bereavement: A Controlled Study of Young Boston Widows and Widowers, Psychosomatic Medicine, Vol. XXXIV, No. 5, Medical Dept., Harper & Row, Publishers, Inc.

Pearse, I.H. and Crocker, L.H. 1943. The Peckham Experiment. London: Allen & Unwin.

Peck, E. and Senderowitz, J. (eds.) 1974. Pronatalism: The Myth of Mom and Apple Pie. New York: T.Y. Crowell.

Pratt, Lois. 1972. Conjugal Organization and Health, Journal of Marriage and the Family, February 1972.

Vincent, Clark. 1973. Sexual and Marital Health. New York: McGraw-Hill.

Other Sources

See Chapter on Parenthood for Associations.

3. Industrial Mental Health

> Health is the working-man's fortune, and he ought to
> watch over it, more than the capitalist over his lar-
> gest investments.
>
> —*William Ellery Channing (1780-1842)*

Industrial mental health may be defined as that branch of community mental health which takes as its functional catchment area the place of work rather than the place of residence. Why should the bedroom rather than the workplace be the geographical base for most community mental health programming? The place of work where individuals spend half their waking hours may become more significant in the coming years for several reasons:

(1) Specific job stresses may be etiologic factors in mental illness. As knowledge increases, the place of work may become important in primary prevention programs.

(2) Ongoing research suggests that the place of work is an effective arena for public education, early casefinding (secondary prevention) and mental health care programming.

(3) If as Freud suggested, the essence of mental health is to be able to love and to work, then control measures for mental illness must be closely tied to work rehabilitation and vocational training (tertiary prevention).

(4) The financing of mental health care may increasingly depend upon the work place. Collective bargaining has already resulted in insured mental health care for some 15 million Americans and their families: There are prospects that national health insurance may, in part, depend upon specific industrial insurance contracts. Health maintenance organizations already depend upon industrial units for much of their benefit marketing.

(5) Finally, emotional disturbance has profound effects on industry ranging from its impact on accident rates, absenteeism, work efficiency, quality and productivity, to blunders in high levels of management. Alcoholism and other forms of substance abuse may be of particular relevance.

ISSUES IN PRIMARY PREVENTION. There has been little research on the effects of specific work environments upon worker mental health. A notable exception is the series of studies on the emotional hazards of coal mining. Halliday (1943) points out that the rate of psychosomatic illness among coal miners is quite high and is specifically related to morale issues. Subsequent studies by Ross et al (1954), Heron and Braithwaite (1953) and Field et al., (1957) all focus on the relationship between hazardous occupations and emotional distress.

This may be compared with studies of soldiers under conditions of combat (see Stouffer et al, 1949 and 1950; Grinker and Spiegel, 1945 and Ginzberg et al, 1959). Studies done under peacetime conditions point out that hazard plus isolation is related to emotional breakdown syndrome among submariners (Ninow, 1963).

A second promising line of inquiry concerns the issues of role stress. Studies on peptic ulcer among executives, craftsmen and foremen by Dunn and Cobb (1962) indicate that the shop foreman caught in the crunch between workers under his charge and the executives to whom he reports has a much higher incidence of the disease. Kahn and Quinn (in McLean, 1970) have suggested a framework for analysis of the mental health of workers in terms of role stress.

Perhaps the richest literature concerns executive stress syndromes. Brady et al (1958) have suggested a highly controversial animal model based upon the occurrence of gastroduodenal ulcers in monkeys charged with the "executive" responsibility of preventing shocks to other monkeys. Holmes (1965) indicates that changing physical locations represents a significant emotional hazard. Many industries are built on frequent forced moves for their executives. Probably the emotional consequences for the executives' families as well as for the executives are negative. (Family Coordinator, 1973). Argyris (1964) has made concrete suggestions for "humanizing the organization." Such efforts could conceivably reduce levels of mental illness within an organization.

Recent lay literature contains frequent allusions to "blue collar blues." This syndrome, allegedly produced by the alienation of industrial line work combined with boredom and esteem loss has not been documented by systematic surveys (Siassi et al., 1974). One of the most comprehensive studies was done on Detroit auto workers: ". . . workers express predominantly favorable feelings toward their job and life situation." (Kornhauser, 1965, page 9.) These gross studies of large populations are not designed to pick out specific mental health hazards of specific work roles: research on this is most needed in the future.

MENTAL HEALTH PROGRAMS IN THE PLACE OF WORK. During the past decade, a series of innovative programs have been developed centering around the place of work (see Noland, 1973; Spiro et al., 1975). Beginning with Phillip Wagner's (1967) cooperative efforts with the Grocery Clerks Union in Los Angeles, these programs in many ways operated as "functional" community mental health center catchment areas. The population is well-defined. The advisory board consists of labor and industrial leaders who can provide strong community input. Prevention programs can take into account both issues of work and issues at home. Treatment methods can be utilized and take into account worker needs. Specific education efforts can be developed involving shop stewards and union committeemen. The programs have been found effective in secondary prevention (early casefinding) and in preventing hospitalization (Spiro et al, 1975).

More traditional is the field of industrial mental health consultation. The industrial psychiatrist usually hired by management engages in casefinding and evaluation. In some settings programs have been developed for the specific problem areas, but in the absence of specific union negotiated benefits, it is difficult to establish a comprehensive mental health care program. Thus patients are generally referred to practitioners in the community (for fuller reviews, see Powles and Ross, 1966; McLean, 1970).

WORK REHABILITATION. The importance of return to work and the rehabilitation of the mentally ill has received increasing emphasis in recent years. Neff's landmark monograph, *Work and Human Behavior* (1968) provides a behavioral science frame of reference for the understanding of work and its significance. Black (1966) provides a survey of industrial therapy for the mentally ill in Europe. Goldstone and Collins (in McLean, 1970) survey current concepts of occupational rehabilitation. Many community mental health centers at the present time include vocational rehabilitation workers or are closely linked to state vocational programs. Along with the development of halfway houses and home care programs for the chronic mentally ill, these rehabilitation programs are vital in tertiary prevention.

THE FINANCING OF MENTAL HEALTH CARE THROUGH INDUSTRIAL PROGRAMS. A relatively recent development has been initiation of mental health services in prepaid programs created through collective bargaining. Glasser (1969), Stone and Caruthers (1972) and Spiro et al (1975) have described procedures which provide viable alternatives to fee-for-service financing and to government financing of community mental health facilities.

The mechanism is similar to the health maintenance organization (HMO) in that it involves prepayment for a defined group of individuals based either on cost financing or capitation based financing. Indeed in some areas, prepaid mental health services have been attached to prepaid health plans (the forerunners of HMO's) to provide a full package of psychiatric benefits (see Tureen and Workman, and Green in Noland, 1973; Fink et al., 1969, and Spiro et al., 1975).

EFFECTS OF MENTAL HEALTH PROBLEMS ON INDUSTRY. Consequences of emotional distress on the job receive considerable attention perhaps because of the significant economic consequences for work establishments. High levels of distress may cause expensive labor turnover (Hakkinen and Toivainen, 1960; Markowe and Barber, 1953), diminished productivity (Schavhter et al, 1961) and absenteeism (Hinkle and Plummer, 1952). The relationship of emotional factors and accidents has received attention since the work of Dunbar (1944). Accident proneness as an etiologic factor remains a disputed issue (Schulzinger, 1956; Froggatt and Smiley, 1964; Selzer et al, 1968 and Hirschfield and Behan, 1963).

The heavy expenses incurred from emotional ill health, alcoholism, and more recently drug abuse may serve as important motivating factors in securing management cooperation and support for industrial mental health programs.

OVERVIEW. Figure I provides a hypothetical schema for the relationship between job factors, illness and job consequences. It seems plausible that job stress, role stress, job insecurity and alienation, specific toxic working conditions and forced geographic mobility may be important contributing causes not only to diminish motivation and the "will to work" but also to syndromes of mental illness and, indirectly, physical illnesses.

Such ill health undoubtedly in turn contributes to absenteeism, diminished productivity, executive and blue collar error with diminished product quality, job turnover, intra-organizational strife and stress and industrial accidents. Additionally, it would seem apparent that these problems lead to personal economic loss, family distress, and personal distress. These clusters of consequences in turn may operate in a vicious cycle both to intensify illness syndrome and increase job stress.

Herzl R. Spiro, M.D.

References

Argyris, C. 1964. Integrating the Individual and the Organization. New York: Wiley.
Brady, J. V., Porter, R. W., Conrad, D. G. and Mason, J. W. 1958. Avoidance behavior and the development of gastroduodenal ulcers. J. of the Experimental Analysis of Behavior, 1:69-72.
Dunbar, Flanders. 1944. Symposium on Psychosomatic Medicine: Susceptibility to Accidents. Medical Clinics of North America, 28:653-662.
Dunn, J. P. and Cobb, S. 1962. Frequency of peptic ulcer among executives, craftsmen and foremen. J. of Occupational Med., 4:343-348.
Field, L. W., Ewing, R. T. and Mayne, D. W. 1957. Observations on the relation of psychosocial factors to psychiatric illness among coal miners. The International J. of Social Psychiatry, 3:2, 133-145.
Fink, R., Shapiro, S. and Goldensohn, S. 1969. The 'filter-down' process to psychotherapy in a group practice medical care program. Am. J. Public Health, 59:245-260.
Froggatt, P. and James, S. 1964. The concept of accident proneness: A review. Brit. J. of Industrial Med., 21:1-12.
Ginzberg, E., et al. 1959. The Ineffective Soldier: Lessons for Management. Vol. I: The Lost Divisions. Vol. II: Breakdown and Recovery. New York: Columbia University Press.

Grinker, R. R. and Spiegel, J. P. 1945. Men Under Stress. Philadelphia: Blakeston.

Hakkinen, S. and Toivainen, Y. 1960. Psychological factors causing labour turnover among undergraduate workers. Occupational Psychology, 34:15-30.

Halliday, J. L. 1943. Dangerous occupation: psychosomatic illness and morale; A study based on the investigation of incapacitating disorders in underground miners. Psychosomatic Med., 5:71-84.

Heron, A. and Braithwaite, D. 1953. Emotional stability in colliery workers. British J. of Industrial Med., 10:27.

Hinkle, L. E. and Plummer, N. 1952. Life stress and industrial absenteeism. Industrial Med. and Surgery, 21:8, 363-375.

Hirschfeld, A. H. and Behan, R. C. 1963. The accident process: I. etiological considerations of industrial injuries. J. of the Am. Med. Assoc., 186:193-199.

Kahn, R. L., Wolfe, D. M., Quinn, R. P., Snoek, J. D. and Rosenthall, R. 1964. Organizational Stress. New York: Wiley.

Kornhauser, A. 1965. Mental Health of the Industrial Worker. New York: Wiley.

Markowe, M. and Barber, L. 1953. Mental health in relation to the labor turnover of unskilled workers in a large industrial establishment. British J. of Preventive and Social Med., 7:205-210.

McLean, A. A. and Taylor, G. C. 1958. Mental Health in Industry. New York: McGraw-Hill.

Neff, W. S. Work and Human Behavior. 1968. New York: Atherton Press.

Ninow, E. H. 1963. Submarine psychiatry (peacetime working conditions). Archives of Environmental Health, 6:579-587.

Noland, R. L., Ed. 1973. Industrial Mental Health and Employee Counselling. New York: Behavioral Public.

Powles, W. E. and Ross, W. D. 1966. Industrial and Occupational Psychiatry. in Arieti, S., Ed. American Handbook of Psychiatry. Vol. 3, New York: Basic Books.

Ross, W. D. 1956. Practical Psychiatry for Industrial Physicians. Springfield, Ill.: Charles C. Thomas.

Ross, W. D., Miller, L. H., Leit, H. H. and Prici, F. 1954. Emotional aspects of respiratory disorders among coal miners. J. of American Med. Assoc. 156:484.

Schachter, S., et al. 1961. Emotional disruption and industrial productivity. J. of Applied Psychology, 45:201-213.

Schulzinger, M. 1956. The Accident Syndrome: The Genesis of Accidental Injury, A Clinical Approach. Springfield, Ill.: Charles C. Thomas.

Selzer, M. L., Rogers, J. E. and Kern, S. 1968. Fatal accidents: the roles of psychopathology, social stress, and acute disturbance. Am. J. of Psychiatry, 124:1028-1036.

Siassi, I., Crocetti, G. and Spiro, H. 1974. Loneliness and dissatisfaction in a blue-collar population. Archives of Gen. Psychiatry. 30:261-265.

Spiro, H., Siassi, I. and Crocetti, G. 1975. Cost financed group practice I, II, and III. J. of Nerv. and Mental Disease. In press.

Spiro, H., Siassi, I. and Crocetti, G. 1975. Fee-for-service insurance versus cost financing. Am. J. of Public Health, 65:2, February.

Stone, J. and Caruthers, V. 1972. Innovations in program and funding of mental health services for blue collar families. Amer. J. of Psychiatry, 128:1375-1380.

Stouffer, S. A., et al. 1950. The American Soldier, Studies in Social Psychology in World War II, Vols. I-IV. Princeton: Princeton University Press, 1949.

Taylor, G. C. 1967. Executive Stress in McLean, A., Ed. To Work is Human. New York: Macmillan Co., 153-160.

Summary Diagram

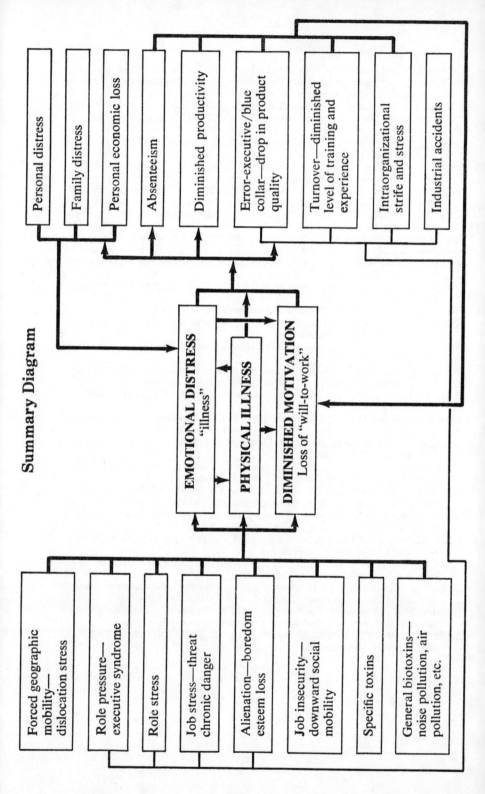

IV. | Meeting Mental Health Needs

1. Treatment

Getting to know someone, entering that new world,
is an ultimate, irretrievable leap into the unknown.
The prospect is terrifying. The stakes are high. The
emotions are overwhelming. The two people are
reluctant really to strip themselves naked in front of
each other, because in doing so they make themselves vulnerable and give enormous power over
themselves to one another.

—*Eldridge Cleaver*
Soul on Ice, 1968

Perhaps 70 percent of patients who come to the office of a general physician suffer from overt or covert emotional disturbances.
Secondary prevention is concerned with the early case finding,
prompt diagnosis and treatment of medical and psychosocial problems. Treatment should start before difficulties overwhelm the person or before they become resistant to early intervention, including
medication, psychotherapy and social support. But many mental
health problems are poorly defined and as yet lack specific treatments; we must therefore rely heavily on non-specific therapy.
Everyone dreams of the kind of practice where a specific diagnosis
is made leading to a specific treatment and, of course, cure or
improvement.

In mental health non-specific treatment is often the only treatment available, and it is a perfectly valid treatment approach, properly monitored and evaluated. Seldom can etiology be related to
treatment in the manner to which the medical profession is generally accustomed. A patient may have schizophrenia, for which we do
not know a specific etiology; phenothiazine medication may help
greatly—and we do not understand how! If further investigation
should reveal that our patient was heavily genetically loaded for
schizophrenia, this would not help much in treating him. Evaluation
of treatment can and often must, therefore, take place independent
of known etiology. As in physical medicine, successful treatment
may be either the first clue or the final proof of etiology.

A child may have a reading disability for which we have no specific treatment. Yet by looking at the child's total life situation and
designing some positive additions to the child's life, such as a big
brother relationship, we may find that we can improve the child's

reading performance. This is an example of the proper use of non-specific therapy. For any patient population then, we must be clear about what specific therapy and what non-specific therapy is available.

Individual psychotherapy, group psychotherapy, family therapy, therapeutic community, and milieu therapy can all be understood from our model of non-specific therapy. Assignment of patients to one modality vs. another is done on the basis of theory, clinical judgment, availability of resources, and cost: accidents of fate more often than knowing which kind of therapy is best for which kind of patient. The treatment received by a particular patient is not so much determined by his illness as by the therapist he or she happens to call on. The only rejoinder to the accusation that therapists mainly "do their own thing" is that good therapists are well acquainted with several modalities and have the acumen and objectivity to determine when someone else's approach may be more beneficial to the patient.

Specific Therapy. Psychopharmacology has added a great deal to this list in the past two decades. Specific therapies include the phenothiazines and other drugs for schizophrenia, the tricyclics and MAO inhibitors for depressive illness, lithium for manic-depressive illness, minor tranquilizers for anxiety reduction, various anti-depressant drugs (paradoxically) for the control of hyperactivity in children and the reduction of learning disability, drugs for the control of alcoholism, and for the control of epilepsy-like syndromes and vitamins for organic brain syndromes, particularly those secondary to alcoholism. Two other modalities of more-or-less specific therapy are electro-convulsive therapy (ECT or shock) for involutional (late life) depression, and behavior modification for the relief of specific symptoms.

Non-Specific Therapy. Psychological or psychodynamic treatment systems include individual (adult, child), group, marital (couple) and family therapy. Various schools or theoretical orientations include psychoanalytic (Freudian et al), client-centered (Rogerian), transactional, and behavioral (operant and classical conditioning). The eclectic therapist, one who absorbs and reflects a variety of influences, and remains open to new evidence, theory and experience, is becoming much more prominent.

Individual psychotherapy predominates over other forms of treatment in this country: recent reports from Community Mental Health Centers indicates a ratio of 4 or 5 to 1 of individual over family or group sessions. By a variety of names—casework, counseling, or therapy—the one-to-one process or "talking cure" has the most emphasis in training and service programs, the most prestige, the most books and articles in professional journals, and the most research—although it is far from being a well-understood process.

A psychotherapy group (Yalom, 1970) usually includes six to ten people meeting one or more times a week with a therapist for either short (less than one year) or long term treatment. Group therapy is efficient in terms of therapist's time. It is reality-based in that problems can be worked through in patients' transactions with each other. The ¬roup provides a generally supportive environment, allows members to give as well as receive help.

In marital or family therapy (Sager and Kaplan, 1972; Slater, 1964) the couple or family is the "patient." The family is seen as a system wherein members are interdependent, the actions of each affecting the others. The identified patient is viewed by the therapist as acting out a family problem; the particular symptoms he presents are seen as indicative of not just his individual difficulties but a dysfunction in the family system as a whole. The therapist helps the family understand established but unrecognized patterns of behavior and maladaptive ways of handling feelings toward one another.

Psychodynamic, or psychoanalytic, theory can be considered the "bedrock" upon which psychotherapeutic interventions rest. The dynamic school contrasted with organic or behavioral approaches relates personal history and subjective experiences to the problems that the individual has now. Transactional therapy is dynamic in a different sense, relying on insight into here-and-now interactions or encounters rather than the uncovering and understanding of past issues and relationships. Psychodynamic and transactional modes of treatment are often combined in individual, family and group psychotherapy.

Behavior therapy (Krumboltz & Thoresen, 1969; Lazarus, 1971), derives its basic theoretical concepts from the learning theories of Skinner and Pavlov. This relatively new, well-researched approach generally uses short-term therapy based on rewarding (reinforcing) desirable patterns and extinguishing (by not reinforcing) undesired behaviors. The approach is generally ahistorical, and insight is not essential in bringing about change. This form of treatment has been most successful when the presenting complaints are highly specific, describable in terms of behavior. Recently behavioral therapy has been applied to the treatment of couples, families, and groups. (Becker, 1971; Stuart, 1970; Patterson, 1971). The foci of such interventions include building skills (couples communications, anxiety management, assertive training) and learning to reinforce desirable behaviors and ignore those which should be extinguished.

Rogers' client centered therapy requires "unconditional positive regard" for the troubled person, whose difficulty is treated as an impediment to growth rather than illness. Techniques of reflection and clarification in a context of empathy and warmth have much in common with other forms of individual psychotherapy.

The highly publicized encounter group movement is a popular

73

and controversial form of psychological growth enhancement or treatment. The types of groups and competence of their leadership vary enormously. Advocates of encounter groups are encouraged and optimistic about the social implications of people learning to listen and respond to each other with feeling (Rogers, 1970). However, the psychological and psychiatric community has been critical because of lack of control over who runs encounter groups, the lack of screening of those who join, and the lack of evaluation of outcomes, a criticism that can apply, however, to most forms of nonspecific treatment.

Whether the clients predominantly served are "ill" is also questionable. Many such groups are offered to enhance self-awareness, etc., without reference to illness or cure. Nevertheless, many people join such efforts because of problems, diagnosable or not, and there have been a few reports of participants suffering ill effects. The same could be said of conventional psychotherapy or psychoanalysis, although more control exists there through licensing, professional associations, and malpractice actions.

Another significant trend in the mental health field is the use of paraprofessionals. This movement has been given great impetus through the work of Carkhuff (1969), Guerney (1969), Reiff and Reissman (1965), and others.

Carkhuff has identified a number of qualities in helpers which have been found to account for much of therapeutic change. These qualities include accurate empathy, nonpossessive warmth, genuineness and ability to confront. Ivey (1972) has operationalized these in a systematic manner in order to train interested lay helpers so that they are able to communicate effectively. Non-professionals can "do the things that the professional cannot do, such as, establish a peer relationship, take an active part in the patient's life situation, empathize with his style of life . . ." (Reiff, 1966, p. 546). Minuchin, Haley and others have trained high school graduates to do family therapy with success.

Under the supervision of professionals, paraprofessionals are being used in a variety of ways including crisis intervention, big brother and other supportive relationships, hotlines, peer counseling, drug and abortion counseling. One of the major challenges to the licensed mental health professional is to learn consultation and training skills so as to more effectively mobilize this potentially large mental health manpower resource.

As new modalities such as family and behavior therapy become more accepted, training programs will broaden their scope and their graduates will have a larger repertoire of therapeutic skills, probably with less allegiance than now to one treatment process or theory. Therapists will intercede in a variety of configurations other than one-to-one, by working with couples, families, and groups.

As specific treatment elements are identified and refined, systematic procedures will be developed and used in both professional and paraprofessional training. The difficulty in instituting major paraprofessional programs will probably center around the emerging relationship between the two groups. Professionals are paid a great deal more, have more power, and are expected to be more competent, although in certain areas paraprofessionals may be more effective, especially if they work with indigent populations, which professionals tend to avoid.

Treatment needs can become obscured by therapists' predispositions, i.e., the bias of the practitioner. The analyst, learning theorist, encounter groupist, medical practitioner, and community worker each view the patient's problem from a limited vantage point. Rarely to be found is an effective treatment system offering coordinated medical, social and psychological services (Huessy, 1973). This problem must be solved, or we will become more isolated and irrelevant to each other and our patients.

Craig Messersmith, D.Ed.
Hans R. Huessy, M.D.

References

Barten, Harvey, H. and Bellak, Leopold (Eds.) 1972. Progress in Community Mental Health, Volume II, New York: Grune & Stratton.

Becker, W.C. 1971. Parents are Teachers. Champaign, Illinois: Research Press.

Bellak, Leopold (Ed.) 1964. Handbook of Community Psychiatry and Community Mental Health, New York: Grune & Stratton.

Carkhuff, R. R. 1969. Helping and Human Relations: A Primer for Lay and Professional Helpers, Vol. I and II. New York: Holt, Rinehart & Winston.

Golann, Stuart E. and Eisdorfer, Carl (Eds.) 1972. Handbook of Community Mental Health, New York: Meredith Corporation.

Guerney, B.G. (Ed.) 1969. Psychotherapeutic Agents: New Roles for Non-professionals, Parents, and Teachers. New York: Holt, Rinehart & Winston.

Huessy, Hans R. (Ed.) 1966. Mental Health with Limited Resources, New York: Grune & Stratton.

Huessy, H. R. 1974. Some historical antecedents of current mental health dilemmas. Psychiatric Annals, Vol. IV, No. 12 (December).

Ivey, A. 1971. Microcounseling: Innovations in Interviewing Training. Springfield, Illinois: Charles C. Thomas.

Krumboltz, J. D. and Thoresen, C. F. 1969. Behavioral Counseling. New York: Holt, Rinehart & Winston.

Lazarus, A. A. 1971. Behavior Therapy and Beyond. New York: McGraw-Hill.

Patterson, G. R. 1971. Families: Application of Social Learning to Family Life. Champaign, Illinois: Research Press.

Reiff, R., Riessman, F. 1965. The indigenous nonprofessional. Community Mental Health Journal Monograph 1.

Reiff, R. 1966. Mental health manpower and institutional change. American Psychologist, Vol. 21, pp. 540-548.

Roberts, Leigh M., Halleck, Seymour L. and Loeb, Martin B. (Eds.) 1966. Community Psychiatry. Madison: Univ. of Wisconsin Press.

Rogers, C. R. 1970. Carl Rogers on Encounter Groups. New York: Harper & Row.

Sager, C. J. and Kaplan, H. S. (Eds.) 1972. Progress in Group and Family Therapy. New York: Brunner/Mazel, Inc.

Satir, V. 1964. Conjoint Family Therapy. California: Science & Behavior Books, Inc.

Stuart, R.B. 1971. Trick or Treatment: How and When Psychotherapy Fail. Champaign, Illinois: Research Press.

Yalom, I. D. 1970. The Theory and Practice of Group Psychotherapy. New York: Basic Books.

2. Rehabilitation

Absence of occupation is not rest;
A mind quite vacant is a mind distress'd.

—William Cowper (1731-1800)

Tertiary prevention is essentially *rehabilitation*, a term that once referred largely to occupational and work therapy undertaken in the hospital in an effort to prevent, to the extent possible, the sequelae of mental disorder and of confinement in an institution. But our concept of rehabilitation has broadened considerably in recent decades. With the advent of community psychiatry and its emphasis on keeping the patient functioning in his own environment, or returning him to that environment as quickly as possible following hospitalization for acute illness, rehabilitation has assumed tremendous importance. It involves the utilization by persons with a wide variety of skills and training, of techniques and tools for helping the patient cope with dysfunction or disability of any kind—mental, emotional, physical, and/or social. It encompasses everything from promoting legislative measures encouraging the hiring of handicapped persons and arranging special work conditions and schedules for them, to helping long-hospitalized patients regain social abilities, to teaching children with learning disorders to read at a level that will enable them to function in a normal school situation. In short, rehabilitation may be regarded as both a means and an end of all mental health intervention; it is a process, a system of methods, an objective, the focus of a wide range of professional activities, and the cornerstone of mental health services.

It is increasingly recognized (WHO, 1967) that rehabilitation is inextricably related to diagnosis and treatment. Lamb (1971) has attempted to differentiate between treatment and rehabilitation suggesting that, whereas the latter focuses on reality factors and is concerned with changing behavior, treatment seeks to modify intrapsychic phenomena and basic character structure. Black (1971), however, sees no necessity for such a distinction, provided adequate mental health services are available to meet the patients' needs: "Perhaps all treatment of mental illness—medical, psychological, or social—is rehabilitation. And perhaps the rehabilitation process is in reality a form of treatment." The preventive aspects of rehabilitation have been underscored by one of the pioneers of community psychiatry, Querido (1966), who noted that rehabilitation could *avert* as

77

well as reduce the sequelae of an illness and help to keep it from becoming chronic.

There is general agreement that rehabilitation is as concerned with overcoming disability and dysfunction as it is with alleviating clinical symptoms. Clinical recovery and social rehabilitation are closely related but not necessarily concomitant achievements. Frequently patients no longer have clinical signs of mental disorder but—because of the length of their illness, social or institutional isolation, or other factors—can no longer function in normal society; or the reverse situation may prevail: patients may be capable of adequate social and economic functioning but continue to show signs of clinical disturbance. We have more or less accepted the reality that we do not have the means of *curing* all or most psychoses; but we can help patients live with or overcome their residual handicaps and maximize their social, familial, physical, psychological, and occupational competencies.

The introduction of the use of psychotropic drugs marked a turning point in mental health care and gave added impetus to rehabilitative efforts. With the aid of the drugs, many patients improved or became more accessible to psychotherapy within the hospital and were eventually able to return to the community. To counteract some of the effects of the institutionalization so aptly described by Goffman (1961), Gruenberg (1967) and Zusman (1966), some hospitals began to alter their structure and practices in an attempt to create therapeutic communities (Jones, 1967) and better prepare patients for life "outside." Rehabilitation thus became an integral part of treatment and the ultimate goal of mental health services.

Work has always been a part of mental hospital life and presumably a means of rehabilitation. Patients have often been assigned to housekeeping duties in the wards, laundry, or kitchens. As Bartlett (1967) has pointed out, this work is a form of peonage and generally is for the benefit of the institution, not the patient. Such duties do little to equip patients with the skills that will help them to reenter the community successfully. Other forms of work in hospitals have been by way of diversion, ways of filling idle hours.

Now, however, efforts are being made to introduce work as therapy that is both practical and constructive. Occupational therapy, once meant to serve as recreation, has gradually developed into a way of preparing patients for more meaningful activity in sheltered workshops and industrial therapy programs. Under the influence of successful Soviet (Ross, 1964) and British (Wing, 1963) experience in preparing patients for a return to normal or sheltered work environments, many U. S. hospitals have begun to change the nature of patients' work activities.

In the United States, vocational rehabilitation agencies that used to deal largely with the physically disabled have begun to serve large numbers of mental patients discharged from hospitals. That their early efforts have been marked by a high rate of failure (Neff, 1968) may be attributed to our appalling lack of transitional and supportive services in the community and to the absence of legislative incentives to hire former mental patients.

Community-based/oriented rehabilitation services have a number of functions. Chief among them are assisting the long-hospitalized patient to adjust to community life and providing treatment and rehabilitation for the acutely ill *within* the community so as to prevent social disruption of their daily lives and thus help to keep their condition from becoming chronic. Community efforts are directed toward overcoming dysfunction, aiding patients to meet crises without breaking down, and teaching them coping skills so that they can function adequately in their normal environment.

A wide variety of community facilities are needed to provide secondary and tertiary prevention: community mental health centers; day, night, and weekend treatment and rehabilitation centers; crises centers, general hospitals with psychiatric departments that offer a full range of patient services; halfway houses and other supervised and subsidized group residences (Rutman, 1970); and sheltered and industrial workshops and patient-oriented businesses (Early and Magnus, 1968).

We still have a long way to go before we can arrive at the kind of community system described by Gruenberg (1972): Community care of the mental patient refers to a particular way of organizing the psychiatric service delivery system. The underlying principle is to arrange mental patient care so as to maximize the preservation of the patient's assets. This is done by paying close attention to his abilities to function as an independent member of his home community. The attention given seeks to preserve, strengthen, fortify and supplement his personal identity with his home community so as to help him continue as a living, working, playing and struggling member of that community.

But we seem to be moving in the direction of establishing networks of supportive services and community-based teams with responsibility for public mental health care within defined geographic areas, adapting to the American scene some aspects of European models (Gittelman, 1972).

The trend, as we have seen, is toward keeping patients in the community, with the aid of the necessary services. Becker (1972) has described the reorganization of one sectorized community mental health service that is striving to provide acute and rehabilitative treatment rather than the usual inpatient and outpatient care. And a recent report by the British Department of Health and Social Services (1972) has stressed the integration of treatment and rehabilitation, aimed at maintaining the patient in his environment, as the principal role of psychiatry. All inpatient, outpatient, and rehabilitative services should be combined in a comprehensive service provided by a single therapeutic team. Whether rehabilitation calls for a specialized function and personnel is a matter for further study.

Research and work are needed in a number of other areas as well. Fairweather and co-workers (1969) have shown that simply returning patients to the community is not enough, that many former mental patients cannot "make it" without special help. The most effective ways of supplying and coordinating that help require further investigation. Attention should also be given to legislative measures for subsidizing support systems for mental patients: reserved jobs, tax incentives for employers who hire handicapped persons, and the establishment of wage subsidies, sheltered workshops, and other aids to keeping patients in the community.

We need more information on what types of habilitative and rehabilitative efforts need to be made to avert dysfunction. Our whole approach to treatment may need rethinking; we should perhaps be concentrating on immediate coping skills and raising functional competence rather than nonspecific therapy. What might be the effects of legislation that would permit mental patients to work fewer hours (with the same compensation); reduce stressful working conditions; and provide home assistance (cooks, housekeepers, child-child workers) where needed? Might the developing French treatment/rehabilitation technique of home treatment by crisis intervention teams (Gittelman, 1973) be applicable in the United States? One can envision that, in the future, rehabilitation concepts—aimed at restoring the patient to maximal functioning—may have an impact on all types of treatment, and that a kind of synergy will take place.

All rehabilitative efforts are bound to be expensive. But weighed against the enormous human suffering endured by the mentally dysfunctional and their families, the cost to society of repeated or prolonged hospitalizations, and the economic and social losses that inadequately functioning mental patients represent, the price may be insignificant.

In summary, people are not getting services that they may need (i.e., medical, mental health, dental, legal, educational, etc.) and some that are given have not been shown to be particularly effective. Services are not always defined in ways that are understandable to the consumer. Needs do not occur in isolation, they occur in clusters. This calls for a human service network devoid of the negative stigma attached to some services, mental health in particular. Services need to be understood in terms of normal life situations. This is a major task for the decades ahead.

Martin Gittelman, Ph.D.
Irving Blumberg

References

Bartlett, F. L. 1967. Present-day requirements for state hospitals joining the community. New Eng. J. Med., 109, 635.

Becker, R. E. 1972. The organization and management of community mental health services. Community Mental Health Journal, 8,292.

Black, B. J. Foreward. In H. R. Lamb, Rehabilitation in the community.

British Department of Health and Social Services. 1972. Rehabilitation: Report of a subcommittee of the Standing Medical Advisory Committee. London:HMSO.

Early, D. F., & Magnus, R. V. 1968. The industrial therapy organization. Brit. J. Psychiat., 114, 335.

Fairweather, G. W., Sanders, D. H., Maynard, H., & Cressler, D. L. 1969. Community Life for the Mentally Ill: An alternative to institutional care. Chicago: Aldine.

Gittelman, M. 1972. Sectorization: the quiet revolution. Amer. J. Orthopsychiat. 42(1), (January).

Gittelman, M. Recent developments in European rehabilitation programs for mental patients. In Handbook of Community Psychiatry, L. Bellak, editor. Vol. III (in press).

Gittelman, M. 1973. Recent developments in French public mental health. Psychiatric Quarterly, Vol. 47, pages 509-520, No. 4.

Gittelman, M. 1974. Coordinating mental health systems: a national and international perspective. American Journal of Public Health, Vol. 64, No. 5, pgs. 496-500.

Goffman, E. 1961. Asylum. Garden City, New York: Doubleday.

Gruenberg, E. 1972. NYSDB A.P.A. Bulletin, (March).

Jones, M. 1967. The current place of therapeutic communities in psychiatric practice. In H. Freeman and J. Farndale (Eds.) New Aspects of the Mental Health Services. London: Pergamon.

Kabanov, M. M. Rehabilitation of the mentally ill. Soviet Neurol. Psychiat. International Arts and Sciences Press, Vol. V, No. 3-4.

Lamb, H. R. 1971. Rehabilitation in Community Mental Health. San Francisco: Jossey-Bass.

Neff, W. G. 1968. Work and Human Behavior. New York: Atherton Press.

Phillips, D. L. 1963. Rejection: a possible consequence of seeking help for mental disorders. American Sociological Review, Vol. 28, 963-972.

Querido, A. 1966. Seminar on rehabilitation and preventive psychiatry. Copen: W.H.O. Cited by Volovik, V. N. (1973) Differentiation of forms and methods of rehabilitation in clinical psychiatry. Sov. Neurol. Psychiat., Vol. 5, No. 17.

Ross, M. 1964. Extramural treatment techniques. In L. Bellak (Ed.), Handbook of Community Psychiatry. New York: Grune & Stratton, Inc.

World Health Organization 1967. Psychiatric Care and Rehabilitation. Copenhagen: W.H.O., Euro 0261.

Wing, J. K. 1963. Rehabilitation of psychiatric patients. Brit. J. Psychiat. 109, 635.

Other Sources

Journals:
Community Mental Health Journal
International Journal of Mental Health
Hospital and Community Psychiatry

Associations:
International Committee Against Mental Illness
National Council of Community Mental Health Centers
National Rehabilitation Association

3. Socio-Cultural Intervention Techniques

> With a basic conviction that only those reasonably
> familiar with the rank and file of recoverable and
> non-recoverable disorders produced by our
> communities can be safe guides, the writer has
> always stood firmly for leadership by hospitals serv-
> ing definite districts, and thus bringing about a first-
> hand knowledge of the acute disorders and also of
> the residuals of what refuses to mend, and maintain-
> ing at the same time a close contact with the
> community.
>
> —*Adolf Meyer, M.D.*
> *First International Congress*
> *on Mental Hygiene, 1930*

There are at least three levels of human functioning that provide intervention strategies for mental health workers. The first is
the physiological level including interventions which, in some way,
alter the physiological makeup of the organism, e.g. drugs and proper nutrition are physiological interventions. The second is the psychological level. At this level interventions would include individual,
group and family therapy. The objective is to alter the thoughts, feelings or behavior of the organism or system through psychological
processes. In the third or socio-cultural level, the organism is seen
as a part of the social network and is viewed synonymously with its
environment. Intervention strategies are aimed at altering the context in which clients or citizens develop positive self concepts, roles
and communication patterns. The rationale is that a change in the
context will help bring about changes in the clients. The first two
levels of intervention and techniques are well known to mental
health workers in contrast to the third, with which this section is
concerned, and which includes community organization, social action and self-help groups.

Community organization has been discussed in the social
science literature, primarily that of applied anthropology, rural sociology and social work (Selig, 1973). Until recently, with the advent
of the Civil Rights Movement, the rediscovery of poverty, and the attempts to organize the American populace in the anti-war movement, community organization has received relatively little attention, except for a celebrated few (Alinsky, 1946). It may be defined

82

as a process in which communities become functional in problem-solving, the values and attitudes of persons in the community become shared, to some extent, and the people feel an increased sense of belonging, participation and power over the course and conduct of their lives.

For mental health workers, community organization can be viewed from at least two standpoints, as a helping strategy and as prevention. Community organization can involve persons in the community regardless of present need for mental health services, thereby decreasing the risk of future need. It may be especially useful in communities that lack well-defined leadership, have poor communication patterns, high rates of crime and delinquency, many broken families, and that are economically depressed (Leighton, 1959). Residents working effectively on local, relevant, real-life problems can help raise their self-esteem and sense of control over their lives and this may decrease the risk of psychosocial difficulty.

Only a small proportion of persons needing some form of mental health intervention are actually receiving it. In addition, the traditional forms of intervention, such as psychotherapy and group therapy, may not be appropriate for some needs and persons, and even if they were, there will probably never be sufficient numbers of practitioners to meet the need. Factors such as ethnic background, religion, sex, age, marital status, definitions of health and illness, attitudes towards the sick role, and social network have all been shown to influence a person's perception of his problems, as well as the actions he may or may not take to deal with them. (Gurin, 1960; Myers, 1968; Richart, 1968; Srole, 1962; Wechsler, 1967). Therefore, it seems timely that mental health workers consider socio-cultural strategies to reach persons who need help but, for a variety of reasons, are not receiving it.

There is also a need for socio-cultural strategies to be applied to prevention. Currently existing programs and strategies, such as Family Life Education, Anticipatory Guidance, Crisis Intervention and Consultation, represent primarily the psychological level of intervention. Mental health workers should intervene at the socio-cultural level as well. Although people argue that major economic and political changes should be the goal, this is not our focus here. Changes in these systems could, however, result from community organization, social action and self-help groups.

Community Organization. There are two main approaches to community organization: the community development model and the conflict model. The following three principles are basic to both approaches; however, they differ in relation to the fourth principle.

1. The organizer must thoroughly and completely understand the values, attitudes, perceptions and lifestyle of his clients whom he hopes to organize.

2. The worker needs to begin his organizing by attempting to meet the felt needs of his clients. People do not respond to vague, theoretical, ideological issues as well as they do to current everyday problems. For example, it might be more effective first to attempt to get a traffic light at a dangerous local intersection, than to organize a program about mental health. Once a group is organized around a relevant visible issue, it is easier to tackle larger or vaguer issues.

3. The organizer needs to use people indigenous to his client group, involving the identified leaders in the community as the front-line organizers. Where leaders don't exist, as in some disintegrated communities, the organizer is to find and develop leadership potential among the people, after which the worker can decrease his role to that of an enabler and supporter.

4. The organizer needs, to some degree, to fit his ideas and/or the organization efforts into existing organizations in the community. In this way, duplication of effort might be avoided, and programs which might threaten certain community people, if they were seen as alien, might have a greater chance of success. This is an evolutionary rather than a revolutionary approach. A more revolutionary approach would differ in its adherence to this principle. The latter approach (conflict model) stresses conflict and differences between the persons to be organized and the external environment. It stresses the need to gain power, which is achieved either by money or by organization, usually the latter. The organization is catalyzed by accentuating divergent aims and interests of local people and others.

Social action is a strategy used to effect change within some limited or specified area of concern. It is not revolution, since it does not seek to alter the entire culture, social structure or community norms. The target of change is usually one issue in a system or community,—e.g. housing, health care, safety—and usually that issue is responsible for some conflict between persons or groups. The same principles that apply in community organization also apply, but the goals are more limited and concrete in social action. There must be an understanding of and consensus on the problem and the objectives, who the opposition and protagonists are, what strategies are appropriate, and what people are prepared or not prepared to do in order to gain their objectives.

Social action techniques are becoming increasingly popular in mental health agencies. Clark (1969) states, "this I believe to be the essence of serious and effective community public therapy. It combines the treatment of individuals, the techniques for the treatment of the society, and a persistence in confronting those aspects of the society, that would resist the changes necessary before effective functioning in mental health becomes possible in the masses of the underprivileged and privileged."

Self-help groups e.g. Alcoholics Annonymous are organizations made up of persons who share a common problem, and who hope, through their joint efforts, to help themselves as well as persons like themselves. Of the many ways to treat problems of alcohol abuse, AA is regarded as one of the best. It is able to reach and effectively help thousands of people who have not responded to other forms of mental health intervention. Self-help groups exist in the areas of alcohol and drug abuse, divorce, parents without partners, tenants' councils, women's groups, ex-convicts' rehabilitation, etc. Basically, two kinds of processes can take place in self-help groups. One is that the group members can engage themselves and others in talking about their problems, their efforts and mutual successes in combatting them, and to develop empathy and solidarity with other members in the organization.

The second basic process concerns an outside task which the group undertakes together.

Andrew L. Selig, M.S.W., Sc.D.

References

Alinsky, Saul D. 1946. Reveille for Radicals, Chicago: Univ. of Chicago Press.

Clark, Kenneth B. 1969. Social Conflict and Problems of Mental Health. Journal of Religion and Health, 8(3).

Cumming, Elaine. 1968. Unsolved Problems of Prevention. Canada's Mental Health, Supplement 56, (January-April).

Goodenough, Ward H. 1963. Cooperation in Change, New York: Russell Sage Foundation.

Gurin, G., J. Veroff and Sheila Feld. 1960. Americans View Their Mental Health. New York: Basic Books.

Leighton, Alexander H. 1959. My Name is Legion. New York: Basic Books.

Leighton, Alexander H. May 1965. "Poverty and Social Change", Scientific American, 212(5).

Myers, Jerome and Lee Bean. 1968. A Decade Later: A Follow-Up of Social Class and Mental Illness. New York: John Wiley & Sons, Inc.

Richart, Robert H. and Lawrence M. Millner, 1968. "Factors Influencing Admission to a Community Mental Health Center." Community Mental Health Journal, 4(1), 27-35.

Ross, Murray A. 1955. Community Organization: Theory and Principles, New York: Harper & Brothers.

Selig, Andrew L. 1973. Prevention of Mental Illness and Community Organization: A Review and Annotated Bibliography. Catalog of Selected Documents in Psychology, Am. Psychol. Association, 3 (Spring).

Srole, Leo, T. S. Langner, S. T. Michael, M. S. Opler and T. A. Rennie. 1962. Mental Health in the Metropolis: The Midtown Manhattan Study, 1, T. A. Rennie Memorial Series in Social Psychiatry. New York: McGraw-Hill.

Wechsler, Henry and Thomas F. Pugh. 1967. Fit of Individual and Community Characteristics and Rates of Psychiatric Hospitalization. American Journal of Sociology, 73(3), 331-338.

Wittenberg, Rudolph M. 1948. Personality Adjustment Through Social Action, American Journal of Orthopsychiatry, 18, 207-221.

4. Economics of Mental Health

> The subject which I treat is not alone humanitarian.
> Its economic importance can hardly be overesti-
> mated. The ravages of insanity cost the world mil-
> lions of dollars and thousands of lives each year.
>
> —Clifford W. Beers
> A Mind that Found Itself (1908)

Mental health problems absorb an appreciable amount of the health care dollars annually expended in the United States. Escalating costs of the medical sector of our economy must be kept in mind when considering the rising costs of providing mental health care.

Total health expenditures have risen between 1950 and 1974 from 6.4% to 7.8% of the gross national product. The rate of increase in medical care costs during recent years has been 10-12%; in recent months, the overall prices of medical care have climbed at a projected annual rate of 17.6%.

The cost of mental illness as conservatively measured in 1971 was $26.2 billion. The cost of mental health services (including the expenses of prepayment through insurance) totaled $10.4 billion—equivalent to 14% of all health care expenditures in the nation. The remainder of the cost is attributable to construction, training, research, and the costs of social welfare and medical care programs and grant and service programs in direct care which are responsive to the needs of the mentally ill.

Additional evidence is now available demonstrating that the rate of mental illness and alcoholism rises with a fall in the economy, such as a recession or depression. Dr. Harvey Brenner's book, Mental Illness and the Economy, concludes that the instabilities in the national economy are the single most important source of fluctuations in mental hospital admissions rates. Finally, the loss to society caused by acute and chronic mental illnesses must be considered in economic terms—loss of productivity, increased dependency—in addition to the human suffering involved.

The last few decades have brought a major change in the attitudes of individuals and governmental policy makers toward mental illness. Increasingly, mental health is regarded as a basic right of all members of society. In the United States, the provision of mental health services has been greatly affected by changes in the role of

TABLE I
The Cost of Mental Illness

Cost Center	Cost
Direct Care	**$10,110,364,000**
State & County Mental Hospitals	2,696,024,000
Other Public Mental Hospitals	412,646,000
Private Mental Hospitals	281,348,000
General Hospitals	980,616,000
Community Mental Health Centers	284,955,000
Freestanding Outpatient Clinics	481,219,000
Drugs	537,590,000
General Medical Services	358,325,000
Nursing Homes	2,666,357,000
Rehabilitation and Halfway House Centers	194,916,000
Children's Programs	303,915,000
Private Practice Psychiatrists	833,117,000
Private Practice Psychologists	79,336,000
Training and Fellowships	**187,053,000**
Research	**398,612,000**
Construction	**603,664,000**
Management	**788,332,000**
Indirect Costs	**14,135,239,000**
Due to Death	3,487,437,000
Due to Disability	7,404,275,000
Due to Patient Care Activities	3,243,527,000
Total Cost	**$26,223,264,000**

Source: The Cost of Mental Illness (NIMH, DHEW Contract No. ADM-42-74-82 (OP)), p. 147.

the federal government in the financing of medical care services generally. The Medicare and Medicaid programs, initiated in 1966 to provide medical care services for the elderly and the poor, are estimated to spend more than $400 million annually on psychiatric services. Established a decade ago, federally supported Community Mental Health Centers now represent an alternative to high cost institutionalization. Training programs for many types of paraprofessionals have helped increase manpower available to provide mental health services at lower unit costs.

While substantial improvements in the financing of mental health care have been made in the United States in the past decade, mental health still takes a back seat in many governmental programs. Several national health insurance proposals presented in the 93rd Congress excluded mental health care. Medicare places major limitations on the extent of coverage for mental illness, and the types of health professionals who will be reimbursed for rendering mental health services.

To ascertain whether adequate financing for mental health care services is worthwhile for governments to undertake, it is useful to summarize the benefits yielded by mental health care. Many economists and mental health professionals have hesitated to apply benefit-cost analysis to mental health care because of the difficulties of gauging the effectiveness of preventive or therapeutic services, and the difficulties of quantifying the benefits of improved mental health. With present levels of knowledge, these difficulties are formidable indeed. However, benefit-cost analysis can indicate what types of social gains are likely to stem from mental health care, and what form of government intervention would help realize them.

As in the case of medical care, mental health services yield benefits to individual consumers and to the society at large. The latter include better-functioning members and the altruistic reward of knowing that those in need of care receive it. Our society has increasingly asserted that medical care is a basic right, not to be denied or regarded as charity. Moreover, people have more than an altruistic interest in seeing that others get medical care. *Maintaining and restoring mental health* leads to a more productive economy—the rewards of which accrue not only to the worker and his family, but to all members of society. A working member of society contributes to all public goods through taxes. Without early and adequate mental health care on the community level, many potential taxpayers could require major investment of public resources in themselves as patients rather than as productive workers. Improving the mental health of parents presumably leads to healthier, happier, and better-adjusted children who will require fewer resources in child guidance programs and later, as adults, less treatment for mental illness. Effective mental health care may contribute to reductions in crime, delinquency, drug abuse, accidents, and suicides. These societal benefits amply justify use of public funds to ensure that all have access to preventive and prompt restorative mental health services.

In addition to the economic benefits to be gained from mental health care, equity grounds also dictate a public policy which recognizes the inability of many individuals to pay for adequate health care. In the absence of government intervention, the lowest income members of society are likely to receive too little or inferior quality care even though these people have the highest incidence of severe mental illness. Financing policies, therefore, must be designed to avoid an inequitable distribution of benefits among income groups.

Studies of prepaid group practice plans indicate that an economic benefit of providing adequate mental health care services is the favorable impact on utilization of other health services. Studies in California, New York, and Washington, D. C. during the 1960's indicated that after brief mental health treatment members of such HMO-like organizations generally saw physicians less frequently and had fewer hospitalization episodes. A recent study shows that counseling during first pregnancy leads to fewer obstetrical and pediatric problems—evidence of the value of a preventive service (Shereshefsky et al, 1974).

Not only do social benefits and goals of mental health services call for a major public role in financing, but the rather unique market for such services requires some special measures. For most goods and services, the government does not tell consumers what, how much, and from whom they should buy. In the case of mental health, many persons receiving services are not in an adequate position to assess the need for treatment, the value of the services rendered, and the best source of treatment. On the supply side of the market, providers of services must act as the patient's agent in making decisions about the amounts and types of care required—but the provider also stands to benefit financially from the decisions made. This conflict of interest may lead to a less than optimal outcome, particularly if the patient equates price of care with quality, and the provider offers a limited range of treatments.

Several policies for dealing with this conflict are possible. One is to provide better information to patients, e.g., on alternative services available from different providers, prices charged for services, and where possible, on effectiveness or patient satisfaction. Another approach is to enhance client involvement in the provision of mental health services by establishing consumer advisory boards, including representatives of the community on hospital boards, review boards, etc. Still another approach used recently with considerable effect is to assert and protect patients' rights through legal means.

Given the imperfections in the mental health market, careful study should be made of the cost-effectiveness of care in different settings. For example, one major shift which has occurred in the last two decades is the change from custodial care in state mental hospitals to earlier, more active care in community hospitals and outpatient clinics. How does maintenance in, or quicker return to, the community affect treatment outcome? What are the cost savings generated by shifting from institutional to outpatient care? Comparative costs of alternative modes of delivering care—for example by professionals in private practice, free-standing clinics, hospitals, and community mental health centers—would be invaluable to policy makers attempting to devise better organizational systems.

Another type of useful investigation concerns the possibilities for substituting different types of medical manpower. What tasks can be adequately, perhaps even more effectively, performed by community-based, specially trained new mental health practitioners, so that scarce specialized manpower may be used more effectively? To what extent will the inclusion of even modest mental health services enhance the awareness and competence of other health professionals, via consultation and collaboration opportunities?

In summary, several features of the mental health care system call for at least three major roles for the public sector. First, it is important that the federal government sponsor research and demonstration for innovative methods of organizing and delivering care—such as the use of paraprofessionals and the establishment of ambulatory centers. Second, the mental health and public health professions should make available a wider range of information on the efficacy of preventive programs (e.g. marital and child development counseling), on different modes of treatment, and on costs and benefits of alternative sources of care. Patients' rights should be enhanced through involvement of consumer groups and adequate legal protection. Third, public financing programs covering mental health benefits must be designed in such a way as to ensure equitable access to mental health care for all persons, avoiding financial burdens to the recipient of treatment, while at the same time encouraging efficiency in the delivery system.

As indicated, the prime locus for mental illness treatment continues to shift from high cost, long-term institutional care to shorter-term, lower-cost outpatient care. This change makes adequate insurance coverage possible, as demonstrated by the Federal Employees Health Benefits Program (FEHBP). Under the Government-wide Service Benefit Plan (Blue Cross-Blue Shield), the mental health benefit consists of unlimited inpatient and outpatient coverage, with a 20% co-insurance for outpatient services after a general $100 deductible. After 1967, when this liberal benefit was implemented, there were small increases in the health benefits as a percent of total medical benefits paid, as would be expected with a new program. Since 1970, that rate of increase has slowed and appears to be leveling off at 7.3%.

Data are also available for 1972 from the Civilian Health and Uniformed Services (CHAMPUS) program, which has an essentially

90

TABLE II
Total Blue Cross-Blue Shield (FEHBP)
Mental and Nervous Benefits Paid
(Amounts in Millions)

	Mental Benefits	Total Benefits	Percent
	Blue Cross-Blue Shield		
1960-65	$40.2	$1040.4	3.9
1966	13.2	277.2	4.8
1967	18.1	336.8	5.4
1968	24.8	405.0	6.1
1969	30.4	480.9	6.3
1970	41.1	601.9	6.8
1971	49.1	698.9	7.0
1972	54.3	760.4	7.1
1973	61.6	848.2	7.3

Source: *Office of the Actuary, U.S. Civil Service Service Commission, 1974.*

unlimited mental health benefit. The average cost per user beneficiary of outpatient mental services was $478; although some patients had many visits, the majority were handled with 15 visits. The average cost per user beneficiary of inpatient services was $2,258; this relatively high cost is affected by the number of youngsters receiving long term care in residential treatment facilities.

Despite the experience of both the FEHBP and CHAMPUS programs, mental illnesses remain inadequately covered by most insurance plans and virtually all National Health Insurance (NHI) proposals.

The most common type of benefit package advocated in proposed legislation provides: (1) 30 days inpatient treatment for mental illness and 60 days partial hospitalization; (2) Outpatient services in a comprehensive community care center equivalent to the costs of 30 visits to a private practitioner, or office services of a private practitioner equal to half the cost of 30 visits; (3) Extended care (day or night hospital, or halfway house) 100 days/year; Home care 100 visits/year; and (4) Cost-sharing: $100-150 general deductible, 25% co-insurance, which may be reduced by additional subsidy for the economically disadvantaged.

Many practitioners believe that this benefit package is inadequate, that it is too arbitrary, discriminates against certain types of patients and, though convenient to actuaries, is dysfunctional to practice. The data on current insurance programs suggest that a benefit package should not be limited in terms of number of days and visits. Instead, it should provide for inpatient and outpatient care boundaried by a careful process of peer review and other quality control mechanisms, that take into account and balance both humanitarian and cost considerations. If cost sharing mechanisms are included to shift a portion of the costs to patients, they should be designed to fall equitably on those able to pay.

Several issues for the mental health field remain to be resolved prior to implementing a sound National Health Insurance program. At present, scarce resources are maldistributed so that only a few areas of the country have adequate manpower and facilities. This could be aggravated by NHI unless there are incentives for practitioners to work in underserved areas. The degree of interchangeability among mental health practitioners is also unresolved, and the use of alternate manpower to alleviate the shortage creates additional problems for planners trying to predict the costs of a large manpower base. Also unresolved is the manner of determining the most cost-effective modality of care, how insurance can be used to shift utilization toward outpatient and preventive rather than inpatient and remedial services.

Peer review, now rapidly developing, should create guidelines for appropriate care without blindly imposing restraints on services through arbitrary limits on benefits.

Whenever NHI is introduced it must address itself to these substantive issues or unforeseen inequities and poor practice will result. Insurance should lessen the barriers to early care, lessen the financial burden of catastrophic illness, and support high standards of quality in service delivery, i.e., ongoing evaluation.

Karen Davis, Ph.D.
Mildred B. Arrill., M.A., M.S.W.
Steven S. Sharfstein, M.D.

References

Auster, Simon. 1969. Insurance coverage for 'mental and nervous conditions:' developments and problems. American Journal of Psychiatry. 126:5, November.

Bennet, A.E., Hargrove, E.A., Engle, B. 1953. Voluntary health insurance and nervous and mental disease. Journal of the American Medical Association. Vol. 151.

Brenner, M. Harvey. 1973. Mental Illness and the Economy. Cambridge, Mass.: Harvard University Press.

Bureau of Community Health Services, Health Services Admin. 1974. Inclusion of Mental Health Services in Health Maintenance and Related Organizations. DHEW. Publication No. (HSA) 75-13019.

Burnell, George. 1971. Financing mental health care: appraisal of various models. Archives of General Psychiatry. Vol. 25, July.

Chodoff, Paul. 1974. Medical insurance and private practice. Psychiatric Annals. 4:1, January.

Cohn, Jerome and Hunter, Harold. 1972. Mental health insurance: a comparison of a fee-for-service indemnity plan and a comprehensive mental health center. American Journal of Orthopsychiatry. 42:1, January.

Cummings, Nicholas, and Follette, William. 1967. Psychiatric services and medical utilization in a prepaid health plan setting. Medical Care. V:1, January-February.

Fink, Raymond. 1970. Financing outpatient mental health care through psychiatric insurance. Mental Hygiene. 55:2, April.

Fink, Raymond, Shapiro, Sam, and Goldensohn, Sidney. 1970. Family physician referrals for psychiatric consultation and patient initiative in seeking care. Social Science and Medicine. 4:3, September.

Fink, Raymond, et al. 1969. Changes in family doctors services for emotional disorders after addition of psychiatric treatment to a prepaid group practice program. Medical Care. 7:3, May-June.

Follman, Joseph. 1970. Insurance Coverage for Mental Illness. New York: American Management Association.

Gibson, Robert W. 1974. The use of financing to control the delivery of services. Psychiatric Annals. 4:1, January.

Gibson, Robert W. 1973. The effect of financing on psychiatric care. American Journal of Orthopsychiatry. 43:3, March.

Gibson, Robert W. 1973. Utilization and costs of psychiatric care: key issues in the coming debate on national health insurance. American Journal of Orthopsychiatry. 43:4, July

Goldberg, Irving, Krantz, Goldie, and Locke, Ben. 1970. Effect of a short-term outpatient psychiatric therapy benefit on the utilization of medical services in a prepaid group practice medical program. Medical Care. 8:5, September-October.

Goldensohn, S.S. and Haar, E. 1972. A prepaid group practice mental health service as part of a health maintenance organization. American Journal of Orthopsychiatry. 42:1, January

Green, Edward L. 1969. Psychiatric services in a California group health plan. The American Journal of Psychiatry. 126:5, November.

Kurzman, Paul A. 1973. Third-party reimbursement. Social Work. 18:6, November.

Muller, Charlotte and Schoenberg, M. 1974. Insurance for mental health: a viewpoint on its scope. Archives of General Psychiatry. Vol. 31, December, pp. 871-878.

Myers, Evelyn S. 1970. Insurance coverage for mental illness: present status and future prospects. American Journal of Public Health. 60:10, October.

National Institute of Mental Health. 1974. Report of the Work Group on Health Insurance. Insurance for Mental Health: Trends in the Delivery and Financing of Mental Illness Services in the United States. (draft report).

NIMH, DHEW publication No. (HSM) 73-9117: Financing mental health care in the United States: a study and assessment of issues and arrangements. 182 pp.

Nelson, Scott H. 1973. A new look at national health insurance for mental health. American Journal of Orthopsychiatry. 43:4, July.

Newman, Donald E. 1974. Peer review: a California model. Psychiatric Annals. 4:1, Jan.

Reed, L.F., Myers, E.S., and Scheidmandel, P.L. 1973. Health insurance and psychiatric care: utilization and cost. Washington, D.C.

Reed, L.S. et al. 1972. Health Insurance and Psychiatric Care: Utilization and Cost. American Psychiatric Association.

Scheidmandel, Patricia L. 1974. Utilization of psychiatric services. Psychiatric Annals. 4:1, January.

Shereshefsky, P.M. and Yarrow, L.J. eds. 1973. Psychological Aspects of a First Pregnancy. New York: Raven Press. 373 pp.

Spiro, H.R., Crocetti, G.M., and Siassi, I. 1975. Fee-for-service insurance versus cost financing: impact on mental health care systems. American Journal of Public Health. Vol. 65, No. 2. pp. 139-143.

U.S. Dept. of Health, Education, and Welfare, National Institute of Mental Health, and the American Hospital Association. 1973. Financing Mental Health Care in the United States: A Study and Assessment of Issues and Arrangements. Wash., D.C.: GPO.

Weiner, Hyman J. et al. 1973. Mental Health Care in the World of Work. New York: Association Press.

V. | The Service System

1. Planning and Administration

> He seemed greater than a private citizen while he
> was one, and by the consent of all would have been
> considered capable of government, if he had not
> governed.
>
> —*Tacitus (c. 60-120)*
> *History, I*

The increasing development of comprehensive community mental health services for the emotionally disturbed and mentally retarded in the mid-twentieth century has initiated dramatic changes in mental health administration and planning, requiring accommodation to community involvement, consumerism, decentralization, new organizational relationships with other public and private human service systems, and new patterns of staffing and manpower. Outcome evaluation of programs has become important for their continued existence and expansion. The dominance of isolated institutions for long-term incarceration of patients has passed, and been replaced by a more complex system with multiple levels of accountability.

The necessity for management skills has increased with the greater diversity and complexity of community mental health centers, clinics, and state hospitals. It is not surprising, therefore, that a study of eight centers indicated that the professionals involved saw administration as the area most needing improvement—this was agreed upon by 50% of the professionals, in contrast to less than 10% citing the need to improve treatment (Glasscote, et al, 1969).

To strengthen administrative planning and competence a variety of new systematic approaches have been introduced but so far have been utilized in only a few mental health facilities. It will take probably another decade before most mental health facilities utilize sophisticated management techniques as standard operating procedure.

One such management technique is Key Factor Analysis. This new technique is an application of general systems theory to mental health in an eight-step process: (1) Statement of purpose of the organization. (2) Derivation of a set of objectives from the statement of purpose in terms of the output expected including target dates and levels of accomplishment. (3) Grouping of objectives for concurrent accomplishment using the same resources. (4) Derivation of key factors, required by management to measure success or failure in meeting objectives. (5) Derivation of key indicators, to document movement within a key factor. (6) Assemble information needed to quantify each key indicator. (7) Statement of goals, or changes sought in a time-specific, content-limited, and action oriented fashion, quantified according to time and level of accomplishment. (8) Program and budget preparation based on goals.

A variety of data systems have also been developed for use in various combinations of management organization of the system and individual patient treatment. These systems include the NIMH-sponsored Multi-State Information System (MSIS) (Rockland State Hospital, New York) focused on individual patients; computerized cost-accounting (Range Mental Health Center, Minnesota); state data systems (Washington) to coordinate and plan state-wide; an event monitoring system (Prairie View Mental Health Center, Kansas) on patients and staff activity; and a management information system (Hall-Mercer Center, Philadelphia) for individual patient monitoring and management planning-research. The introduction of such information systems has led to systematic management procedures in some organizations, e.g., continuity of care and emergency service procedures, use of case mangers to ensure continuity of care for individual patients, systematic periodic review of cases, and billing procedures to ensure sustaining revenue. All too few mental health facilities, however, are at the point where they are using these and other sophisticated information systems.

Operations research, a process long used in industry, including the health industry, is employed in a few mental health operations for balancing resource allocation, component staffing, planning, individual patient scheduling and routing, centralized supply and pharmacy services, facility design, optimum data processing services, facility location, program effectiveness and community impact analysis, treatment versus prevention cost-effectiveness, etc. Operations research involves the use of mathematical models to arrive at optimal solutions in situations involving conflicting goals. The steps in operation research problem solving are: (1) defining the problem; (2) constructing the model; (3) deriving a solution from the model; (4) testing the model; (5) implementing the solution; and (6) observing the effects of changes on the actual operation of the system. Such an approach is ideally suited to gaming problems or simulation of situations where there is a conflict of interest, allocation problems for limited resources, inventory problems, scheduling difficulties, equipment and facility replacement problems, search problems to maximize the probability of detection with the use of a given set of resources, and sequencing or routing problems to order the sequence of events to minimize time and effort needed to perform a set of given tasks.

Too many administrators are either inadequately trained or do not like administrative tasks, or both. The clinician-turned-administrator often views program management as a mechanistic process lacking in human contact. In recent years, serious attempts have been made to resolve this problem through NIMH-sponsored university programs. More trained administrators have been appointed as directors of facilities regardless of discipline, a move which the American Psychiatric Association approved in 1973, recognizing that administrative skill does not inhere in a particular mental health profession.

With Community Mental Health Center (CMHC) legislation in 1963 came federally-mandated catchment area planning for geographic sectors of 75,000-200,000 people. Catchment planning often produced arbitrary designs which ignored existing medical or health care trade areas, local political boundaries, community cohesiveness, and transportation networks.

While catchmenting did stimulate state mental health planning to an unprecedented degree, the creation of "poverty" catchment areas to receive a greater share of federal funding resulted in boundaries conflicting with local political and community realities. Catchmenting across health planning regions and health service trade areas further estranged mental health from general health and made more difficult the inclusion of mental health in long-range health planning.

Some areas have endeavored to come to grips with these vexing dichotomies. In Connecticut, for example, a state-sponsored task force recommended the development of "functional service catchment areas." Under this concept, state plan catchments, meeting federal standards as to size, would fit within larger service areas to conform with community boundaries. Most states however, adhere to their original catchment plans, forcing local level planning to follow an unrealistic formula.

The major issue in mental health administration involves the structure and organization of mental health services in the future, inasmuch as the CMHC is viewed by many as a transitory stage. The present Center model only prescribes required and optional services, not organizational dimensions. So, a wide variety of Center formats have developed over the past decade, with far too little research on which formats are successful, and what new systems might be developed.

Regarding the role of community mental health, the past decade brought much controversy over the "medical model" versus a nonmedical or "social model." Advocates of the medical model acknowledge that community mental health has ventured afield from traditional medical-psychiatric operations. Inasmuch as mental "illness" and mental retardation have been correlated with everything from poverty to anomie to air pollution, we can expect growth of social models and social action in community mental health.

To deal with conflict among the primary mental health professionals—nurses, psychiatrists, psychologists, and social workers—the administrator must create good egalitarian teamwork to control rivalry, while ensuring that in any potential struggle for dominance among the disciplines, each will not promise more than it can do, only to leave a disappointing gap in actual services.

Mental health professionals are trained to operate on the basis of rather subjective judgment, but there must be objective evaluation of programs if they are going to continue to receive support for their existence and development. Evaluation remains the weakest link in present-day mental health operations. As more evaluation and applied research is undertaken, and the paths of dissemination of information become better defined, mental health services will become increasingly systematized. With the increasing number of trained administrators, mental health services will become more viable in planning and effective in operation.

The advent of a national health insurance plan with mental health coverage, the broader development of Health Maintenance Organizations with mental health services, and the establishment of regional health authorities as advocated by the Council on Economic Development, will serve to link mental health with both physical health and broader human services, in a more rational and more humane system.

Gare Le Compte, Ph.D.

References

Ackoff, Russell L. and P. Rivett, A Manager's Guide To Operations Research. New York: Wiley, 1967.

Barton, W., Administration In Psychiatry. Springfield, Illinois: Charles Thomas, 1962.

Bellak, L. (editor), Handbook Of Community Psychiatry and Community Mental Health. New York: Grune and Stratton, 1971.

Halpert, H. P., N. J. Horvath, and J. P. Young, An Administrator's Handbook On The Application Of Operations Research To The Management Of Mental Health Systems. Washington, D.C., NIMH.

Feldman, Saul. Administration of Mental Health Services. Springfield, Ill.: Charles C. Thomas.

Glasscote, R. M., J. N. Sussex, E. Cumming, and L. H. Smith. The Community Mental Health Center: An Interim Appraisal, Washington, D.C. Joint Information Service of the American Psychiatric Association of National Association for Mental Health, 1969.

Golann, S. E. Coordinate Index Reference Guide To Community Mental Health. New York: Behavioral Publications, 1969.

Lamb, H. R., D. Heath, and J. P. Downing (editors), Handbook of Community Mental Health Practice. San Francisco: Jossey-Bass, 1969.

Pierson, P. H. A Statistical Information System For Community Mental Health Centers. Washington: Public Health Service Publication 1963, 1969.

Taube, C.A. Community Mental Health Center Data Systems: A Description Of Existing Programs. Washington, D. C.: Public Health Service Publication 1960, 1969.

Other Sources

Journals:
Community Mental Health Journal (Behavioral Publications, New York City)
Administration in Mental Health (NIMH publication)
Abstracts of Hospital Management Studies (University of Michigan)
Administrative Science Quarterly (Cornell University)
Behavioral Science (University of Michigan)
Evaluation: A Forum for Human Service Decision-Makers (Program Evaluation Project, Minneapolis)
Health Services Research (Hospital Research and Education Trust)
Hospital and Community Psychiatry (American Psychiatric Association
Journal of Health and Social Behavior (American Sociological Association)

Associations:
Association of Mental Health Administrators
National Council of Community Mental Health Centers

2. Evaluation Research and Its Utilization

Them as won't be ruled by the rudder must be ruled
by the rock.

—*Eden Phillpotts (Eng. 1862—1960)*

Evaluation is a small but vital part of the overall system of care, which, formerly neglected, is now receiving extraordinary emphasis. As conceptualized by Edward Suchman (1967, p. 33) evaluation is a continuous, circular process starting and ending with the formation of values. Assuming that certain therapeutic activities have value, objectives are set, then criteria are formulated for the measurement of these objectives, programs are planned and put in operation. Then evaluation takes place, leading to possible changes in the value assumptions, and the entire process repeats itself.

Rational input into policy formulation—i.e. scientific confirmation or modification of working hypotheses—is one major benefit of this process. Evaluation plays an essential role in administrative decision-making, permitting the program to meet the requirements of accountability to funding sources and to the public it serves. At the program level itself, evaluation demonstrates the merits of a specific methodology and, in the case of a program in difficulty, points out problem areas. This, in turn, should lead to improvement of services.

Various levels of government, i.e. federal, state, and local, both contract for and perform evaluative work. Service programs themselves may assume responsibility for evaluation, which frequently involves input from users of service, as well as from other sources.

Evaluation may be done by one person within a program or by teams of researchers, who may be responsible to an outside agency, frequently the one which has funded the program.

Suchman defines evaluation ". . . as the determination (whether based on opinions, records, subjective or objective data) of the results (whether desirable or undesirable; transient or permanent; immediate or delayed) attained by some activity (whether a program, or part of a program, a drug or a therapy, an ongoing or one-shot approach) designed to accomplish some valued goal or objective (whether ultimate, intermediate or immediate, effort or performance, long or short range)" (p. 31).

The following outline summarizes the major approaches to evaluation that are presently in use:

I. *Subjective Appraisals*—Judgments made by experienced professionals via: (a) on-site visits, (b) peer review studies, (c) case studies.

II. *Monitoring*—Methodical checking on financial and program matters for accountability to licensing or funding agencies by the following methods. (A) *Audit;* (1) financial: income, allocations of funds, and expenditures, (2) program: records pertaining to patient movement through a program; (B) *Inspections;* to ascertain if a program meets standards, (C) *Budget Systems;* Program Planning Budgeting System (PPBS) uses cost figures and measurable goals on a projected time framework.

III. *Evaluation Research Models*—(A) *Goal-Attainment Model* (long-range, intermediate, or immediate goals) can be measured according to the following criteria: (1) effort: input, e.g. man-hours of work, number of patients seen, qualifications of personnel; (2) effectiveness: program output, i.e. accomplishments; (3) efficiency (alternatives in terms of costs): i.e. money, time, number and qualifications of personnel and public convenience. Cost benefit analysis and cost-effectiveness analysis are specific methodologies used to measure efficiency; (4) adequacy of performance: how well a program meets the total need; (5) process criteria: reasons for success or failure; (Suchman, 1967); Systems model is often used. (B) *Testing Models* (1) demonstration projects: time-limited with ongoing evaluation, (2) operations research: ". . . the application of scientific method to the study of alternatives in a problem situation, with a view of providing a quantitative basis for arriving at an optimum solution in terms of the goals sought." (Koontz & O'Donnell, 1972, p. 182).

IV. *Combined Approach*—Combines subjective appraisals with objective data.

Given the difficulty of the challenge and the large assortment of evaluation methods available, it is understandable that there are areas of uncertainty and controversy. Problems arise, about the methods to be utilized and the role of the researcher. Some administrators wish to evaluate programs by subjective appraisal, generally made during site visits, rather than by the use of objective research models. Sometimes administrators feel that a description of the patterns of service will provide an evaluation, failing to understand that such description provides background material only.

Differences arise, also, between researchers themselves. Does the goal-attainment or the systems model provide better results? These two concepts are not really in opposition to one another; the systems model is simply an extension of the goal-attainment model which includes background information and interrelationships within the program.

What is the ideal status or role of the evaluator? Should this

103

person belong to the organization being evaluated or be an outsider? Should he be "staff" or "line." i.e. have an administrative role? Also, should the evaluator be involved in writing the goals to be evaluated? These differences of opinion, although controversial now, may well lead to better solutions to problems.

Evaluation has in the past decade received an increasing amount of attention: from public and private funding agencies, researchers, legislators, administrators, providers and consumers. Limited money and personnel make it essential to learn which programs are proving most successful in order to obtain the most productive use of these resources. Both on the state and federal levels, steps have been taken to require evaluations of mental health services: e.g., the amendment to the Lanterman-Petris-Short Act of California, the newly enacted law in Massachusetts, and the evaluation mandate for HEW.

This trend occurs in response to increased demands for accountability from funding agencies, both governmental and private, by the tax-paying public and by consumers of the services. In addition to these pressures from outside is the desire of the people employed in the field to monitor and improve their performance. Evaluation is moving from subjective to objective methods and from the evaluation of effort, or input measures only, to the measurement of effectiveness (outcome measures) and the process which leads to success or failure. A further movement favors the use of the systems model concept of operations research to provide more comprehensive information, leading to better use of the results. Professional evaluators want better quality, more sophisticated methodology, and more application of the findings.

Research utilization is one of the major problems to be solved in the coming years. Many reasons are given to explain the frequent lack of utilization of research findings, e.g., a lack of well-oriented and interested personnel, methodological problems, mediocre quality of the evaluation, and work of insufficient depth to lead to acceptable recommendations. Poor timing is another serious problem that interferes with the use of evaluative data to make program changes; it may be that at the time of evaluation the program has not yet had an opportunity to have a positive impact because it has not been in operation long enough; large programs frequently take many years before they are working at full capacity. However, when an evaluation research design is implemented, it may take several years before results are available, and changes may have already been made.

Changes in policy for political reasons, especially at governmental levels, act as a deterrent to use of evaluative recommendations. A program may be functioning well and show very positive results from an evaluation, but may not be funded for reasons far re-

104

moved from the basic considerations. Also, a program may be approved and funded by legislators without provision for evaluation, because the lawmakers had to be assured beforehand that the program's value was already proven.

There are also the usual problems involved in any planned change, such as the difficulties encountered when trying to change the perceptions, beliefs, attitudes and behavior of any group of people. These problems start at the inception of the evaluative work and have implications not only for the final quality of the research but also for the acceptance of the results. Included in this area are a lack of understanding by the administrators and other personnel, aspects of the findings which threaten the program itself, resentment of the administrators and other personnel, and resistance of the recipient of the service.

Based on the outline given above, what are some of the questions that an administrator should expect to have answered from an evaluation? This depends in large part on the extent and focus of the evaluative work. A limited effort might include these questions: Are the staff members working the required amount of time? Are they qualified for the work? How many patients are being treated during a specified time period and at what cost per patient? How many patients have improved to a specified level during a one year period? What proportion cancel appointments, or quit treatment dissatisfied?

More extensive work might answer these questions: Which of several treatment methods gives the best results, as measured by patient improvement, for the cost? What is the distribution of a condition (e.g. drug abuse, schizophrenia) in the population? How well has this program met the need in the community for the treatment of a specific condition? This is a small sample of the information that can be gathered by evaluators. The questions to be asked, and answered, depend upon the investment of time, money and personnel that is made in the evaluative effort. This, in turn, often depends on the desire of the administrator for evaluative findings of high quality.

Evelyn L. Goldberg, Sc.D.

References

Caro, Francis G. 1971. Readings in Evaluation Research. New York: Russell Sage Foundation.

Koontz, Harold and O'Donnell, Cyril. 1972. Principles of Management: An Analysis of Managerial Functions. New York: McGraw-Hill Book Company. p. 182.

Schulberg, Herbert C., Sheldon, Alan, Baker, Frank, (eds.). 1969. Program Evaluation in the Health Fields. New York: Behavioral Publications. 582 pp.

Suchman, Edward. 1967. Evaluative Research. New York: Russell Sage Foundation.

U. S. Dept. of HEW, Public Health Service, Health Service and Mental Health Admin., NIMH. 1972. Planning for Creative Change in Mental Health Services: Use of Program Evaluation. pp. 3-12.

Weiss, Carol H. 1972. Evaluation Research: Methods of Assessing Program Effectiveness. Englewood Cliffs, N. J.: Prentice Hall.

Wing, J.K. and Hafner, H. (eds.) 1973. Roots of Evaluation. London: Oxford U. Press. 360 pp.

World Health Organization 1971. Statistical Indications for the Planning and Evaluation of Public Health Programmers. Geneva: Who Technical Report Series. No. 472.

3. Community Mental Health Centers and Health Maintenance Organizations

The CMHC and the HMO are not mutually exclusive; a small HMO might contract with a CMHC for all mental health services; a CMHC might develop features common to HMO's. This discussion is simplified as a conceptual introductory analysis of currently operating CMHCs and prototype HMOs. Ideally, HMO planners will provide an adequately funded in-house mental health program for their members, although this has not been the case in most prototype HMOs.

The late 1950's and early 1960's were a time of change in mental health care delivery. The state mental hospital "system" was woefully inadequate to meet the mental health need. A Joint Commission on Mental Illness and Health was formed by Congress to evaluate U. S. mental health resources and systems of care and make recommendations for the future. The Commission recommended increased availability of psychiatric services by moving the base for provision of care from large, outlying state mental hospitals to the community. (JCMIH, 1961)

In 1963 President John F. Kennedy became the first President to present to the Congress a message devoted entirely to mental health and mental retardation, recommending CMHC development. Congress responded with federal monies for CMHC planning, construction and staffing over several years. To be eligible for funds the CMHC had to serve a geographic area with a population of 75,000 to 200,000 persons and had to provide at least five essential services—inpatient, outpatient, 24-hour emergency, partial hospitalization, and consultation and education (e.g. to schools, parents, law enforcement and social service agencies). Recent CMHC legislation calls for services to children, the aged, and those afflicted with drug abuse problems and alcoholism. Federal funds through NIMH were matched by states according to a formula of decreasing federal participation. The original goal was for the establishment of 2,000 centers by 1980—a nationwide community-based care system.

Prepaid group practice is not a new concept. It developed in the 1930's and 1940's demonstrating certain advantages in guaranteeing access to, assuring quality and containing costs of comprehensive medical care. The prepaid systems put a premium on competent administration and lent themselves to newer management techniques.

By contrast the Medicare-Medicaid experience since 1965 demonstrated that increasing the effective demand for health services without a better system of supply only leads to medical cost inflation. Prepaid group practice (the HMO) is designed to be a better health care delivery system. The government defines an HMO as a four-way arrangement between: 1) an organized health care delivery system which includes health manpower and facilities; 2) a voluntarily enrolled population; 3) a financial plan which meets the cost of services on a pre-negotiated and prepaid per-person or per-family basis; and 4) a managing organization which assures legal, fiscal, public and professional accountability.

Federal funds for the development of new HMOs were voted in 1973 and are likely to be continued. HMOs will need to develop their own mental health services and it is instructive to compare the advantages and disadvantages of CMHCs and HMOs as mental health delivery systems.

1. *System Characteristics:* The CMHC is open to all residing in the catchment area (some use the CMHC, some use private practitioners or other resources). The HMO by contrast is open only to members enrolled on a prepaid basis and to others only on a time-available fee-for-service basis. The HMO contracts in writing with the consumer, binding one to the other. The HMO must provide the services it has agreed to deliver and the enrollee pays twice if he uses other than HMO care.

The CMHC has no such contract with the catchment area resident; however, the CMHC is supposed to serve those who seek care. In program planning and evaluation the CMHC must use aggregated information to describe the population it is serving (usually census data of the catchment area). These data may or may not describe the population actually using the center. The act of enrollment allows the HMO to describe its population from a demographic standpoint and establish a denominator from which meaningful incidence and prevalence figures can be derived. In an HMO one can ascertain, for instance, that "the incidence of suicide is 12 per 100,000 per annum for a population with these demographic characteristics." The CMHC, however, can develop area-wide data on health and social needs as a basis for program planning and evaluation.

2. *Administrative Issues:* The CHMC is usually operated with federal, state and local budgetary support with a small percentage of medicare, medicaid and private insurance dollars. The HMO, once established, operates on enrollment premiums, both governmental "soft" monies and "hard" monies derived from membership premiums are subject to vagaries of economic change. Longer range planning is more possible in the HMO since patterns of use are easier to predict. Staff in HMOs are often on a risk-sharing arrange-

ment which may increase stability and thereby enhance continuity of care.

3. *Mental Health Delivery Characteristics:* The CMHC tends toward a human service orientation compared with the medically-oriented HMO. Such consultation and education efforts as exist in the CMHC are directed toward catchment area schools, law enforcement agencies, churches, and social agencies more than to health care providers. By contrast the HMO is a health care institution with mental health care as a part of general health care delivery. Mental health consultation and education efforts are directed primarily toward the medical staff of the HMO and the enrollee family. The HMO offers better integrated medical mental health services whereas the CMHC helps integrate mental health services into the social and human services of the catchment community.

Continuity of care is particularly important in the delivery of mental health services and in this area HMOs appear to have more advantages. There is better "medical" continuity in the HMO. Here the mental health staff has direct access to primary physicians and medical charts. However, most HMOs do not have long-term care benefits and have less ability to treat the chronically mentally ill than the CMHC. The HMO tends to treat the middle class to a greater extent than the CMHC. The CMHC has attempted to intervene in the social arena where the mental health problems of the poor often have their roots. The U. S. population has been described as a mobile population, but most moves are local. Moves across CMHC catchment boundaries could disrupt CMHC continuity of care but would not affect that of an HMO.

Since HMOs will probably not provide long-term psychiatric hospitalization or treatment of addictive diseases, the CMHC can often provide continuity in these areas better than the HMO.

Incentives for prevention activities differ in CMHC and HMO. Notwithstanding the regulatory requirement to engage in consultation and education activities, the CMHC does so only to the extent the staff is so inclined: such activities can be community-wide, not limited to enrolled patients. In the HMO there are direct financial incentives to engage in mental illness prevention activities among its enrollees. However, since the HMO must justify its expenditures out of limited premium dollars, it tends to be more conservative in developing primary preventive programs than the CMHC. Cost-effective prevention techniques, free premium dollars for additional services, and with more experience the HMO can develop better strategies for mental health maintenance.

Daniel Y. Patterson, M.D., M.P.H.

109

References

Crawford, J. W., Crawford S. 1973. Psychiatry and group medical practice: the diagnostic process, referral patterns, and utilization of services. Am J Psychiatry 130: 637-642.

Follette W., Cummings N. A. 1967. Psychiatric services and medical utilization in a pre-paid health plan setting. Med Care 5:25-41.

Goldensohn, S. S. 1972. A pre-paid group practice mental health service as part of a health maintenance organization. Am J Orthopsychiatry 42:154-158.

Goldensohn, S. S., Fink R., Shapiro S. 1969. Referral, utilization and staffing patterns of a mental health service in a pre-paid group practice program in New York. Am J Psychiatry 126:689-697.

Joint Commission on Mental Illness and Health. 1961. Action for Mental Health: Final Report of Joint Commission on Mental Illness and Health. New York: Science Editions, Inc.

Locke, B. Z., Krantz, G., Kramer, M. 1966. Psychiatric need and demand in a pre-paid practice program. Am J Public Health 56:895-904.

U. S. Dept. of Health, Education and Welfare. 1974. Inclusion of Mental Health Services in Health Maintenance and Related Organizations. DHEW Pub. No. (HSA) 75-13019. USGPO.

Other Sources

Journals:
Administration in Mental Health

110

4. Public Psychiatric Hospitals and County Clinics

A man is deemed a lunatic; a certificate has been
signed, to the effect that confinement in a lunatic
asylum is necessary to his recovery: The patient is
taken away from his family; abandoned by his usual
medical attendant; waited upon by strangers, and
his whole management confided to a person whose
profession it is to cure lunatics; to one who, if he is a
medical practitioner, seldom professes to think the
mind worthy of particular consideration; or, it may
be to one who is altogether ignorant both of bodily
and mental disease.

—John Conolly (1830)

Mental health facilities, other than Community Mental Health
Centers, Health Maintenance Organizations and the private sector,
include: Veterans Administration neuropsychiatric hospitals, VA
and other general hospitals with separate psychiatric services,
state and county mental hospitals and psychiatric services, residential treatment centers for emotionally disturbed children, psychiatric day treatment facilities, and outpatient psychiatric clinics.

Such hospitals and clinics are not bound by the federal catchment area requirement or the five mandated services of the Community Mental Health Center Act. They do exist as elements in state
systems, for example, and meet the requirements, of state statutes.
The hospital districts cross county lines, and may serve areas greater than 200,000 people. The county clinics are usually bound by
county lines, and generally serve less than 200,000 persons. In larger counties, such as Los Angeles, the county may be divided into
catchment areas.

Private hospitals may have open or closed staffs, serve a limited
number of diagnostic categories, are usually concerned with short-
term treatment, and charge fees which exclude much of the population. State hospitals for the mentally ill follow a century old tradition
of admitting all diagnostic categories, including the dangerous, suicidal, manic, deeply depressed, chronic recurrent, and neurologic.
For most people with limited funds, state mental hospitals represent
the last or only resort.

Mental health care is also provided by professionals in private

111

practice, neighborhood health centers, nursing homes, and often by hospitals without separate psychiatric services. Informal estimates from some data supplied by the American Psychiatric Association indicate that approximately 750,000 to 1,000,000 people receive services through these facilities annually.

As of January, 1973, there were 3,200 mental health facilities in the United States. Of these, 1,123 (35%), were free-standing outpatient clinics; 770 (24%) were general hospitals with separate psychiatric services; 482 (15%) were psychiatric hospitals; 344 (11%) were residential centers for emotionally disturbed children; and 295 (9%) were federally funded Community Mental Health Centers. Of the total mental health facilities in the country, 46% were public and the remaining 54% were under non-public auspices.

In 1971, of the 2.54 million inpatient and outpatient admission episodes, 48 percent were inpatient and 52 percent were outpatient admissions. The inpatient admission rate was 597 per 100,000 population, while the outpatient admission rate was 642 per 100,000 population. Inpatient admissions predominate after 45 years of age. In the 45-64 year age group, there were three inpatients to two outpatients, and after 65 years, there were three inpatients to every outpatient admission. Two-thirds of admissions were to public facilities.

County and municipal clinics are primarily for ambulatory patients, not in need of hospitalization, and generally unable to afford private mental health care. Such patients will often respond to short term therapy, but may also require therapy for one or more years.

The county or municipal clinic, and state hospitals, are supported by varying combinations of state and local tax monies. Combinations of state and local government exercise control and annual review of the qualification of staff, rules and regulations, budget, and projected planning.

Governmental social service agencies and insurance plans often assist in paying for the treatment of some patients in clinics and state hospitals. There is no pre-enrollment of patients in these facilities inasmuch as any resident of the specific county or municipal area or state is considered to be eligible to receive services.

According to data derived from six independent NIMH surveys between June 1970 and July 1971, males accounted for 52 percent of the total admissions in all categories. Non-white admissions constituted 17 percent of the total, or 45 percent higher than the rate for whites.

A recent trend, in a number of states, has been to reduce the census of patients in state hospitals, and refer as many as possible back to local public clinics for follow-up care. The result has been an increase in the size and scope, as well as the responsibilities, of county clinics with a proportionate increase in their budgets.

112

Nationally, of the 1.2 million inpatient admissions in 1971, 33% were to state and county mental hospitals; 25% to private hospital psychiatric services; 18% to public general hospital psychiatric services; 11% to Veterans Administration hospitals; 7% to private mental hospitals; and 6% to federally-funded Community Mental Health Center inpatient services.

Considering outpatient psychiatric clinics, the free-standing clinics account for over one-third (37%) of the outpatient admissions in 1971. Community Mental Health Center outpatient services account for approximately one-quarter (26%), and general hospital outpatient psychiatric services for a little over one-fifth (22%). About half of all outpatients admitted to the free-standing clinics were under 18 years of age.

Since 1955, the locus of patient care has changed considerably, and this change is still notable. The total number of episodes of care has increased 142% from 1.7 million in 1955 to 4.0 million in 1971. Patient care episodes in inpatient services, 77% in 1955, dropped to 43% in 1971. However, outpatient psychiatric services increased from 23% to 57%. Patient care episodes in Community Mental Health Centers doubled between 1969 and 1971. State and county mental hospitals, which accounted for about half of the patient care episodes in 1955, accounted for only one-fifth in 1971.

With the change in the locus of patient care, county and municipal clinics have had not only to expand their services, but often reach subcontracting agreements with existing agencies in the mental health field to enable them to meet the rising service demands. These arrangements have not only provided private services with public funds to permit their survival, but also opportunities for consultation, education, supervision, sharing of staff, libraries, and special equipment with the local public mental health service agency. The result is a better coordinated mental health service effort at the local level, with more understanding, teamwork and referral. Duplication of effort may thereby be reduced, resulting in better community-wide service to an expanding needy clientele.

The state hospitals, due to a reduced census in recent years, have been able to develop a better doctor-to-patient ratio, and thus provide better service to the hospitalized patient. As a consequence, state hospitals have developed better community resources for referral of patients, as well as arrangements with other services for cooperative follow-up, day care, and sharing of resources. In addition, New York and other states have passed legislation permitting and encouraging shared services and costs between state and local government facilities, and joint planning efforts to meet projected needs in a systematic way.

Regarding psychiatric hospitals, county and municipal clinics, and related services, the major needs are: to acquire more and better trained personnel; to secure adequate funding for staff and facilities; to coordinate state and local facilities to provide more effective and efficient service.

The future for all mental health service institutions remains an open question as government at all levels struggles to determine its long-term investment in mental health care. Community Mental Health Centers are growing too slowly, both in terms of geographic coverage and ability to meet the needs of most Americans. Health Maintenance Organizations are too recent and too few to be fairly judged in a national context. State hospitals are changing from being isolated "human warehouses" to becoming small community-centered, community-oriented treatment units and back-up for the local agencies. County and municipal clinics will continue to expand, primarily because they are closer to the people and their local government, and provide faster, cheaper, and widely-diversified treatment to an ambulatory population.

Joseph J. Friedman, M.D.

Summary Table

	County and Municipal Clinics	State Mental Hospitals
Origins of Movement	Local government needs during the last quarter century.	19th century state needs responding to "poor houses" with flagrant social presures.
Governmental Support	State and local support, frequent sliding fee scale (insurance and personal payment based on income).	Total state support.
Essential to Concept	Catchment area of one county or less. Out-patient services. Focus on people who cannot afford private care.	State-wide catchment, or divided between several state centers. Primarily inpatient services. Focus on people who cannot afford private care.
Type of System	Open	Open
Patient Population	Involuntarily Assigned	Involuntarily Assigned
Contract with Patient	Usually none. Possible court-ordered treatment and probation.	Usually none. Possible court-ordered commitment for variable time.

114

Demographic Description of Population	Same as CMHC's—indirectly described via census data and sampling procedures.	Same as CMHC's—indirectly described via census data and sampling procedures.
Operating Funds	Hard governmental funds	Hard governmental funds
Bureaucratic Encumbrance	Moderate	Severe
Orientation and Integration	Combination of medical model and human service model.	Medical
Consultation and Education	Subcontracted human service agencies, schools, welfare, and criminal justice system.	Limited but developing in the past decade.
Incentive of Prevention	Regulatory requirement and philosophical commitment.	Regulatory requirement and philosophical commitment.

References

Barton, W. 1962. Administration in Psychiatry. Springfield, Illinois: Thomas.

Bellak, L. (ed.) 1971. Handbook of Community Psychiatry and Community Mental Health. N. Y., Grune and Stratton.

Lamb, H. R., Heath, D., Downing, J. P. (eds.) 1969. Handbook of Community Mental Health Practice. San Francisco: Josseu-Bass.

Pierson, P. H. 1969. A Statistical Information System for Community Mental Health Centers. Washington, D. C.: Public Health Service (Publication 1963).

The Dimension of Community Psychiatry. 1968. New York. Group for the Advancement of Psychiatry. (Report 69).

Strupp, H. H., and Lubarsky, L. (eds.) 1962. Research in Psychotherapy. Vol. 2. American Psychological Assoc., Inc., Wash., D. C.

Tulipan, A. B., Feldman, S. (eds.) 1969. Psychiatric Clinics in Transition. POCA perspectives: No. 1. Brunner/Mazel, Publishers, New York.

Roberts, L. M., Halleck, S. L., Loeb, M. B. (eds.) 1966. Community Psychiatry. University of Wisconsin Press. Milwaukee.

Glasscote, R., Sanders, D., Forstenzer, H. M., Foley, A. R. 1964. The Community Mental Health Center. The Joint Information Center, 1700 18th Street, N. W., Washington, D. C.

Glasscote, R., Kraft, A. M., Glassman, S., Jepson, W. W. 1969. Partial Hospitalization for the Mentally Ill. A Study of Programs and Problems. The Joint Information Service. 1700 18th Street, N. W., Washington, D. C.

Other Sources

The NIMH is the primary source of national data on mental health services.

Journals:
Community Mental Health Journal (Behavioral Publications, N.Y.)
Hospital and Community Psychiatry (American Psychiatric Assoc.)
Administration in Mental Health (NIMH HSM 73-9050)

Associations:
National Council of Community Mental Health Centers.
National Association of State Mental Health Program Directors.

116

5. Private Mental Health Treatment Programs

Now, 'tis e'er the wont of simple folk to prize the deed and o'erlook the motive, and of learned folk to discount the deed and lay open the soul of the doer ... the difference 'twixt sour pessimist and proper gentleman lies just here: That the one will judge good deeds by a morality of motive and ill by a morality of deed, and so condemn the twain together, whereas your gentleman doth the reverse, and hath always grounds to pardon his wayward fellows.

—John Barth
the Sot-Weed Factor (1960)

Institutional providers of mental health services in the United States have traditionally been governmental or nonprofit in nature. Only the mental health practitioner in the private sector has characteristically operated on a "for-profit" basis. The last few years, however, have seen the emergence of corporate ventures in health, and more recently investor-financed private mental health systems have appeared, due to several factors. 1) Analysis of economic trends in the United States indicates that the growth era for the next decade will be in the area of personal services, rather than goods, thereby stimulating investor interest in service organizations of all types. 2) There is a conviction that such ventures will be treated equitably in federal reimbursement schemes. 3) National health insurance will help. 4) The development of a cadre of competent mental health administrators, a result of the proliferation of community mental health centers, provides a new manpower resource for such ventures. 5) Disillusionment with the capability of government and non-profit entities to deliver services that meet the simultaneous demands of economy and quality is widespread among consumers, providers, and third-party payers alike. 6) New technology for assessing outcome has been developed so that reward systems can be constructed to reward not only quantity of clinical work performed but also quality. This provides a long-missing tool for effective management of mental health services. 7) The increasing complexity of reimbursement systems, and the pressures for improved record-keeping for peer review and utilization review by third-party payers, makes the development of organized, broadly integrated

117

practices more attractive. 8) More different types of problems are now seen as disorders that can be treated by mental health professionals. This makes demands that the solo practitioners are ill equipped to meet. 9) Over-utilization of psychiatric inpatient beds in this country, in spite of clinical ineffectiveness and excessive cost, has motivated some innovators to develop efficient, economic alternatives to hospitalization.

Supporters of the new private mental health system believe that equivalent or better quality of service can be delivered for equivalent or lower costs than those prevailing in the existing private or public sectors. Furthermore, through improved clinical management and general administration, a profit can still be generated to deliver a fair return on the investor's money.

There are a number of different models currently on national trial. One system, the Institutes of Human Resources, is a subsidiary of National Medical Care, Inc., which developed a system of renal dialysis centers as its first venture. The Institute of Human Resources operates free-standing psychiatric hospitals on the east coast, and psychiatric day and evening centers west of the Mississippi River, emphasizing day hospital as an alternative to inpatient care.

Psychiatric Institutes of America, headquartered in Washington, D.C., assists groups of private practicing psychiatrists to develop a psychiatric hospital. The local psychiatrists co-venture in providing the capital, as well as benefiting from the profits. Psychiatric Institutes of America also provides management assistance in conducting the financial affairs of the psychiatric group.

Psychiatric Research Associates, operating primarily in the northeast section of the country, is in the process of developing both traditional and innovative psychiatric programs. Community Psychiatric Centers, Inc., is a west coast operation which develops and operates private psychiatric hospitals located primarily in the rapidly growing suburban fringes of major metropolitan areas.

In addition, most of the corporate general hospital systems have one or more psychiatric hospitals, or psychiatric units in their general hospitals, although none of them apparently sees the development of psychiatric facilities as a primary thrust of their future development. Some existing psychiatric facilities, such as the Carrier Clinic in Belle Meade, New Jersey, have been acquired by other corporate enterprises.

The development of privately financed mental health systems offers great potential. It has hazards for exploitation, as does any new profit-making venture. The third-party payers, already a major factor and certain to increase with the enactment of national health insurance, are, or should be, a major safeguard against abuse.

In the great wave of reform following the Flexner Report, American medicine hurriedly abandoned the proprietary or private-

118

for-profit institutional medical provider as inherently corrupt and providing inferior service. This was probably an unwarranted conclusion then and now. Private operations, because of the greater degree of freedom and access to greater supplies of capital, have a great potential for good or evil. We must remember that many of the outstanding psychiatric institutions in the United States, such as the Menninger Clinic, began their existence as proprietary mental health operations.

In the next few years, private mental health services should provide, as a minimum, a useful stimulus for innovative, healthy competition for the existing public and non-profit mental health entities.

H.G. Whittington, M.D.

Other Resources

Journal of the National Association of Private Psychiatric Hospitals

6. Comprehensive Mental Health Through a Neighborhood Health Center

> It may seem a strange principle to enunciate as the
> very first requirement in a hospital that it should do
> the sick no harm.
>
> —*Florence Nightingale (1820-1910)*

The human services and civil rights push of the 1960's has spawned a growing new front for health care delivery, the comprehensive health center in a neighborhood location (Renthal, 1971; Sparer, 1971). While these have been gaining in acceptance, the mental health professions have been preoccupied with building their Community Mental Health Centers (CMHC) and have been slow to realize the inherent advantages of delivery through this new Neighborhood Health Center (NHC) setting.

These NHCs have arisen through a hodgepodge of funding sources in the last decade: Maternal and Infant Care, Migrant Health, Children and Youth, Family Planning, Office of Economic Opportunity (OEO), Model Cities, Health, Education and Welfare (HEW), Municipal Government, and others. Gradually the more categorical of these have added the full spectrum of health care, often at the urging of consumer boards involved before or after the fact. Most are now giving a combination of adult medicine, pediatrics, pre-and post-natal care, and gynecology. The disciplines of public health nursing, community health workers, social work, family planing, and nutrition are often included. The centers pride themselves on their neighborhood location, consumer boards, and continuity and comprehensiveness of care. Decreases in categorical federal funding recently have caused many of them to plan conversion to a prepaid group practice or Health Maintenance Organization (HMO).

Where and how does mental health fit into this? Initially few of these programs had mental health input other than a very part-time consultant or liaison relationship with a backup psychiatric facility. (Lowenkopf & Werling, 1971) The early exceptions included some of the more heavily funded demonstration projects by OEO or academic centers. These were able to hire full-time mental health staff for comprehensive outpatient services, unlike most HMOs which have had to offer limited mental health services to fit within their

120

budget. (Morrill, 1972; Morrill, in press) The idea that true comprehensiveness includes mental health and social services as well as medical has spread and the more limited health centers have gradually added mental health programming.

The advantages of the NHC are due to two basic factors, the decentralized neighborhood location (Macht, 1974) and the comprehensive primary health care setting. (Roche, 1973) At the mental health-patient interface in a NHC, it is apparent that the staff see fewer patients "pushed through the door," as is often the case with a strictly mental health facility. There are more personal, earlier, less traumatic referrals at a NHC. Why? There is much less stigma attached to the program by potential patients, the program is more physically accessible and less formidable and psychologically forbidding to patients, and the great drawing power of the comprehensive services assures mental health staff of working in a setting where people *want* to receive services and by and large have trust in and depend on those services.

Thus by working through such a setting, the mental health program can increase its effectiveness in the area of primary prevention (i.e., prenatal and postnatal couples groups), secondary prevention (i.e., early detection of developmental arrest in children through a screening program with pediatrics), tertiary prevention (i.e., less patient resistance to posthospital follow-up of chronic psychosis at a NHC). Primary and tertiary prevention are both effected when a patient who has major mental illness is helped to function effectively as a mother by the provision of social and psychological support. Thus, tertiary prevention for the mother becomes primary prevention for the children.

The realization of these advantages, however, depends on the quality of the second key interface, that between mental health staff and the other health care providers. The closeness of staff in such a NHC leads to a striking increase in informal communication about patients, referrals, and knowledge about each others' capabilities. (Plesset, 1969; Fink et. al., 1969) When the health centers grow in size, teams become necessary to prevent "health care cliques" or fractionation of care along disciplinary lines.

This horizontally organized interdisciplinary family care team can coexist and complement the usual vertical hierarchy. Through the team, interdisciplinary respect, communication, and joint planning can occur. Without this, the NHC remains in danger of becoming a small version of the City Hospital clinics transferred to a neighborhood site. In practicing in such a setting, mental health staff have "rediscovered" the mental health role of the doctor and nurse and have the opportunity to enhance this in a consultative role through their close contact. Joint psychosomatic programs naturally develop, such as group therapy for hypertensives with the medical

121

nurse as a co-leader with the mental health group leader.

After some experience in a comprehensive neighborhood health setting, most mental health staff have been quite impressed with the way this begins to shape their practice towards a family orientation, a willingness to "despecialize" into more of a "general practitioner" of mental health, and towards better utilization of vastly increased information about family life, milestones, and crises of the patient and his family through the other staff.

In Massachusetts, the League of Neighborhood Health Centers through their Mental Health Task Force has been a leader in pulling together experiences from twenty varied NHC settings and has found a high consensus on certain programmatic principles which have enhanced development of mental health programs within NHC settings. (Borus, et. al., 1974) These include: 1. Neighborhood location for greater accessibility and acceptability. 2. Full range of mental health and social services with a family and community orientation including evaluation, treatment, consultation, and education for children and adults. 3. Mental health staff include paraprofessionals from the community as well as the full range of professionals. The full staff should be eligible for third-party reimbursement. 4. Mental health staff should be full-time, or nearly so, and housed with other services to improve the relationship between them and other health care staff. 5. The mental health program should be oriented towards working through the NHC as a system of care of which they are an integral part—not a "program within a program".

Our experience leads us to predict that the NHC, operating as a prepaid group, might well become the main locus for most mental health care. The CMHC, however, would still be needed to provide certain more specialized back-up services, a legally responsible program to ensure adequate services and planning for a larger catchment area, and services for those who may want a more anonymous facility than the one in their neighborhood. At least four types of relationships between CMHC and NHC can be envisioned: (1) The NHC patients needing mental health services are sent to the separate CMHC; (2) A pseudopod of the CMHC extends into the NHC; (3) Part of the CMHC funds or staff are allocated to the NHC to be used to deliver the mental health services for that neighborhood through the NHC; (4) The NHC receives separate mental health funding from whatever source (capitation, state grant, third party) and then associates itself with the local CMHC to ensure coordination of service. Experience shows that only through the last two models will a mental health service emerge that can effectively utilize all that a Comprehensive Neighborhood Health Center has to offer for better mental health service to the consumer.

CMHCs in Boston are beginning to assign some of their staff to

NHCs and in two such situations are finding that the "no show" rates for patients are lower in the neighborhood sites. As this shift progresses, questions begin to be raised about the relationship between the two parties. We have found that the mental health staff operates more effectively in a NHC if they are seen as belonging to it, which in turn encourages their commitment to work through its system. On the other hand, the CMHC must maintain performance standards and coordination for its personnel if they are to operate in different neighborhood sites. One resolution for these apparently conflicting interests is to contract out CMHC services to comprehensive health centers in various neighborhoods of the CMHC catchment area. The NHC can thus regard such staff as being within their program administratively and psychologically.

To ensure coordination with the backup CMHC, these staff can spend part of their time delivering services or attending coordination meetings at the central CMHC site to tie them into the network.

This tie between CMHCs and NHCs seems quite complementary. The NHC has the access to and relationship with the consumer but currently has only limited means of funding mental health services, either through restrictive third party funds, or prepaid benefits package which cannot pay for full ambulatory mental health care.

The CMHC, on the other hand, lacks the access to patients and families of the NHC but has the governmental responsibility and funding for all mental health care in that catchment area. Utilization of some of these CMHC funds through the NHC programs will thus bring together the NHC's access to patients and the CMHC's full service funding. This seems a logical next step for improved service to the consumer, meeting the goals of both the CMHC and NHC.

Richard G. Morrill, M.D.

References

Renthal, A.G., 1971, Comprehensive Health Centers in large U.S. cities, A.J.P.H. 61,324 (Feb.).

Sparer, G., 1971. Evaluation of OEO Neighborhood Health Centers. A.J.P.H. 61,931 (May).

Lowenkopf, E.L. and Zwerling, I., 1971, Psychiatric service in a Neighborhood Health Center. Am. J. Psychiat. 127,916 (Jan.)

Morrill, R.G., 1972. A new mental health services model for the Comprehensive Neighborhood Health Center. Am. J. Pub. Health. 62,8,1108-1111.

Morrill, R.G., Integration of Mental Health and Comprehensive Health Services in a Neighborhood Health Center. In process of publication.

Macht, Lee B., 1974. Neighborhood psychiatry, Psychiatric Annals 4, 9, (Sept.)

Health Center Setting Cited as Best for Patients, Psychiatrists. 1973. Roche Report, Frontiers of Psychiatry, 3, 1-11.

Plesset, M.R., 1969. The role of a psychiatrist in a medical group. Group Practice, 18,39 (Aug.)

Fink, R., Shapiro, S., Goldensohn, S.S., and Daily, E.F., 1969. The "Filter-Down" Process to psychiatry in a group practice medical care program. Am. J. Pub. Health. 59, 245-260.

Neighborhood Health Center; The Mental Health Delivery System of the Future, Authors: Johathan Borus, M.D.; Lawrence A. Ganowitz, M.S.; Frances Kieffer, M.A.; Richard G. Morrill, M.D.; Lee Reich, PhD.; Edward Simone, M.A.; Lyla Towle, M.S.W. Presented at American Public Health Association Convention, New Orleans 1974.

Other Sources

Journals:

American Journal of Public Health
American Journal of Psychiatry
Medical Care
American Journal of Orthopsychiatry

124

VI. | Categorical Needs and Services

1. Child Mental Health: Prevention and Early Intervention

> If we had paid no more attention to plants than we
> have to our children, we would now be living in a
> jungle of weeds.
>
> —*Luther Burbank (1849-1926)*

Primary prevention of and early intervention into children's diseases and disorders can only occur on a mass basis in a system which is already geared to professional involvement with children. Recent child development studies indicate that these efforts must begin very early in life. This has led many educators, developmentalists, pediatricians and child mental health professionals to advocate the downward extension of universal education to age three. They are joined by social psychologists and epidemiologists who note the increase of previously undetected minimal brain damage and of severe emotional disturbance, the latter resulting from depersonalizations due to rapid technological changes, population mobility, enormous ghettos, and the former from extensive poverty, pre-and post-natal malnutrition, and general poor health care.

The enormous number of depressed young parents both in poverty areas and in suburbia also means that they and their infants and young children require help. Early stimulation and developmentally oriented programs for young children are especially important.

Several studies have proven that the use of public health nurses and home community aides to work with mothers and infants has increased the mothers' capacity to interact with their children, resulting in improved responsiveness of infants. Toy libraries have been used to help babies and young children and their mothers to find age-appropriate toys and to learn the kind of mutual play that promotes curiosity, stimulates further play and engages the mother with her child.

School as a Child Development Resource. Equally important is the education of teachers in preschool, primary and secondary grades in practical application of child development knowledge. Such knowledge must also become part of the present teachers' armamentarium through inservice training.

As Bower (1963) and others have emphasized, teachers with

127

minimal additional help can become very effective in the detection of emotional disturbances in young children. They need much more help, however, in understanding the developmental needs of children, both psychological and physical, and in developing curricula to reflect developmental changes throughout the school contact with a child. Such curricula will help teachers protect children at times of developmental stress and take advantage of developmental competences and informational input in our video-oriented, maturation-speeding society.

School as an Identification Center. Regular screening of children as they enter preschool at age three, and at developmental milestones: at entry into first grade (ages 5-6), about third grade (ages 8-9) with increased capacities and pressures for learning, and at pubescence, as well as throughout the adolescent years, would lead to early identification of disease and disorder. Mental health problems identified early can often be remedied, leading to the prevention of severe emotional disorders. Many children with minimal brain damage function relatively well until they need to utilize their coordination skills in more complex behaviors and are compared with age mates. At that time (age four to five), these obvious lacks begin to become psychologically troublesome. The coordination and perceptual motor problems can be worked on and the difficulty ameliorated. Often its psychological consequences can be prevented. Hyperactivity picked up early in preschool is better corrected then. When behavior patterns have stabilized, the learning and behavior problems which accompany hyperactivity often become severe and result in the students' dropping out or being expelled from school.

Prevention and early intervention in health, mental health and learning problems require that preschools and elementary schools become the site of both early screening and remediation or treatment. The importance of learning as a means of feeling competent, effective and worthwhile cannot be overemphasized in preventive mental health. Millions of children are deprived nutritionally and emotionally and therefore cannot learn. Millions more are not taught adequately, especially if they are poor, or handicapped.

Parents' Role in School Home Learning. Recent research reveals that the single most important factor in school achievement is the interest of parents in the child's learning in school. Several studies showed that socioeconomic level was less important in school achievement than parental attitudes (Children of Kauai). Children with the same IQ in preschool years showed, by the fifth grade, a differential of minus two years for those of lower socioeconomic class or whose parents were unconcerned about education. The Plowden Report and Head Start data confirm other large studies.

How can parents become relevant parts of the school to influence their child's learning and implement teachers' methods and curriculum? Several studies show that parents can very early be engaged in learning about their own child's growth and development and thus be involved in the necessary interaction and stimulation which lead to attachment, security, curiosity and investigativeness as delineated by Bowlby. Other studies reveal that parents of children in kindergarten and primary grades can be involved in the use of games to help their children learn concepts, acquire reading skills and thus become related to the child's learning. Parents concerned with problems of the school can become effective observers, gather data about the classroom, and arrive at relevant methods of enhancing teaching and learning. One intervention is the regular use of parents as helpers in the classroom. Thus, the alienation of parent from school, almost universal in our country, can be reduced.

Problem Solving: Educational and Life Goal. Some new, experimental programs are being mounted that are geared to finding alternative ways of engaging students in learning. Most schools are still a century behind in basic attitudes toward developmentally-based learning and teaching methods. The most encouraging efforts from the mental health viewpoint are those that involve students in learning to collect data, to assess them and to reason about how problems can be solved. Inherent in a problem-solving approach is the evolution of participatory democracy in the classroom. Students so prepared can become effective citizens who can assess problems independently and derive from the data what is important. Project learning where students cooperatively pick a topic to be researched, evaluate data and make recommendations has proven to be effective. In this process adults are faciliators of the process, not sources of facts or ultimate truth.

Education for a Real World of Relationships and Work. Of great interest also are programs which involve young adolescents in learning child development with a practicum in child care. These efforts have led to seminars on relations between people; how feelings can be expressed; human development; and discussions of human sexuality. The eventual openness of communication is exciting to both teachers and adolescents. Educators are beginning to look at school as a place to help young people to learn those skills which lead to employment and the capacity for making relationships and learning to live in a rapidly changing society. Those few programs in junior and senior high schools which offer practical experience in several occupations, most notably in human services, deal with another pervasive mental health and health problem. Many young people are not trained for and cannot find work. Productive and meaningful or valued work is important to health and mental health. Unemployment means the streets, crime and delinquency for

129

youth of all socioeconomic classes but especially the poor and minorities. For some students, peer counseling of others can be the first eye-opening experience, both enjoyable and socially important.

In a few schools, affective learning is stressed. Feelings engendered by interactions between students and students and teachers by their reading of the literature, history, or current events, become opportunities to learn that feelings can be expressed. They then learn that full and non-destructive expression of feeling rather than suppression of feelings or precipitous action is an aid to thinking processes. Affective learning so long neglected in the school today is critical to the development of human relations and greater awareness of the depth and range of feelings in oneself and others.

Mental Health Consultation. The purpose of mental health consultation is to help teachers and administrators have greater impact on school problems, and to help educators to become more aware of the behavioral consequences of birth trauma and of environment, both past and present, in schools and out. Consultation can help them discover how each of them can be more helpful to their troubled and troublesome students. With 10 to 20% of our students requiring mental health interventions, mental health professionals cannot cope alone. Educators can with consultation enhance children's learning and decrease behavior problems. Mental health consultation recognizes that every person involved with children in the schools is a potential aide in diagnosis and remediation of health and mental health problems.

Future shock is here; the problems of a complex society require involvement of people and concern with a future. Early mother-infant interaction and stimulation must be supported. Feelings and how they are safely and humanely communicated must become part of curricula. We must help students relate to each other with compassion, concern and a sense of dignity and equality. In an ever-more indifferent, dehumanized and even hostile impersonal world, concern with prevention of health and mental health and learning problems inevitably leads to a concerned action by adults which in quality and persistence provides children with a model for their interactions with others.

Irving N. Berlin, M.D.

References

Bower, E. M. 1963. Primary prevention of mental and emotional disorders. Am. Journal of Orthopsychiatry, Vol. 33, 832-848.

Berlin, I.N. and Berlin, R. 1975. Parents' advocate role in education as primary prevention in I.N. Berlin (ed.) Advocacy for Child Mental Health. New York: Brunner/Mazel.

Bowlby, J. (ed.). 1969. Attachment. New York: Brunner/Mazel.

Hetznecker, W. and Forman, M.A. 1974. On Behalf of Children. New York: Grune & Stratton.

Werner, E.D., Bierman, J.M. and French, F.E. 1971. The Children of Kauai. Honolulu: University of Hawaii Press.

2. Parenthood

> All marriages without a visible or probable means of
> subsistence are founded in madness. All premature
> attachments between the sexes which obstruct the
> pursuits of business are likewise the offspring of the
> love mania. The expenses of a family, like a blister-
> ing plaster between the shoulders, never fail of cur-
> ing this species of madness.
>
> —Benjamin Rush, M.D. (1745-1813)
> On The Different Species of Mania

Parenthood, simply stated, involves the responsibility of rearing children—natural or adopted. Unfortunately, parenthood and its many implications are not simple; it requires that numerous behavioral adaptations be made.

Historically, conception has been widely viewed as an automatic introduction to parenthood; that is, if a child were conceived, the female involved had little choice but to bear the child and subsequently to enter into childrearing. There have, however, been many socio-cultural and psychological changes relevant to parenthood in the last decade. These changes have been manifested in what society, institutions (e.g., the legal system, the schools, and the churches), and individuals recognize as "acceptable" views about parenthood. Thus alternatives to "automatic" parenthood have developed, and the alternatives have, in turn, resulted in conflicting positions on many issues relating to parenthood; consequently, there is a pressing need for efficacious behavioral adaptations.

The basic problem areas relating to parenthood encompass many "family tasks" relating to the parents' responsibility to meet the family's basic needs for food, clothing, and shelter, to meet their own social and emotional needs and to foster appropriate development and socialization for their children. Meeting these various needs is no easy matter in the highly complex socio-cultural system that is contemporary society. Many parents must struggle to provide basic economic and emotional support, and virtually all parents experience conflict between meeting their own needs and those of their children. Parents must make significant adjustments when the first child is born and must continue to make different adjustments with each additional child, as well as other adaptations as their children grow and the family moves into new familial stages.

Clear-cut behavioral boundaries, such as would be derived from traditional values and mores, belong to a bygone era; today's parents must, to a large extent, derive their own set of values, behavioral goals, and guidelines for childrearing. This task is a challenge to all and is overwhelming to some people. Furthermore, each person must confront his or her personal preferences for pleasure, recreation, social activities, educational plans, and vocational aspirations and be able to resolve the inevitable conflicts between one's personal need system and the responsibilities of parenthood. Here, mental health services may be needed (perhaps in the form of education, counseling, and/or psychotherapy). As might be anticipated, comprehensive Community Mental Health Centers, special community agencies, and private practitioners are devoting more time and resources to parent education and to counseling for such essential behavioral adaptations as accomplishing family tasks, and functioning in a complex, rapidly changing socio-cultural system.

The family as a social system inevitably experiences change and conflict, and parents learn to resolve conflicts so that adult needs are fulfilled at the same time that children's needs are being met. Parental responsibility is clearly manifested in such actions as nurturance, discipline, and facilitative communication. Parents must make life adaptations to meet the responsibilities of parenthood; yet there are many persons who cannot or do not assume responsibility for their own actions and who have greater difficulty with the added responsibility of parenthood. Thus it has become a major mental health objective to help parents adjust to the responsibility of effectively managing their own lives while effectively contributing to the management of the family system.

The seemingly rapid changes relating to parenting have resulted in numerous controversies in both lay and professional communities. Three problematic areas involve personal decisions that are made regarding parenthood. First, with the changes in attitudes toward "automatic" parenthood and greater opportunities for women to find fulfillment through educational and vocational channels, the question arises whether or not to become a parent. There is a small but growing segment of the population that believes that their own self-fulfillment clearly dictates that they should not have children. In addition, the population explosion has lent support to having fewer or no children. These cultural facts and their philosophical concomitants are reflected in changing legislation about parenthood, particularly legalized abortion. Second, with advances in behavioral science, more theories of human development have emerged; parents are faced with choices of methods of childrearing. Third, there are more families in which both parents are employed. This introduces the need for a parent surrogate, and raises the issues of part-time parenting and the use of day-care programs.

133

Beyond these issues of primarily personal concerns there are three major areas of controversy having important social implications: first, the opinion that our society needs a stated national policy with regard to family life. Such a policy would acknowledge society's responsibility in maximizing the quality of human resources by providing support for optimal child devolopment, family stability, and other facets of family life. The second is the issue of population; controversial areas relating to this issue are sex education programs and liberalized contraceptive and abortion services. The third is the need for parents to have specific knowledge about child development and the methods they, as parents, will use in childrearing. The controversy results from proposals for licensing for parenthood, which would require prospective parents to demonstrate their ability to make adaptations required by childrearing.

Only tentative future predictions can be made. Apparently the recent low birth rate will continue and the birth of children will be purposefully planned and controlled by most couples. There will probably be an increase in voluntary non-parenthood and in the number of one-parent families resulting from a continued high divorce rate as well as increased social approval for single parenthood. It seems likely that the number of working mothers will continue to increase, and that there will be, consequently, an increased usage of day-care facilities and surrogate parents (i.e., full-time childcare workers, perhaps living in the home) and a salutory sharing of childrearing responsibility between the father and the mother.

Priority should be given to establishing a national family policy that will insure standards for mental and physical health and general well-being for all citizens. Helpful at the local level would be a comprehensive mental/physical health education program from preschool through university programs that encompasses education for parenthood.

Participation in such a program might be a prerequisite for a marriage license or for some economic or other incentive. There might be legislation requiring a family impact assessment for all major federal funding projects, akin to environmental impact statements assessments now required.

Robert Henley Woody, Ph.D.
Jane Divita Woody, Ph.D., M.S.W.

References

Anthony, E. James, and Benedek, Therese (eds.) 1970. Parenthood: Its Psychology and Psychopathology. Boston: Little, Brown and Co.

Deibert, Alvin N. and Harmon, Alice J. 1970. New Tools for Changing Behavior. Champaign, Il.: Research Press Co.

Driekus, Rudolf and Cassel, Pearl, 1973. Discipline Without Tears. New York: Hawthorn Books, Inc.,

Ginott, Haim. 1965. Between Parent and Child. New York: Macmillan Publishing Co., Inc.

Gordon, Thomas. 1970. Parent Effectiveness Training: The No-Lose Program for Raising Responsible Children. New York: Peter H. Wyden, Inc.

Knox, David. 1971. Marriage Happiness: A Behavioral Approach to Counseling. Champaign, Il.: Research Press Co.

McIntire, Roger W. 1970. For Love of Children: Behavioral Psychology for Parents. Del Mar, Ca.: CRM Bks.

Madsen, Chas. H., Jr. and Madsen, Clifford K. 1971. Parents—Children—Discipline: A Positive Way. Boston: Allyn & Bacon, Inc.

Patterson, Gerald R. and Gullion, M. Elizabeth. 1971. Living with Children: New Methods for Parents and Teachers. Champaign, Il.: Research Press Co.

Patterson, Gerald R. 1971. Families: Applications of Social Learning to Family Life. Champaign, Il.: Research Press Co.

Satir, Virginia M. 1972. Peoplemaking. Palo Alto, Calif.: Science & Behavior Books, Inc.

Woody, Robert H. and Woody, Jane D. 1973. Sexual, Marital and Familial Relations. Springfield, Il.: Charles C. Thomas, Pubs.

Other Sources

Journals:
Journal of Marriage and Family Counseling (AAMFC)
Journal of Marriage and the Family (NCFR)

Associations:
Planned Parenthood-World Population
Sex Information and Education Council of the U.S. (SIECUS)
National Council on Family Relations
Office of Child Development, DHEW
American Home Economics Association
American Association of Marriage and Family Counselors
Child Welfare League of America
Family Service Association of America

3. Aging

Don't think of retiring from the world until the world
will be sorry that you retire.

—Samuel Johnson (1709-1784)

The Senate Special Committee on Aging, in anticipation of the White House Conference on Aging in 1971, issued the report, *Mental Health Care and the Elderly: Shortcomings in Public Policy*, which stated, "widespread confusions and contradictions in public health policy on mental health of the elderly are causing heavy economic, social and psychological costs among older Americans and their offspring." These costs are paid by the elderly who are misplaced in institutions when they could, with appropriate services, return to the community. Others pay that cost by remaining in their own homes, "in confusion or despair, denied access to services which help others but not them."

Psychopathology in general and depression in particular rises sharply with age. Suicide reaches its zenith in elderly white males. The elderly need a social life, good health care, special housing arrangements or assistance in maintaining themselves in their own homes—all elements of a continuum of which mental health is a part and to which it is linked. Mental health program achievement depends on the maintenance of that continuum and the interrelationships on which it is built.

A primary problem is the scarcity of community resources, including mental health services, limiting the range of service choice. Should current trends of mental health service continue through 1980, it is projected that 80 % of elderly persons in need of mental health services will go without them. Contributing to the problem are severe limitations in service programs all too often imposed by the financing source.

Recent research findings suggest that functional (non-organic) mental impairment in older persons is as responsive to treatment as that in younger patients, and that apathy, isolation, and regressed behavior can be reduced by adequate diagnosis and intervention (Butler & Lewis, 1973).

Considerable research has dealt with negative attitudes that permeate the area of geriatrics. It was found that both administrative and treatment staff inappropriately fear that the elderly are unresponsive to treatment and rehabilitation. Such misconception

136

often delays help-seeking until a crisis, or permanent disability, develops.

A major factor causing society to turn away from the elderly is the reality of death which is associated with the older person, and our cultural denial of this reality. In a study of 348 elderly patients at a New York State mental hospital, Markson (1970) concluded that mental hospitals are being used as an "easy out" for terminal patients: easy for the society perhaps, at the expense of the patients. Elderly persons referred to the geriatric services of mental hospitals tend to be from socioeconomically deprived levels. Their low status leads to unnecessary hospitalization. This could be controlled by diminishing the number of cursory psychiatric examinations and by improved psychiatric screening. Education directed at the public and professionals to understand the rights of the elderly to die in the comfort of their homes with the emotional support of their families was suggested by the study.

Changing directions in service delivery systems provide opportunity and potential for a flexible array of training approaches, both in the existing core mental health disciplines and with new hybrids. The service needs suggest helpers who can find rewards in more modest therapeutic gains than the traditional goals of training programs oriented almost entirely to younger patients.

Suitable mental health service models for the elderly must be administratively feasible and oriented to the priorities of the elderly. Criteria for useful program models include: (1) availability of services to the elderly either in their own neighborhoods or with the help of adequate transportation; (2) high payoff in achieving specified, tangible albeit modest objectives; (3) responsiveness to the demands and needs of the elderly and the community; (4) administrative accountability for measurable program results, including those in longterm care facilities.

Good programs should involve their recipients along with related community service providers in developing and maintaining quality policy and practice. The elderly need a strong element of outreach. Collaboration in the delivery of service is essential at the agency or consumer level, regardless of the separate purpose of the agencies that may be involved. There must be a "critical mass" of adequacy and quality of service.

There is much to learn about how to improve systems of care. Yet too large a gap remains between our knowledge and its application. If, somehow, we could succeed in applying on behalf of the elderly that which we already know, it could bring about a whole new era for our older Americans, and their descendants.

Nathan Sloate, M.S.

References

Butler, Robert N. and Lewis, Myrna I. 1973. Aging and Mental Health—Positive Psychosocial Approaches. St. Louis, Mo.: The C.V. Mosby Company.

Group for the Advancement of Psychiatry. 1970. Toward a Public Policy on Mental Health Care of the Elderly. New York: Group for the Advancement of Psychiatry.

Kasl, S.V. 1972. Physical and mental health effects of involuntary relocation and institutionalization on the elderly: a review. American Journal of Public Health, 62:377-383.

Lowenthal, M.F. 1967. Aging and Mental Disorders in San Francisco. San Francisco: Jossey-Bass, Inc.

Lutz, C. and Gaitz, C.M. 1972. Psychiatrists' attitudes toward the aged and aging. Gerontologist, 12(2):163:167.

Markson, E.W. and Hand, J. 1970. Referral for death: low status of the aged and referral for psychiatric hospitalization. Aging and Human Development, 1(3):261-272.

The President's Task Force on the Aging. 1971. Toward a Brighter Future for the Elderly. Washington, D.C.: GPO.

The President's Task Force on the Mentally Handicapped. 1970. Washington, D.C.: GPO.

U.S. Senate Special Committee on Aging. 1971. Mental Health Care and the Elderly: Shortcomings in Public Policy. Washington, D.C.: GPO.

White House Conference on Aging. 1971. Report to the delegates from the conference sections and special concerns sessions. Washington, D.C.: GPO.

Wolk, R.L. and Goldfarb, A.K. 1967. The response to group psychotherapy of aged recent admisssons compared with long-term mental hospital patients. American Journal of Psychiatry, 10:1252-1256.

Other Sources

Journals:
The International Journal of Aging and Human Development (Baywood Publishing Co.)
Journal of Gerontology (Gerontological Society)
The Gerontologist (Gerontological Society)

Associations:
Group for Geriatric Psychiatry

138

4. Mental Retardation

I find the great thing in this world is not so much
where we stand as in what direction we are moving
. . . We must sail sometimes with the the wind and
sometimes against it, but we must sail, and not drift,
not lie at anchor.

Justice O.W. Holmes (1841-1935)

Mental retardation refers to "significantly sub-average general intellectual functioning, existing concurrently with deficits in
adaptive behavior, and manifested during the developmental
periods." (American Association of Mental Deficienty, 1973). In this
recent definition the word "significantly" is important, removing the
borderline category as did the World Health Organization. Hence-
forth, "borderline," refers only to intelligence, not mental retardation. This change reduces the stigma of labeling a large group of
people as retarded, and defines functioning more reasonably. This
brings together statistical usage with the functional definition (18 %
of the population was included in the borderline retarded group as
opposed to 1%-3% as now defined). Also, the term "adaptive behavior" in the definition prevents a person being labeled MR solely
on the basis of IQ scores. As has been repeatedly documented, IQ
scores frequently do not show the ability of a person to function in
society, but may lead to unfair, discriminatory placements in
schools.

In the history of past attitudes toward the retarded there have
been periods of tolerance and abuse, but a general tendency to put
these individuals "out-of-sight and out-of-mind." Originally, care of
the retarded was dominated by physicians. Not until the latter part
of the 19th century was the term "custodial" care used. This negative trend was aggravated by the eugenics approach in the early
1900's. With the development of the parents' movement, President
Kennedy's Panel Report on Mental Retardation, (GPO, 1962) and the
many changes in the fields of genetics, education, and rehabilitation
in recent years, another look was taken at the situation. Most recently, concern with human rights and human dignity have further
substantiated the need for a new approach to the individual with
problems of mental retardation.

The development of the National Association of Retarded Children (a parent's group), about 1948, produced a stimulus towards development of community services (on a very limited scale due to lack of funds). Although some special education was in process, most of it was a type of classroom captivity for the educable retardate. Not until the 1960's was there a major movement toward keeping mentally-retarded children at home, with community support for the children and parents; this is often the most productive approach, for less isolation brings positive change in many mentally retarded persons, regardless of IQ. This movement grew rapidly, accompanied by a concern to eliminate institutional dehumanization; concurrently there was movement towards normalization, keeping the retarded in the normal life stream with use of generic services, i.e. those not geared especially for the mentally retarded. Increased appreciation of human rights, and examples from other countries, have created a trend away from institutionalization towards small group homes, foster care, and other alternate residential situations. More emphasis needs to be placed on parent training, counseling, availability of a wider range of community services and, when possible, involvement of the person with the handicap in his or her program decisions. Interestingly enough, this parallels movement in the mental health field in many respects.

Until recently, it was thought that about 3% of the total population was mentally retarded, including the classifications of mild, moderate, severe, and profound retardation. Now it is recognized that adaptive behavior can be modified so that mental retardation is no longer as large a problem. Today, those who are really mentally retarded probably consist of only one-half to 1% of the total population. It is this figure that is used to determine the number who need highly specialized services. This figure is also in keeping with the experience of the Scandinavian countries who are considered more advanced in treating people with this handicap. The approach of looking to see how far one can go, instead of accepting barriers, enhances the progress of many people with problems of mental retardation and brings dramatic changes. Large institutions, by their very nature, (i.e., their lack of financial support, the frequent lack of availability of skills, and even their locations) often make impossible what can be achieved in smaller settings.

At various times in the history of this field, the trend has gone from the medical to a strong psychiatric, then to an educational, and finally to an interdisciplinary type of intervention approach. We now recognize that each individual is unique and needs helping disciplines at different times. This view has nurtured development of a wide variety of skills from the mental health specialties. Balancing the involvement of these skills requires combined agency planning as opposed to a unilateral single disciplinary approach. The recognition of this fact has produced considerable improvement

140

of individualized program planning and has been reflected in progress of many mentally retarded people.

There are still major controversies in this field. One is the idea that this field belongs primarily to either education, psychiatry, pediatrics, or social services. In reality, none of these predominate across the board. Any particular department or agency can have major responsibility for MR, but should realize that today its role is that of a team member with a variety of disciplines and agencies. Also, the movement towards the increased use of generic services, with their new responsibility to serve also the retarded, has reduced the numbers who require residential care or need special services. The fact still remains, however, that the need for agencies to get together to plan for MR is essential and was the purpose of the Developmental Disability Legislation of 1971 which created state councils and provided them with funds to supply grants to close gaps between services and/or agencies, as well as to provide a planning process to continue the comprehensive mental retardation planning efforts of 1963-68.

A second area of controversy involves mental health and mental retardation. This is far less intense than it used to be. Since the individual with mental retardation has the same chance to become mentally ill as the non-MR, he or she should be eligible for treatment in mental health facilities. These two disabilities—mental illness and mental retardation—are neither the same nor mutually exclusive, but overlap considerably. Unfortunately, the training of most people in the area of mental health, as well as other areas such as law, has not been adequate to enable these professionals to handle clients who are mentally retarded: the generalized approach of mental health professions to MR will not be successful unless MR concepts are well-covered in training for all human services. Here the various university-affiliated mental retardation training centers should be of great help.

Most admissions to MR institutions are on the basis of emotional disturbances or social factors, both of which can be controlled and handled. The mental health component is handled from a developmental perspective and with behavior modification rather than from traditional mental health approaches since most of the patients are non-verbal, multiply-handicapped, or severely retarded.

A major controversy concerns the right of a person, particularly an adult, to decide his degree of freedom and participation in treatment. To what extent does an adult with limited understanding of voluntary versus involuntary commitment have decision rights? The development of necessary guardianship and protective services, which should vary according to the capabilities of each individual as opposed to an all-or-none approach, is easier to recommend than to define.

A new controversial area is the matter of permitting the mentally retarded individual to experience the same risks as well as the same benefits to which anybody else is entitled. There is still a tendency to be overprotective of people with mental retardation, which is not part of the "normalization" aspect; protection must be relative to the individual's capabilities. Since this is a new area, better guidelines are required.

In the future, more services should be provided by generic community agencies. Parents and governmental agencies should be primarily involved in standard setting, program evaluation, and making sure that people with MR get a fair share of human service resources. There should be a move completely away from institutions, as they presently are structured, and into alternate residential situations. These include foster care, group homes and some selected environments in which specialized health services for the multiply handicapped are present, e.g. in rehabilitation centers or chronic nursing homes. At present, most nursing homes will not take the more severly handicapped because of cost, although the prospects are improving. Joint endeavors for residential services between mental retardation agencies and others such as penal or juvenile delinquency agencies, health departments, and social services would be an improvement over exaggerated separatism. Agencies geared for the mentally retarded are better able than generic agencies to keep up with the field and thus they should supply consultation, training, and evaluation support, particularly in program areas. This combination should provide a much richer program with better utilization of the available tax money and person-power, and should group people more on a functional ability rather than on the basis of a particular etiological or diagnostic label.

There will always be concerns with the mentally retarded getting services when other people are not, and the feeling of many that the money should be used towards the greatest good for the greatest number. This dilemma will never be solved short of solving all the problems of society. On the way to this utopia, getting a fair share of help and treating people with mental handicaps as human beings will require major advances not just in science and technology, but also in human relations.

Robert I. Jaslow, M.D.

References

Bowlby, J.: Maternal Care and Mental Health; World Health Organization, Geneva, 1952

Changing Patterns in Residential Services for the Mentally Retarded; R. B. Kugel and W. Wolfensberger (Eds.), President's Committee on Mental Retardation; Wash., D.C., 1969

Davies, Stanley P. 1959. The Mentally Retarded in Society. New York: Columbia University Press.

Grossman, Herbert, (Ed.), 1973. Manual on Terminology and Classification in Mental Retardation—Rev. Ed. American Association on Mental Deficiency, Special Publication Series, No. 2, p. 11.

Kanner, Leo, 1964. The History of the Care and Study of the Mentally Retarded. Springfield, Ill.: Charles C. Thomas.

The Mentally Retarded Child and His Family; A Multidisciplinary Handbook; Richard Koch, M.D. and James C. Dobson, Ph.D. (Eds.), Brunner/Mazel Publishers; N.Y., N.Y., 1971

The President's Panel on Mental Retardation. A Proposed Program for National Action to Combat Mental Retardation, Washington, D.C., 1962

A Proposed Program for National Action to Combat Mental Retardation, Oct. 1962, U.S. Government Printing Office, Washington, D.C.

The Right to Choose, National Association for Retarded Citizens; Residential Services Committee; 1973

Standards for Community Agencies; Joint Commission on Accreditation of Hospitals, Chicago, Ill., 1973

Standards for Residential Facilities for the Mentally Retarded; Joint Commission on Accreditation of Hospitals, Chicago, Ill., 1971

Woody, R. H., 1974, Legal Aspects of Mental Retardation: A Search for Reliability. Springfield, Ill.: Charles C. Thomas

Other Sources

Journals:
The American Journal of Mental Deficiency (AAMD)
Mental Retardation (AAMD)

Associations:
American Association of Mental Deficiency
American Academy on Mental Retardation
National Association for Retarded Children

143

5. Risk-Taking and Suicide

The preservation of health is a duty. Few seem conscious that there is such a thing as physical morality.

—Herbert Spencer (1820-1903)

Risk-taking, initially brings to mind activities which involve the prospect of physical danger to a person, such as motorcycle driving, mountain climbing, hunting, and skydiving. Other risk-taking activity includes all forms of gambling, and even stock market and other investing. In addition, activities such as cigarette smoking, dangerous driving, the habitual use of alcohol, chronic obesity, attempted suicide, multiple drug use, and failure to undergo a periodic physical examination are also examples of risk-taking.

Risk-taking has been defined as the selection of a course of action from several alternatives in which the consequences of that choice could leave the individual in a worse situation than if he had made another selection or perhaps not selected at all. More simply, risk-taking may be viewed as embarking on a task without being certain of success.

Behavioral scientists have not been able to agree fully on an accepted definition of risk-taking, perhaps because the concept of risk can be applied to nearly every major area of human activity. Developmentally, it is an integral part of human experience and personality growth from birth to death. Infants explore and interact with their environment, causing parents concern. This risk-taking reflects an innate drive rather than the selection of a course of action involving the weighing of consequences and alternatives. Yet we can view this behavior as the initial experience of action and consequence upon which later choices are based.

Efforts to organize the concept of risk-taking have resulted to four major components or categories of situations: 1) financial gambles or monetary risks; 2) chances of bodily harm or physical injury; 3) ethical risk; and 4) situations involving a person's esteem in the eyes of others, or social risk.

Research to date suggests: 1) that there is no general risk-taking disposition; 2) that some of the numerous instruments (primarily personality tests) used to measure risk tap only a few dimensions; 3) that these instruments fail to provide the subject with a true atmosphere of risk. The data support the view that risk-taking is a multidimensional and transitional phenomenon. Furthermore, individuals

144

are inclined, in varying degrees, to take risks, and this universal tendency must be differentiated in relation to the situational context.

An examination of the risk-taking behavior of groups compared with the individual group members has revealed a "Group Shift" phenomenon; that is, group choices tend to be either more risky or more conservative than individual choices. These differences may be explained on the basis of conformity to the cultural norms of that group, anonymity afforded by the group, and a decreased sense of personal responsibility for outcome.

Because of its special significance, we will focus on suicidal behavior, a serious public health problem taking at least 20,000 lives annually, and injuring many more. In the United States, the national suicide rate is 10.5 per 100,000. It is the tenth leading cause of death among adults and the third among youth. Suicide *attempts* are estimated to occur at a rate of 100/100,000 or approximately ten times as often as the fatal act. These figures are woefully inaccurate for several reasons. Suicidal behavior is associated with a severe social stigma. As a result, many incidents are not reported or are erroneously reported, and evidence may be altered or destroyed.

Suicidal behavior may be defined as the performance of acts of a self-damaging nature, which may be lethal or potentially so. A suicide attempt may be considered to be any non-fatal act with self-destructive intention, including long-standing behavior patterns, such as alcoholism, cigarette smoking and dangerous driving; these behaviors have been described as "slow" or "chronic" suicide. The outcome of suicidal behavior depends upon a variety of factors, some but not all being controlled by the individual.

Studies have shown that eighty percent of people at one time or another contemplate suicide. Approximately two million individuals now living in the United States have a history of at least one unsuccessful suicide attempt. No single group, race, or class of people fails to contribute to this number. The "wish to die" is frequently found in children, and "suicidal fantasies" are common in normal adults.

The frequency of suicidal behavior increases with age. It is rare in children but is the third-leading cause of death in teenagers and young adults not counting automobile accidents, many of which are disguised suicides. During the middle years decreasing physical vigor, unfulfilled dreams and various familial conflicts may produce a mid-life crisis with ominous implications. Yet, the suicide problem is greatest among elderly citizens who, if they choose to attempt suicide, usually succeed.

Economic conditions and occupations both seem to influence suicidal behavior, as evidenced by the increased rate of suicide noted during periods of economic instability. Women have always outnumbered men in *attempted* suicides in a fairly stable ratio of three to one. For *completed* suicides, the result and ratio are reversed; that is, one female to three males. Men often seek self-destruction by the use of highly lethal methods, such as firearms and hanging, while women prefer more passive and less lethal methods, such as sleeping pills, poison, or gas.

Marriage is associated with decreased suicidal behavior, with the exception of the young, i.e. those under 25. Urban rates are higher than rural. Spring and the Christmas period have the highest suicide rates. Catholics and Jews have lower rates than Protestants.

The repudiation of life which accompanies suicidal behavior is invariably shocking and raises the question, "Why?" The many theories which attempt to explain this phenomenon cite unresolved intrapsychic conflict, e.g. unresolved anger at a deceased parent; defects in personality development; environmental pressures; physical illness; and a combination of factors. Generally, the suicidal episode occurs in the form *of a crisis of limited duration* during which the person has ambivalent feelings marked by hopelessness and a wish to be rescued. This is borne out 1) by the fact that 80% of those who engage in suicidal behavior communicate their intentions in one or more ways to other people, and 2) by the discrepancy between the rates of attempted and completed suicides. This is significant from a public health point of view because it indicates the potential value of programs designed to identify individuals at risk, to provide assistance during periods of crisis, to provide intervention by appropriate personnel, and to provide follow-up on individuals who are judged to be suicidal. This form of risk-taking will continue, and comprehensive programs will not be developed, unless: 1) the social stigma attached to suicide is alleviated; 2) there is an adoption of humane legal attitudes; and 3) the many forms that self destructive behavior assumes can be more effectively diagnosed and classified.

Risk-taking of all types is a large public health problem with grave consequences for risk-takers, for their families, and for society. Its protean forms go largely unobserved, but its price in human suffering is nevertheless extracted. Superstition, moral judgments, and laissez-faire attitudes combine to form a quagmire in which scientific investigation has floundered. Neither the positive nor the negative aspects of risk-taking behavior have received the attention they deserve.

Melvin W. Williams, M.D., M.P.H.

References

Carney, Richard E. 1971. Risk-taking Behavior. Springfield, Il.: C.C. Thomas.

Cohn, John. 1960. Chance, Skill and Luck. Baltimore: Pelican Books.

Hafen, B.Q. and Faux, E.J. 1972. Self-destructive Behavior. Minneapolis: Burgess.

Kramer, M., Pollack, E.S., Redick, R.W., Locke, B.Z. 1972. Mental Disorders/Suicide. Cambridge, Mass: Harvard Univ. Press.

Lester, G. and Lester, D. 1971. Suicide: The Gamble with Death. Englewood Cliffs, N.J.: Prentice Hall.

Moran, E. 1970. Proceedings of the Royal Society of Medicine. 63: 1273-75.

Resnick, H.L. P. editor. 1968. Suicidal Behaviors. Boston: Little Brown & Co.

Wallach, M.A. and Kogan, N. 1967. New Directions in Psychology III. New York: Holt, Rinehart and Winston.

Other Sources

Journal articles are listed in Index Medicus under gambling, behavioral adaptations (psychological), suicide, and a variety of cross-referenced headings.

6. Substance Abuse: Alcohol, Drugs, Tobacco and Food

My very chains and I grew friends,
So much a long communion tends
To make us what we are.

—Lord Byron (1788-1824)
Prisoner of Chillon

The abused substances investigated herein are alcohol, drugs, tobacco and food. The definition of *substance abuse,* adapted from one on alcoholism, is: *repeated implicative use of alcoholic beverages, drugs, tobacco, or food so as to cause injury to the user's health or to his social or economic functioning* (Keller, 1960). Injury to the user's health is a likely consequence of frequent, excessive use of any of the four substances, whereas social and economic malfunctioning are more likely to occur as a result of drug or alcohol abuse.

Some still unresolved issues related to definition are: severity, recency, and reversibility. First, should any use constitute abuse, or if not, at what point does use become sufficiently excessive to be considered abuse? Second, shall persons with previous but no current problems due to substance abuse be considered positive subjects, or if not, how long an interval of freedom from such problems should be required? Third, if persons having only previous problems are *not* to be considered positive subjects, is total abstinence (except from food) or moderate consumption necessary to indicate freedom from addiction or habituation?

Considerable evidence of cross-substance abuse exists, supporting theories of an "addictive personality" (Haberman, 1969). Cigarette smoking, for example, has been observed to vary directly with drinking and with drug use to a marked extent, and drug users not infrequently have a history of excessive alcohol use (Haberman and Baden, 1974A).

Alcohol—About 70% of adults in the United States drink alcoholic beverages, although perhaps only half of these drink more than once a month; a majority of teen-agers have consumed alcoholic beverages on more than one occasion. About four-fifths of men and three-fifths of women are drinkers, with the proportion of males relatively constant for the past 20 years or so, while drinking among

148

women has increased. The proportion of drinkers is directly related to social class and inversely related to age—particularly among women. By color, white and black men vary little in the proportion of drinkers, whereas black women are much less likely to drink than are white women.

About one-tenth of all drinkers are alcoholics or problem drinkers; men are perhaps three to four times more likely to have drinking-related problems than are women, but this sex difference has been diminishing. Blacks, and in particular black women, are alcoholics much more frequently than their white counterparts. The rates of alcoholism among ethnoreligious groups vary considerably. By social class, there does not seem to be a clear trend in rates of alcoholism; but since fewer lower class persons drink, drinker-specific rates vary inversely with class i.e., among lower class drinkers there is a higher rate of alcoholism. (Bailey et al., 1965; Cahalan et al., 1970; Public Health Service, 1967).

Drugs—According to recent national surveys, almost one-sixth of youths aged 12 to 17 and adults have used marijuana at least once, with half as many being current users. Other illegal drugs, as well as legal drugs taken nonmedically, are used by much smaller proportions of youths and adults, ranging from no more than one percent who ever used heroin, to between three percent and six percent for LSD or other hallucinogens, amphetamines, barbiturates and minor tranquilizers (Josephson, 1974; National Commission on Marijuana and Drug Abuse, 1973).

Males are more likely than females to have used marijuana, as well as hallucinogens, amphetamines, barbiturates, and tranquilizers nonmedically; and use varies directly with class as indicated by education and family income. Whites more often than blacks tend to use these drugs. (McGlothlin, 1974). Opiate use, in contrast, is greatest among blacks and other minority and poor groups (Chambers, 1974). Women are more likely than men to have used prescribed psychotherapeutic drugs, most of which are prescribed by non-psychiatrist physicians. Prescribed use is most prevalent in the highest social class, but heavy use occurs most often among the poor, who are least likely to receive psychotherapy (Mellinger et al., 1974).

Tobacco—In 1970, more than two-fifths of American men smoked cigarettes—a decrease of eight percent from 1965. Among women, 30 percent reported smoking in 1970—a substantial increase since the 1950's, but a slight decrease since 1965 (Department of Health, Education and Welfare, 1972A). The prevalence of smoking is highest in the 20-29 age group for black and white men and women; blacks of both sexes have shown higher proportions of smokers than have whites (Friedman, 1972). Among men, smoking is inversely related to social class, although the converse appears to

149

be true for amount smoked. For women, smoking is less related to social class (Department of Health, Education and Welfare, 1972B). Nationally, in 1972, one-sixth of male teenagers aged 12 to 18 smoked regularly, a decline from the peak of one-fifth in 1970. One-eighth of youths 12 to 18 reported smoking regularly; however, the prevalence of smoking among teenage girls has continued to rise steadily from eight percent in 1968 and 12 percent in 1970 (Department of Health, Education and Welfare, 1972C).

Food—Sex, age, color and class differences in proportions of overweight persons have been discerned. One-quarter of women in their third decade have been found to be 20 percent or more above their ideal weight and one-half in their fifth decade were similarly overweight. About one-third of 15-year-old girls have been identified as being overweight. Males are less likely to be overweight than females at almost every age; the proportion being 20 percent above ideal weight increases from one-quarter to one-third between the ages of 30 and 59. There is a marked inverse correlation between class and obesity, particularly among females; 30 percent of poor women and 5 percent of non-poor are overweight (Department of Health, Education and Welfare, 1966; Stunkard et al., 1972; Goldblatt et al., 1965). One-fifth of black women and one in twenty white women are 20 percent above their ideal weight (Public Health Reports, 1954). The differences for men are in the same direction, but less. Finally, there is evidence that up to four-fifths of overweight girls and boys retain this condition as adults, and that diet during childhood is important in establishing later metabolic patterns (Abraham and Nordsieck, 1960).

Morbidity and Mortality—Substance abuse is associated with excess morbidity and mortality. Abuse of tobacco and food, for example, greatly increases the risk of cardiovascular disease. Other known conditions related to substance abuse include: cirrhosis of the liver, tuberculosis, and lobar pneumonia associated with alcoholism; lung cancer, emphysema, bronchitis, and circulatory diseases associated with cigarette abuse; diabetes, hypertension, and renal disease associated with obesity; and infectious diseases, e.g., hepatitis, tetanus and bacterial endocarditis associated with drug abuse.

The linkage between excess alcohol use and accidents is well-known. A definite relationship between narcotism, alcoholism or recent excessive alcohol ingestion and violent death, i.e., homicide, traffic fatality, other fatal accident or suicide has been consistently observed (Haberman and Baden, 1974B). Drug addicts often resort to crime to support their habits; crimes may also be committed because of the effects of certain drugs; and a substantial minority of drug addicts are also alcoholics.

Treatment and Prevention—There are several different approaches to the treatment of substance abuse. Self-help groups (e.g., Alcoholics Anonymous or Weight Watchers) and self-regulatory therapeutic communities (e.g., Synanon, Odyssey House, or Daytop Village for narcotic addicts) rely primarily on counseling by non-professional ex-abusers. Aversion therapy techniques or other forms of behavior modification, including use of deterrents or antagonists (such as, Antabuse for alcoholics and cyclazocine or Naloxene for narcotic addicts), are used to reduce the craving for specific substances. Methadone maintenance is used to block the effects of heroin; and medically supervised distribution of certain narcotic drugs is practiced in England. More traditional psychotherapeutic techniques alone have not generally been as effective as those methods which are directed specifically at symptom relief (Public Health Service, 1967; Jaffe, 1971; Guildford, 1972).

Efforts to prevent alcohol, drug, and tobacco abuse fall into two categories. Programs primarily within school systems are aimed at informing, persuading and less frequently, scaring. Sales restrictions for alcohol and tobacco products include limitations on business hours and on the age of buyers or users, taxation, and the licensing of outlets. Restrictions on advertising, and recently, counter-advertising are also employed.

There are three major areas of controversy in respect to substance abuse. First, is substance abuse due mainly to illness or to "moral weakness," and if the former, are the different kinds of substance abuse separate, or one disease classification, or varied symptoms of one underlying disturbance? Second, what policy alternatives should be pursued with regard to certain illicit drugs, e.g., marijuana, which are widely used and considered by many to be no more harmful than legal substances, e.g., alcohol and tobacco? Third, what type of treatment for substance abuse should be utilized, and should treatment deal primarily with symptom relief or the understanding of underlying causes?

In the United States since mid-century, there is majority acceptance that alcoholism and drug addiction are due mainly to illness rather than to "moral weakness," although some of this sentiment may be little more than lip service. (Haberman and Sheinberg, 1969). Whether substance abuse is a disease or symptom of underlying disturbance, the extent to which it is a somatic or psychosomatic condition, and the etiology are still unresolved questions, with opinion varying according to specific substances.

On marijuana, the proportion in favor of legalization is increasing, but the consensus at present seems to be more in favor of penalty reduction for the private use of small amounts ("decriminalization"). With regard to the treatment of narcotics abuse, there is much debate about programs that keep persons drug-dependent by dispensing either less harmful drugs, e.g., methadone, or the addicts' choice of drug, as is common in England. Another unresolved question is whether treatment should stop at symptom relief or attempt to get at the presumed underlying causes of the problem; a related issue is the role of ex-abusers and trained professionals in treatment. Regarding alcohol abuse, there is some discord about whether complete abstinence should be the goal as it is for Alcoholics Anonymous or whether moderate social drinking indicates an equal or better adjustment, even though this apparently can be maintained only by a small minority of alcoholics (Bailey and Stewart, 1967).

The prognosis, it would seem, is that drug, alcohol, tobacco, and food abuse in the U. S. should tend to stabilize. The use of marijuana under certain circumstances will probably have increasing public support. Substance abuses in general will increasingly be viewed as due to illness and as stemming from similar underlying causes, with the choice of substance being related to availability and sociocultural factors, especially peer group usage. Treatment will probably emphasize the multimodal approach, utilizing several different but complementary techniques.

Paul W. Haberman, M.B.A.
Loretta Hervey

References

Abraham, S. and Nordsieck, M. 1960. Relationship of excess weight in children and adults. Public Health Reports, 75:263-273.

Bailey, M. B., et. al. 1965. The epidemiology of alcoholism in an urban residential area. Quarterly Journal of Studies on Alcohol, 26:19-40.

Bailey, M. B. and Stewart J. 1967. Normal drinking by persons reporting previous drinking problems. Quarterly Journal of Studies on Alcohol, 28:305-315.

Cahalan, D., et. al. 1969. American Drinking Practices. New Brunswick: Rutgers Center of Alcohol Studies.

Chambers, C. 1974. Some Epidemiological Considerations of Onset of Opiate Use in the United States. In Josephson, E. and Carroll E. (Eds.) Drug Use: Epidemiological and Sociological Approaches. Washington, D. C.: Hemisphere-Wiley.

Department of Health, Education and Welfare. 1972A. Cigarette Smoking: United States, 1970. Health Interview Survey—Provisional Data from the National Center for Health Statistics, Publication No. (HSM) 72-1132, Vol. 21, No. 3, Supplement, June 2.

Department of Health, Education and Welfare. 1972B. (Rev. Ed.) Chart Book of Smoking, Tobacco, and Health. National Clearinghouse for Smoking and Health, Publication No. (HSM) 72-7511.

Department of Health, Education and Welfare. 1972C. Patterns and Prevalence of Teenage Cigarette Smoking: 1968, 1970, and 1972. National Clearinghouse for Smoking and Health, Publication No. (HSM) 73-8701, August 6.

Department of Health, Education and Welfare. 1966. Obesity and Health. National Center for Chronic Disease Control.

Friedman, G. 1972. Smoking among white, black, and yellow men and women. American Journal of Epidemiology, 96:23-35.

Goldblatt, P., et. al. 1965. Social factors in obesity. Journal of the American Medical Association, 192:1039-1044, June 21.

Guildford, Joan. 1972. Group treatment vs. individual initiative in the cessation of smoking. Journal of Applied Health, 56:162-167.
Haberman, P. W. and Sheinberg, J. 1969. Public attitudes toward alcoholism as an illness. American Journal of Public Health, 59:1209-1216.
Haberman, P. W. and Baden, M. M. 1974A. Drinking, drugs and death. International Journal of the Addictions, 9:761-773.
Haberman, P. W. and Baden, M. M. 1974B. Alcoholism and violent death. Quarterly Journal of Studies on Alcohol, 35:221-231.
Haberman, P. W. 1969. Drinking and other self-indulgencies: complements or counterattractions? International Journal of the Addictions, 4:157-167.
Jaffe, J. 1971. The status quo. Hospitals, 45:40-43.
Josephson, E. 1974. Adolescent marijuana use, 1971-1972: findings from two national surveys. Addictive Diseases: An International Journal. 1(10): 55-72.
Keller, M. Definition of alcoholism. 1960. Quarterly Journal of Studies on Alcohol, 21:125-134.
McGlothlin, W. 1974. The Epidemiology of Hallucinogenic Drug Use. In Josephson, E. and Carroll, E. (Eds.) Drug Use: Epidemiological and Sociological Approaches. Washington, D. C.: Hemisphere-Wiley.
Mellinger, G., et. al. 1974. An Overview of Psychotherapeutic Drug Use in the United States. In Josephson, E. and Carroll, E. (Eds.) Drug Use: Epidemiological and Sociological Approaches. Washington, D. C.: Hemisphere-Wiley.
National Commission on Marijuana and Drug Abuse. 1973. Drug Use in America: Problem in Perspective. Second Report (March).
Public Health Reports. 1954. Estimated Prevalence of Overweight in the U. S., 69:1084.
Public Health Service. 1967. Alcohol and Alcoholism. Publication No. 1640.
Stunkard, A., et. al. 1972. Influence of social class on obesity and thinness in children. Journal of the American Medical Association, 221:579-584, (August 7).

Other Sources

Journals:
Quarterly Journal of Studies on Alcohol
International Journal of the Addictions (drugs, alcohol and tobacco)
National Drug Reporter
Smoking and Health Bulletin
Obesity and Bariatric Medicine

Associations:
Alcoholics Anonymous (General Service Office)
National Council on Alcoholism
Rutgers Center of Alcohol Studies
National Clearinghouse for Alcohol Information of the National Institute on Alcohol Abuse and Alcoholism
Alcohol and Drug Problems Association of North America
Addiction Research Foundation (Canada-Drugs and Alcohol)
Bureau of Narcotics and Dangerous Drugs
National Clearinghouse for Drug Abuse Information of the National Institute on Drug Abuse
National Clearinghouse for Smoking and Health
American Cancer Society
National Interagency Council on Smoking and Health
American Society of Bariatric Physicians
Weight Watchers International

7. Crime and Delinquency: The Corrections System

We have many boys who have been addicted to
habits of stealing, running away from home, playing
truant from school, etc., for four or five years, and
some, even, who have never regularly attended
school, and could not even give the name of a single
letter of the alphabet, who were sixteen years old,
and have always lived in this State. There are many
such among us, growing up in idleness, ignorance
and crime.

—*Annual Report of Superintendent
State Reform School (Maine)
in Portland Advertiser (January 26,
1858)*

The corrections system, as it exists in America today, is one of
the most misunderstood and little known aspects of the criminal justice system. Even corrections workers tend only to be aware of their
own special area of responsibility. We are dealing with complex
phenomena. For example, why should the crime/delinquency rate
vary from one population to another, and what effect will the corrections system have upon the offenders in each group?

To approach the issue of the corrections system and its effect
upon crime and delinquency, the following terms are defined:

(I) *Anomie* or "normlessness." The French sociologist Emile
Durkheim (1858-1917) contributed the theory of anomie to the study
of deviant behavior, specifically suicide. Robert K. Merton (1938)
expanded the theory of anomie to the societal level. On the one hand
a society develops a continually refined structure generally consistent with its goals, but on the other hand, it must have a means of incorporating change in a socially approved manner. A smoothly running society may be said to have institutionalized its most effective
norms and values. This means an individual, as a contributing and
accepted member of his society, may progress, achieve, and work toward the values in which he believes. The reverse of this situation
occurs when societal norms and values are poorly coordinated. The
consequence is a highly ineffective society where individuals are unable to work productively in a socially approved manner. Herein, a
state of anomie (normlessness) exists. A consequence of anomie is

154

deviant behavior, which may be either constructive or destructive to the society and/or the individual. Crime and delinquency is an example of the destructive effects of anomie.

Gibbons (1973, p. 183) returned to Durkheim's original theory, maintaining that mankind must be regulated within a social organization or collective order to control his unlimited aspirations. Otherwise, a state of normlessness will emerge from a loss of rules. The normlessness of anomie exists whenever the rules of order in a society break down (e.g., during periods of unexpected prosperity, unexpected depression, or rapid technological change) and when people are "misled into aspiring to goals extremely difficult if not impossible to achieve."

(II) *Delinquency.* Woodmansey (1971, p. 155) defines delinquency as, "a mental state specifically characterized by a tendency to behave without regard for, or in active opposition to, the welfare of others." This definition is not the same as generally applied to the act of law-breaking, although in practice it may be the principal cause thereof.

(III) *Crime.* "A crime is any wrong which the government deems injurious to the public at large, and punishes through a judicial proceeding in its own name." (1 Bish. Crim. Law, 32.) In a general sense, a crime "implies any act done or committed in violation of public law, and for which the person is liable to punishment by indictment, presentment, or impeachment." (Smith v. Smith, 2 Sneed-Tenn.-473.)

There is a wide variability in the manner in which individuals define criminality. Not only those convicted in the courts of criminal violations are criminals; each individual has an internalized conceptualization of law allowing him, in a personal way, to determine what level of behavior constitutes a crime and who is a criminal.

With social change the response to crime has been modified over the years. For example, Marshall and Clark (1952) have traced developments in legal history in terms of the shifts from the old self-help (i.e., private vengeance) law of crimes to the present where personal action to achieve retribution is unreasonable. In other words, society has not coded its laws and set specific penalties for their violation. During the centuries of legal change the concept of crime and criminality has not been altered appreciably, but the concept of punishment has undergone constant revision. Also, new crimes have been formulated over time and occasionally punishment has been altered to fit the criminal instead of the crime; nevertheless the concept of crime itself has remained constant: ". . . crime concerns transgressions against the public order, rather than against the moral or private orders" (Marshall & Clark, 1952, p. 14).

(IV) *The Corrections System.* The corrections system is composed of various settings (penitentiaries, prisons, jails, work-release centers, etc.) and processes, both in and outside the community, by which an individual convicted of a crime is made to pay his debt to society. This payment may take several forms. Institutionalization of offenders accounts for one-third of the convicted criminal population, with the remaining two-thirds under supervision in the community. On an average day adults comprise about three-quarters of those under custody or in community treatment programs, with the majority of them classified as felons.

In the case of juveniles (persons usually under 18 but ranging from under 16 to 21 in some jurisdictions) the commission of serious crimes may place the offender in an adult category, where they will be treated with other adult offenders. However, juveniles are generally processed in special juvenile courts which employ procedures and treatments unique to this population.

In the overall picture of the corrections system certain characteristics predominate. In one recent study, the average sentence for all first offenses was 38.6 months with the average time served being 19.7 months. Thus, the average offender served 51 percent of his total sentence in a correctional institution. (Task Force Report: Corrections, 1967, p. 1-2, 45).

About 95% of all offenders in the United States corrections system are males between the ages of 15 and 30. Federal Bureau of Investigation figures for 1970 show that 1.6 million juveniles were arrested, and 60% of those convicted were found guilty of violations in three areas of criminal law: (1) drug laws, 12%; (2) larceny-theft, 28%, and (3) transportation, etc. of stolen motor vehicles, 20% (Statistical Abstract, 1971, p. 158). In addition, 40% of all armed robberies and assaults were committed by juveniles under the age of 18 and the proportion is rising. When these convicted juveniles are placed in the corrections system they comprise nearly a third of the inmate population of this country. In 1965, 63,000 juveniles were in institutions and 285,000 were in some form of community treatment. The 1975 FBI statistical forecast predicts a juvenile inmate population of 108,000 (Task Force Report: Corrections, 1967, p. 2).

(V) *Community Treatment and Halfway Homes.* Community treatment is a viable alternative to incarceration for many first offenders. The community approach draws heavily on local resources (mental health teams and other professional, as well as volunteer organizations). The primary purpose of community treatment and halfway homes is to offer an alternative to institutionalization, and to remove its "isolating effects" while at the same time providing a vehicle for re-entry back into the community at large.

The widespread lack of knowledge and understanding of the corrections system has produced for the offender, and the society of which he is a part, an institution which does not correct. In fact, rehabilitation is impossible in some cases and severely impaired in others. This is due in large part to a societal attitude that does not want to look at its deviant members, especially in a way which makes the deviant more human, since society generally categorized deviants in an "other" class by themselves.

Every juvenile delinquent, failure, misfit, and otherwise deviant member of society has had to face a corrections system, the traditional role of which has been one of confinement, segregation, and punishment. Many people still feel this is the way the system should work.

During the last fifteen years the concept of true rehabilitation has become the primary aim of the corrections system. Rehabilitation at first was limited to the idea of teaching new job skills, so that a man might gain useful employment upon his release. But, what was called rehabilitation was merely retraining. With the entry of specialists from all phases of mental health into the corrections system, rehabilitation is in the process of becoming a meaningful concept.

New programs in corrections include the familiar foster homes and group homes for adults and juveniles, plus halfway houses where guided group interaction sessions may take place. Finally, intensive community treatments have been created, such as the California Youth Authority's Treatment Project, prerelease guidance centers, reception center parole, the Highfields project in New Jersey, and the Pinehills project in Provo, Utah (Task Force Report: Corrections, 1967, p. 38-44).

Problems encountered in new programs include: (1) the need to make administrators and legislators aware of the programs in an atmosphere favorable for development; (2) the replication of successful parallel alternatives to institutionalization in different parts of the country; (3) the need to secure new sources of funding, and (4) the need for trained manpower to staff these programs and projects (Task Force Report: Corrections, 1967, p. 38-44).

One major controversy centers around institutionalization of offenders as opposed to community treatment since the rehabilitation philosophy is a relatively recent development in this field. According to Gibbons (1973), history shows that offenders have had to suffer so that society may feel the criminal has paid for his crime, and so that future lawbreakers might be deterred. The notion that punishment prevents recurrence of deviant behavior through the offender's effort to avoid pain has a long history, whereas the view that the correctional process should attempt to reform, resocialize, modify, or remake the offender so that he will avoid future lawbreaking is of recent origin, but is gaining research and administrative support.

A second issue is the need for articulation among the various allied service agencies which serve the offender. It is essential that members of allied service agencies, e.g., social services and mental health, be consulted during the planning of community programs.

This consultation is necessary since many specialized community programs in corrections place demands upon the same resources as do mental health agencies. Only through inter-agency cooperation will the corrections and mental health fields form an effective functional relationship (Task Force Report: Corrections, 1967, p. 44). This functional relationship depends in part upon community involvement and participation. Too often new models from the mental health field (e.g., halfway houses) have failed because the community refused to accept them. To promote this acceptance, it is essential that citizens be included in the planning of any treatment facility located in their community, not just for program acceptance, but to enable the community to help in the rehabilitation process.

In the past few years many people have questioned whether higher rates of crime and delinquency reflected an actual increase or better reporting procedures and computerized record keeping. Bersani (1970) feels the reasons behind the rising crime rate make little difference since the outcome is generally the same: people act and react based upon what they believe to be real, and crime and delinquency generate fear, hostility and disgust in our society. These feelings produce public pressure for the maximum use of the corrections system, particularly institutionalization of offenders. Supposedly, imprisonment of the criminal or delinquent assures public safety and deters future deviant behavior.

It is important to remember that what the public believes to be real determines public opinion, regardless of whether or not such belief is based upon fact or fiction. Thus, today's society focuses attention more on the police function and the court system than upon activities within the corrections system. Therefore, the corrections system and its efforts to rehabilitate the offender may ironically conflict with the traditional goal of the criminal justice system which has been to deter or arrest, and punish the offender.

Improvements in the corrections system must meet several fundamental conditions before the system can achieve its rehabilitation goals. These include: improved and efficient organizations; more and better-trained staff; community education and community services for the offender; better decision-making at all levels, and extended research and evaluation. Finally, the criminal justice system must not mete out excessively harsh penalties to offenders because the corrections system then must deal with two opposing forces: (1) the offender's despair and hostility generated by the harsh penalty, and (2) help for the individual's return as a productive and contributing member of the community.

As the President's Commission on Law Enforcement and Administration of Justice points out, "The most conspicuous problems in corrections today are the lack of knowledge and an unsystematic approach to the development of programs and techniques"

(Task Force Report: Corrections, 1967, p. 13). All too often a stop-gap approach has been applied to the problems of the corrections system, resulting in small lifeless programs which add little to the effort to produce decisive and effective rehabilitation programs. On a more holistic level, what is needed is a plan that attempts to deal systematically with all the interlocking facets of the corrections system. Additional basic research and evaluation of current programs may help avoid wasteful repetitive error and demoralizing redundancy.

B. James Naberhuis, Jr.

References

Alexander, Myrl E. 1960. Current Concepts in Corrections. Tacoma, Wash.: Pacific Lutheran University.

Amos, William E., & Wellford, Charles F., (eds.) 1967. Delinquency Prevention, Theory and Practice. Englewood Cliffs, New Jersey: Prentice-Hall.

Barnes, Harry E., & Teeters, Negley K. 1959. New Horizons in Criminology. (3rd. ed.), Englewood Cliffs, New Jersey: Prentice-Hall.

Benjamin, Judith G., Freedman, Marcia K., & Lynton, Edith F. 1965. Pros and Cons: New Roles for Nonprofessionals in Corrections. New York: National Committee on Employment of Youth.

Chambliss, William J. 1966. "The Deterrent influence of punishment," Crime and Delinquency, 12 (January).

Clinard, Marshall B., (ed.) 1964. Anomie and Deviant Behavior: A Discussion and Critique. New York: Free Press of Glencoe, Inc.

Cloward, Richard A., & Ohlin, Lloyd E. 1960. Delinquency and Opportunity. New York: The Free Press.

Conrad, John P. 1967. Crime and Its Correction. Berkeley: University of California Press.

Gibbons, Don C. 1973. Society, Crime, and Criminal Careers (2nd. ed.). Englewood Cliffs, New Jersey: Prentice-Hall.

Gibbons, Don C. 1965. Changing the Lawbreaker. Englewood Cliffs, New Jersey: Prentice-Hall.

Hoebel, E. Adamson. 1954. The Law of Primitive Man. Cambridge, Mass.: Harvard University Press.

Lofland, John. 1969. Deviance and Identity. Englewood Cliffs, New Jersey: Prentice-Hall.

Menninger, Karl. 1968. The Crime of Punishment. New York: The Viking Press.

Packer, Herbert L. 1968. The Limits of the Criminal Sanction. Stanford University Press.

Radzinowicz, Leon. 1948-1957. A History of English Criminal Law and Its Administration From 1750. 3 vols. New York: The Macmillan Co.

Robinson, Louis N. 1921. Penology in the United States. Philadelphia: John C. Winston.

Rothman, David J. 1971. The Discovery of the Asylum. Boston: Little, Brown and Co.

Rubin, Sol. 1963. The Law of Criminal Correction. St. Paul, Minn.: West Publishing Co.

Sellin, Thorsten, (ed.). 1967. Capital Punishment. New York: Harper & Row.

Sykes, Gresham M. 1958. The Society of Captives. Princeton, New Jersey: Princeton University Press.

Tappan, Paul W. 1960. Crime, Justice, and Correction. New York: McGraw-Hill.

Vold, George B. 1958. Theoretical Criminology. New York: Oxford University Press.

The President's Commission on Law Enforcement and Administration of Justice. 1967. The Challenge of Crime in a Free Society Washington, D. C.: U.S. Government Printing Office.

The President's Commission on Law Enforcement and Administration of Justice. 1967. Task Force Report: Corrections Washington, D. C.: U.S. Government Printing Office.

The President's Commission on Law Enforcement and Administration of Justice. 1967. Task Force Report: Juvenile Delinquency and Youth Crime Washington, D. C.: U.S. Government Printing Office.

VII. Professional Training

1. Distribution and Utilization of Mental Health Services Personnel

All persons employed in the care of the insane should be active, vigilant, cheerful, and in good health. They should be of a kind and benevolent disposition; be educated, and in all respects trustworthy; and their compensation should be sufficiently liberal to secure the services of individuals of this description.

—*Thomas Kirkbride, M.D. (1809-1883)*

One of the eleven supporting studies behind *Action for Mental Health,* the final report of the Joint Commission on Mental Illness and Health, was devoted to mental health manpower (Albee, 1959). The Report provided the foundation for a major shift in mental health manpower policy as this was related to changes in the services delivery system. The provision of care, treatment, and rehabilitation services for the mentally ill had undergone significant changes with the advent of psychotropic drugs and with the transitional shifts in the nature of community care for the mentally ill. A wider range of comprehensive services was provided through the establishment of expanded free-standing mental health and child guidance clinics not directly related to hospitals as institutions. Mental health personnel took on many responsibilities for community education and prevention not normally included in the scope of state and local mental hospitals. In a sense, therefore, the distribution of mental health personnel tended to "follow the patient" from the hospital into the community. *Continuity of care* as a concept emerged during this period as one of the aspects of comprehensive mental health services which implied that long-term treatment could be provided outside the walls of the state mental hospital (Kahn, 1969).

The problems of manpower for mental health services were never fully addressed until the passage of the National Mental Health Act of 1946 (Public Law 487, 79th Congress) Section 2 therein, outlining the major objectives of this legislation, includes "training of personnel in matters relating to mental health." The Act went on to modify Section 301 of Public Law 410 (Public Health Service Act) to provide for training of personnel to assist in the diagnosis, treatment, and rehabilitation of the mentally ill. Under this authority

163

the first training grants were made available in the core mental health disciplines (psychiatry, psychology, nursing, and social work) to permit the expansion of professional schools and to further the establishment of new training programs in states where these did not exist. There followed steady growth in the number of graduates in all four fields. The training program was later expanded to include biological and social scientists as well as a range of personnel requiring technical education for services in mental health. In-service training and continuing education programs were added later.

The initial objective was to improve the staffing of state mental hospitals and the growing number of mental health clinics and child guidance centers (Williams, 1972). The direction of manpower development was significantly influenced by the Community Mental Health Centers legislation of 1963, with its new approach to care, treatment, and rehabilitation of the mentally ill and prevention of mental illness in the United States. Over 500 mental health centers are now in operation around the country, with staff of over 42,000 mental health personnel, or 6.6% of the national mental health manpower pool.

According to the most recent manpower statistics (NIMH, 1972), there are about 429,000 positions in mental health facilities. Of these, 358,000 were full time, 52,000 were part time, and there were 19,000 trainee positions. In a sample week during January 1972, this staff provided over 15 million manhours of service, with most (13.8 million) being provided by full-time personnel.

The largest manpower category is classified "other mental health workers" (less than the AA degree or two year college level), which includes 27.2% of all staff. The next largest is the registered nurse group, 8.5% of the total; social workers are 5.4%; other mental health professions (BA and above, vocational counselors, occupational therapists, teachers) 5.0%, psychiatrists 4.9%, and psychologists 3.3% of total staff. Of the total number of staff, 66% were listed as directly involved in patient care; the rest were devoted to other related activity.

Of all professionals, psychiatrists constitute 16.1%, psychologists 10.8%, social workers 17.5%, registered nurses 27.7%; all other (BA or above) 16.3%, and physical health professionals and assistants 6.9% (dentists, pharmacists, dieticians, etc.).

It is possible to predict a gradual thinning out of staff in state and city mental hospitals as these are reduced in size and eventually phased out or over to other purposes than housing long-term mental patients. The trend toward community care reflects diminishing proportions of the population in mental hospitals each year. As more community facilities are built, staff will shift to these new centers of service (Survey and Reports, 1973).

164

The distribution of mental health personnel by type of facility in the United States has been reported as follows (NIMH, 1972):

	Percent
State and City Mental Hospitals	59.5
Veterans Administration Psychiatric Services	11.3
General Hospital Psychiatric Services	8.2
Federally Funded Community Mental Health Centers	6.6
Private Mental Hospitals	5.7
Residential Treatment Centers	4.5
Free Standing Outpatient Clinics	4.2
	100.0

The guidelines for the development of community mental health centers require five essential services: outpatient and inpatient services, day-care or partial hospitalization, emergency services, and consultation and educational activities. Five additional services are recommended but not required: pre-care and after-care, diagnostic services, rehabilitation, and research and training activities (Levenson, 1972). Various other mandates or priorities have emerged as time has moved forward. Many Centers have undertaken extensive programs in alcohol and drug addiction or in child mental health. A few programs have been directed toward minority communities where an effort has been made to deploy minority mental health manpower. However, traditional patterns of entrance into and completion of preparation for the mental health professions have limited the development of minority manpower especially needed to provide effective services to communities with ethnic enclaves (Smith and Wittman, 1974).

Some significant results have been accomplished by such organizations as the Chicano Training Center in Houston, Texas and the Asian American Mental Health Training Center in Los Angeles which prepare minority students for work in social and mental health services. A number of models for the special preparation of minority manpower have been developed to recruit and train students needed in the several ethnic communities.

One current critical issue is the problem of division of labor in mental health manpower (Arnhoff, Rubinstein, Speisman, 1969). The work of mental health personnel can be seen as having two aspects, the provision of clinical services and of community services. The former requires sound clinical preparation to provide effective treatment for a person or a family having psychosocial problems. The workers who wish to undertake the coordination of community services or the development of social and public health resources in rural, urban or suburban areas, also require relevant training, e.g.

165

in community organization, planning and administration (Austin, et al., 1974).

There has been an enormous growth of nonprofessional manpower in the mental health field (Sobey, 1970). New career workers (also called paraprofessionals or new professionals) have undertaken important outreach functions and have conducted a good deal of community education and liaison (Grosser et al. 1969). Manpower development over the last decade has encouraged the diversification of training to accommodate the several levels of practice and wide range of skills needed for delivery of mental health service (Barker and Briggs, 1968). There is, as well, growing attention to the value of training programs in primary care that aim to integrate the physical and psychosocial aspects of health care. The special requirements for service in rural mental health programs and those which serve the inner city are being added to curricula in mental health training centers, but with serious limitations deriving from lack of well-equipped teaching personnel. There is a continuing need to keep education for the mental health professions related to practice issues.

Milton Wittman, D.S.W.

References

Action for Mental Health: Final Report of the Joint Commission on Mental Illness and Health, New York: Basic Books, 1961.

Albee, George W., Mental Health Manpower Trends, New York: Basic Books, 1959.

Arnhoff, F. N., Rubinstein, E. A., and Speisman, J. C., Manpower for Mental Health, Chicago: Aldine, 1969.

Austin, Michael J., Ashcraft, John, and Simons, Paulette, 1974. Working Papers in Mental Health Administration, Florida State University, Tallahassee, FL. (October).

Barker, Robert L. and Briggs, Thomas G., Differential Use of Social Work Manpower, New York, National Association of Social Workers, 1968.

Grosser, Charles, Henry, William E., and Kelly, James G., Nonprofessionals in the Health Services, San Francisco: Jossey-Bass, 1969.

Kahn, Alfred J., "Community Psychiatry: Boundaries and Intergovernmental Relations in Planning," in Studies in Social Policy and Planning, New York: Russell Sage Foundation, 1969, pp. 194-242.

Levenson, Alan I., "The Community Mental Health Centers Programs" in Handbook of Community Mental Health, Stuart E. Golann and Carl Eisdorfer, eds., New York: Appleton-Century-Crofts, 1972, pp. 687-698.

National Institute of Mental Health, Staffing of Mental Health Facilities, United States, 1972, DHEW Publication No. (ADM) 74-28, U. S. Government Printing Office, Washington, D. C., 1972.

Smith, Neilson F. and Wittman, Milton, "New Roles and Services in the Community Mental Health Center" in A Design for Social Work Practice, F. D. Perlmutter, ed., New York, Columbia University Press, 1974, pp. 74-100.

Sobey, Francine, The Nonprofessional Revolution in Mental Health, New York: Columbia University Press, 1970.

Survey and Reports Section, Biometry Branch, National Institute of Mental Health, Descriptive Data on Federally Funded Community Mental Health Centers, Rockville, Maryland, May, 1973.

Williams, R. H., Perspectives in the Field of Mental Health, "Part III Training, Roles and Manpower", Rockville, Maryland, NIMH, 1972. pp. 117-140.

2. Traditional Mental Health Professionals — Changing Roles

A. Psychiatry and Clinical Psychology

I love doctors and hate their medicine.
—*Walt Whitman (1819-1892)*

The psychiatrist is a physician specializing in the study and treatment of diseases or disorders manifested primarily by disturbed deviant behavior and thought to be mental in origin. After internship, a three year residency training program in hospitals and clinics is required. Supervised work with patients is the major training technique, accompanied by seminars, lectures and reading; personal psychotherapy or analysis is often encouraged as part of training. Training analysis is required for those who go on to specialize in psychoanalysis.

Psychiatric thinking in the past century has come almost full circle. Formerly based on "moral" and somatic theories of disordered behavior, treatment included a variety of environmental and somatic therapies, from an improved and humane milieu to shock therapies. The psychodynamic approaches which emphasized unconscious psychic mechanisms primarily instinctual and interpersonal in origin were first introduced by the work of Freud and his predecessors, Charcot, Janet, and Bernheim. Subsequently, in this country, there was Adolph Meyer and his psychobiological approach, based on the view that behavioral disorders can be understood only by considering the whole person's reactions to both environment and biological endowment; Harry Stack Sullivan developed the earliest and most pervasive neo-Freudian ideas of psychotherapy and the view of the therapist as a participant observer in the process. Erich Fromm, a psychoanalyst, early emphasized the social factors in normal and aberrant human development.

World Wars I and II greatly influenced the course of psychiatry. The first World War, with its many "shell shock" victims, hysterical paralyses, etc., brought out the need for practical psychodynamic approaches to mental illness. World War II saw many draftees rejected because of psychiatric illness, especially schizophrenia and severe psychosomatic diseases. The psychiatric casualty rates were high. These facts plus the exodus into the United States of many German and Viennese psychoanalysts after the rise of

168

Hitler made available a large core of psychoanalytic teachers available to medical schools, clinics, and state hospitals.

In a wealthy country like the United States, psychoanalysis as an intensive treatment modality became a private practice model with high prestige. Psychotherapy, which borrowed from psychoanalytic and other psychodynamic theories was the primary method of treatment taught in most psychiatric residency programs.

With the discovery of electroshock treatment in the 1940s, involutional (late-life) depressions and some forms of psychosis became more treatable. The discovery of the first psychotropic drugs to affect psychosis in the mid-1930s began the search for chemical methods of treating schizophrenia and manic depressive psychosis. The startling effectiveness of chlorpromazine (Thorazine) on chronic and acute schizophrenic reactions, the efficacy of other psychotropic drugs and in the last decade of the tricyclic antidepressants in psychotic depressions and lithium in manic depressive psychosis has ushered in a new push toward understanding brain-behavior mechanisms from a new physiologic-biochemical framework.

A second development since World War II was the birth and growth of child psychiatry into a distinct specialty and a subspecialty recognized by the certifying board. It is now a part of the training of most psychiatrists. Family therapy is another new approach with a number of different schools of practice developed over the last twenty years.

The Joint Commission on Mental Health published *Action for Mental Health* in 1960. It emphasized social factors in etiology of mental illness and helped in the enactment of the Community Mental Health Act of 1965. The professions began to emphasize the need to view patients in the context of their environment and to recognize that neither drugs nor psychotherapy by themselves could cure serious psychiatric disorder if the social environs in the home and community were ignored. Thus, community psychiatry became operational.

Methods of working in the community emphasized not only the need to find the mentally ill early but to utilize workers from the community to provide therapeutic support to the ill. They helped use the community networks of religious, social, and neighborhood groups as a way of encouraging psychiatrically ill people to make a better, more integrative adjustment to living and working in the community.

The experiences from community psychiatry suggest that unless the social forces which influence disease are dealt with, long-term amelioration of disease and restoration of function will not occur for many patients. Current trends in psychiatric training emphasize generalist concepts, influenced by the growing body of knowledge from several disciplines. We are at the threshhold of a synthesis of genetic, biological (neurochemical), psychodynamic, and social psychiatric factors which promises a more holistic approach to training for psychiatrists and other mental health workers of the next decade.

Broadly speaking, clinical psychology is the branch of psychology concerned with personality maladjustment and the modification of maladaptive behavior. The clinical psychologist is trained within doctoral programs usually housed in university departments of psychology. In addition to course work in major areas of psychology, these programs offer a variety of clerkships and practicum experiences, as well as a one year internship.

Clinical psychology was a relatively small discipline before World War II. Because of their contributions to handling the mental health problems of servicemen and increased recognition of these problems in civilian life, clinical psychologists were in demand after the war. The doctoral programs that were set up adhered by and large to the "scientist-practitioner" model. This model represented something of a compromise between the traditional stress on scientific inquiry within psychology and the need to apply the results of these inquiries.

The scientist-practitioner remains the predominant product of doctoral programs in clinical psychology, with training in research as well as in diagnosis and therapy. The graduate may pursue a research or clinical career, or a combination of these. Many clinical psychologists are employed by non-profit clinical agencies such as medical schools and community mental health clinics; others are employed by universities and colleges as teachers, researchers, and trainers; and still others—a small, but growing minority—are engaged in private practice, either as office practitioners or as consultants to agencies.

Two of the traditionally important activities of the clinical psychologist are assessment of individual differences and research. Students learn how psychological tests are constructed and evaluated, with intensive study of the problems of reliability and validity. Clinical psychologists administer intelligence and personality tests and questionnaires in order to contribute to the diagnosis of personal problems. During recent years, increasing efforts have been made to develop techniques of behavioral assessment, in which the subject's behavior is observed under specified conditions, i.e. classroom, and coded quantitatively. Recent years have seen a growth of interest in program evaluation, i.e., assessment of the effectiveness and efficiency of clinical and social programs.

Perhaps the most influential developments reflected in training during the past decade are those of behavior analysis modification, or therapy. Methods of operant conditioning, classical conditioning, and observational learning are effective and efficient means of treatment of certain types of problems. These methods have been used more or less effectively with mute psychotics, phobic and highly anxious neurotics, and juvenile delinquents. Paralleling similar developments in psychiatry is the growth of community psychology, something of a hybrid mixture of clinical and social psychology. Community psychologists seek to understand deviations in the behavior of individuals as a function of social, cultural, and economic factors, and are especially interested in the prevention of mental illness. On the research front, there is a trend toward large scale collaborative and interdisciplinary investigations.

One of the most fruitful cross-fertilizations between research and clinical practice has occurred in the field of developmental psychology. The application of research data to clinical practice at every age and stage of development has occurred within the last decade. Observations of the neonate, stimulation programs for deprived infants, compensatory education, stress on cognitive and emotional development of preschoolers in such programs as parent-child centers are examples of such application.

In the future, combination of research and clinical practice will extend to more systematic work with large institutions such as schools and industry. Community psychology and developmental psychology are still in their infancy. Behavior modification, a powerful tool, may see its limits clarified. Neuropsychology, integrating physiological and clinical tools is growing in use. Psychological, behavioral manifestations of discrete and generalized brain lesions are being mapped out with increasing precision. Training in all of these areas will be part of future curricula.

Irving N. Berlin, M.D.
Irwin G. Sarason, Ph.D.

References

Comer, J. P. 1973. Discussion of Dr. Meyer's paper. In. V.B.O. Hammet and N. Hansell (Eds.), Psychiatric residency in service settings. Proceedings of the Aspen Conference, Snowmass-at-Aspen, Colorado. Hillsdale, New Jersey: The Town House Press, Inc. pp. 36-40.

Deutsch, A. 1937. The Mentally Ill in America: A History of their Care and Treatment from Colonial Times. New York: Doubleday.

Kanner, L. 1945. The origins and growth of child psychiatry. Am. J. Psychiat. 101, pp. 139-143.

Kerwin, E. 1945. Contribution of Adolf Meyer and psychobiology to child guidance. Ment. Hyg. 29, p. 575.

Lewis, N. D.C., 1959. American psychiatry from its beginnings to World War II. In S. Arieti (Ed.), American Handbook of Psychiatry. pp. 3-17.

Marmor, J. 1974. Changing trends in psychotherapy. In G. Usdin (Ed.), Psychiatry: Education and Image. New York: Brunner/Mazel. pp. 84-104.

Mora, G. 1967. Adolph Meyer. In A. M. Freedman and H. I. Kaplan (Eds.), Comprehensive Textbook of Psychiatry. Baltimore: Williams & Wilkins. pp. 363-366.

Mora, G. 1959. Recent American psychiatry developments. In S. Arieti (Ed.), American Handbook of Psychiatry. pp. 19-57.

Murphy, G. 1959. Social psychology. In S. Arieti (Ed.), American Handbook of Psychiatry. pp. 1733-1742.

Sargent, H. D. and Mayman, M. 1959. Clinical psychology. In S. Arieti (Ed.), American Handbook of Psychiatry. pp. 1711-1732.

B. Social Work

If we admit that in education it is necessary to begin
with the experiences which the child already has
and to use his spontaneous and social activity. Then
the city streets begin this education for him in a
more national way than does the school.

—*Jane Addams*
Democracy and Social Ethics, 1903

Social workers occupy direct service, administrative and policy
positions in a wide range of health and welfare programs and
institutions in our communities. In its practice, social work is concerned with "the interaction between people and their environment
which affects the ability of people to accomplish their life tasks,
alleviate distress, and realize their aspirations and values. The purpose of social work therefore is to (1) enhance the problem-solving
and coping capacities of people, (2) link people with systems that
provide them with resources, services, and opportunities, (3) promote the effectiveness and humane operation of these systems, and
(4) contribute to the development and improvement of social policy"
(Pincus and Minahan, 1973).

Two models of social work practice have emerged: (1) direct
service to individuals and families, and (2) development of the systems in which services are located. This distinction, not entirely new
to social work, is reflected in the traditional practice methods of
social casework, group work and community organization. Social
casework aims at improvement and enhancement of individual
social functioning via counseling therapy. In addition it involves linking and case advocacy, i.e., case referral, and perseverence on behalf of the client so that rights are honored and needs are met. The
social group work method aims at assisting small groups to function
in a manner which enhances the well being of individual group members, and also helps groups to achieve their goals. Community
organization or community work involves two separate but related
processes: program development and organizing. The former concerns program goals, the analysis of policy options, and the specifi-
cation of programs which enact policy. Organizing is the inter-
actional aspect of community work. This may involve organizing at
the neighborhood level or organizing planning structures such as
committees, commissions or program planning units. Distinctions

between these traditional social work methods are less sharply drawn in contemporary practice. Some educational programs, attempt to combine elements of casework and group work into an integrated method of social work practice. Recent attempts to combine common knowledge and common skills into a more generic practice arise from the recognition that solutions to complex individual and social problems require techniques of more than one type.

The master's degree of social work, the traditional cornerstone of social work education, is acquired at graduate schools of social work, and is required for many social work positions. Classroom instruction consists of courses in social welfare policy, research and human growth and development. These foundation areas of knowledge provide the background for curriculum which includes concepts and principles of casework, group work, community organization and social administration. In response to the increasing need for social workers in management positions in health and welfare agencies, a number of graduate schools of social work have added specializations in social administration and planning.

Field experience is central to social work education at the master's level. Through cooperative arrangements with community agencies, all social work students spend a specified number of hours in direct practice training under a qualified field instructor. Involving students in learning through doing is a key objective of field instruction, through which students master a body of theory and apply their knowledge and skills to human problems. Field work provides an opportunity to integrate, utilize and apply classroom content to problems in practice.

Social work education is becoming increasingly stratified, with four levels of formal training: associate, baccalaureate, master's and doctoral. The associate degree is offered in two-year community colleges; it prepares the student for community and social service technician roles. The baccalaureate degree, offered in four year colleges and universities, prepares the student for beginning professional social work practice. The master's degree is offered in graduate schools of social work; it prepares the students for direct counseling-therapeutic service, administration, policy and planning. The doctor's degree is also offered at graduate schools of social work. It prepares the student for leadership roles in policy development, administration, planning, advanced counseling-therapy, social research and teaching (Boehm, 1971).

In recent years, considerable expansion of undergraduate social work education has taken place. In large measure, it aims at improving the quality of services offered in large public service systems, e.g., welfare, juvenile services and public hospitals. These had traditionally accepted a baccalaureate degree in any area for their direct service positions. As a result, many of our major public ser-

174

vice programs are staffed with individuals lacking specific social work skills or formal training. Professional social work education at the baccalaureate level creates a supply of better-trained candidates for direct service in these public programs.

Many other public and voluntary agencies are attempting to sort out direct practice skills that could be performed by individuals possessing levels of education below the master's level. In fact, recent trends show that direct service to individuals and families has become a smaller proportion of social worker's activities at the master's level. In 1969, only 36.5% of the members of the National Association of Social Workers (NASW) were classified as direct service practitioners (Meyer, 1971). The trend has been toward the employment of master's level social workers in positions associated with supervision, administration and policy. The emergence of two models of practice, one aimed at direct service and the other at broader social approaches, presents a dilemma to the profession. It will be increasingly necessary to find ways to integrate two very different views of practice into a single social work profession.

Recent surveys show a concentration of social workers in mental health, medical and child welfare settings. Three-fifths of the master's level social workers are employed in government agencies primarily at the state and local levels. In recent years, however, an increasing number of social workers are entering private practice; they tend to be the more experienced social workers drawn from voluntary family agencies and psychiatric settings. The increasing interest in fee-for-service, private practice has generated considerable controversy because traditionally, social work has been an agency-based profession (Meyer, 1971).

Since the establishment of the first school of social work at the turn of the twentieth century, the profession has grown and diversified. While it is impossible to predict the future, trends indicate continued expansion and the development of specializations in both direct practice and broader social approaches aimed at prevention of social problems. Interest in social work as a career, among students at the baccalaureate and master's level, significantly increased in the early 1970's when applications for admission to educational programs in social work reached their highest levels. The long-range trend toward the expansion and institutionalization of social services in urban, industrial society suggests an increasing role for the profession in modern society.

Donald V. Fandetti, D.S.W.

References

Pincus, Allen and Anne Minahan. 1973. Social Work Practice: Models and Methods, Illinois: F.E. Peacock Publishers, Inc.

Encyclopedia of Social Work. 1971. New York: National Association of Social Workers, (16th edition).

Boehm, Werner, W., "Education for Social Work," Encyclopedia of Social Work, New York: National Association of Social Workers, 1971, p. 259.

Brager, George and Specht, Harry. 1973. Community Organizing, New York: Columbia University Press.

Meyer, Carol H. 1970. Social Work Practice, New York: The Free Press.

Meyer, Henry, J., "Profession of Social Work: Contemporary Characteristics," Encyclopedia of Social Work, New York: National Association of Social Workers, 1971, p. 964.

Roberts, Robert W. and Nee, Robert H. 1970. Theories of Social Casework, Chicago: University of Chicago Press.

Reid, William J. and Epstein, Laura. 1972. Task-Centered Casework, New York: Columbia University Press.

Northen, Helen. 1969. Social Work with Groups, New York: Columbia University Press.

Kahn, Alfred J. 1973. Social Policy and Social Services, New York: Random House.

Klein, Alan. 1972. Effective Groupwork: An Introduction to Principle and Method, New York: Association Press.

Kahn, Alfred J. 1969. Theory and Practice of Social Planning, New York: Russell Sage Foundation.

Other Sources

Journals:
Social Casework
Social Work
Social Service Review
Child Welfare
Children
Public Welfare
Social Security Bulletin
Journal of Education for Social Work
Journal of Social Policy

Associations:
National Association of Social Workers, 2 Park Ave., New York, New York, 10017
Council on Social Work Education, 345 E. 46th St., New York, New York, 10017.

C. Psychiatric Nursing

> It seems a commonly received idea among men and
> even among women themselves that it requires noth-
> ing but a disappointment in love, the want of an
> object, a general disgust, or incapacity for other
> things to turn a woman into a good nurse.
>
> —*Florence Nightingale (1820-1910)*
> *Notes on Nursing*

Psychiatric nursing is a specialized area of practice in the science and art of nursing. The scientific aspect is the application of
new and complex knowledge of human life based on the natural and
behavioral sciences. The art of psychiatric nursing is derived from
the purposeful use of self in the practice of the profession.

Psychiatric nursing thus utilizes a broad spectrum of general
and specialized nursing knowledge and skill in a variety of settings
with different psychiatric approaches to patient care. The settings
for psychiatric nursing services vary widely in purpose, size, type,
location, and auspices under which they are operated. They include
hospitals, public health agencies, community mental health centers,
emergency care units, clinics, day and night care centers, offices,
homes, schools, camps, and industrial centers.

Nursing care of psychiatric patients is provided by registered
nurses with varying levels of preparation. Basic schools of nursing
prepare nurses for generic (general) practice and provide basic
principles and skills for continual professional development. Graduate programs prepare clinical specialists for more advanced nursing practice.

The registered nurse prepared in a two year associate degree,
three year diploma, or four year baccalaureate program, is able to
observe and to distinguish a broad range of problems of a physical
and socio-psychological nature. These basic nursing programs provide a combination of theory and practicum of various lengths. Continuing in-service education to enhance the basic nursing education
is necessary to provide the opportunity for the nurse to acquire certain knowledge and skills in the care of psychiatric patients.

Clinical specialization in psychiatric nursing is based upon the
knowledge and skills obtained through completion of a program of
graduate study in a university with clinical specialization in psychiatric-mental health nursing. The master's degree is the basis of clin-

ical specialization. Therapeutic skills are developed through academically supervised study and clinical practice.

The clinical specialist in psychiatric nursing is prepared to practice individual therapy, group therapy, family therapy, and to function in indirect nursing care roles such as administration, supervision, staff development, consultation, and research.

There are approximately 37,000 registered nurses who designate psychiatric nursing as their major area of practice. Of these about 10% have graduate degrees (masters, doctoral). Most, or 85% psychiatric nurses report their field of employment as the hospital.

The scope of nursing is remarkably different today than it was a few decades ago. Then nursing consisted primarily of comfort and cleanliness measures together with whatever technical tasks might be delegated by the physician. Now nursing practice encompasses compensating for man's inadequacies and sustaining and supporting him throughout periods of temporary or permanent dependence caused by infirmity, disease, or dysfunction.

The trend in nursing education is toward increasing specialization. Preparation of the nurse specialist may focus on the family or on the individual with an illness. The nurse practitioner, as a primary care-giver, can be described as a health counselor for the family and its members, initiating the first diagnostic and assessment procedures, teaching, and strengthening the family's ability to cope with health problems. The nurse practitioner helps the family modify behavior to enhance their level of wellness, collaborates with other health and related personnel involved in assisting the family, and at the same time provides those nursing services that are indicated. The nurse is a family health practitioner who can fill a well-recognized gap in our present system of delivery of health services.

The other major area of specialization within psychiatric nursing practice is on the individual with an illness; the primary concern and the focus in nursing is on restoration and rehabilitation. Here the nurse initiates therapeutic care plans, teaches the patient, involves him in his own care, and collaborates with other medical and health-related personnel in assessing, planning, implementing, and evaluating the care of the patient.

For those nurse practitioners who are prepared in more traditional programs there must be a program of continuing education which includes short-term intensive training programs. There must also be some way of identifying, for the public and professional colleagues, those nurse practitioners who excel in psychiatric and mental health nursing practice. Such a program of certification for excellence in practice was established in 1973 by the American Nurses' Association.

Ruth V. Lewis, R.N., M.A.

References

Burd, S.F. and Marshall, M.A. 1963. Some Clinical Approaches to Psychiatric Nursing. New York: Macmillan.

Fagin, C.M. 1970. Family-Centered Nursing in Community Psychiatry: Treatment in the Home. Philadelphia: Davis.

Group for the Advancement of Psychiatry. 1952. Committee on Psychiatric Nursing and the Committee on Hospitals. The Psychiatric Nurse in the Mental Hospital. GAP Report No. 422.

Mereness, D.A. and Taylor, C.M. 1974. Essentials of Psychiatric Nursing. 9th Ed., St. Louis: Mosby.

Peplau, H. E. 1952. Interpersonal Relations in Nursing: A Conceptual Frame of Reference for Psychodynamic Nursing. New York: Putnam.

Stokes, G.H., et al. 1969. The Roles of Psychiatric Nurses in Community Health Practice: A Giant Step. Brooklyn, N.Y., Faculty Press.

American Nurses' Association. 1967. Statement of Psychiatric Nursing Practice, ANA Publication Number S-85, 10M, Kansas City, Mo.

American Nurses' Association and U.S. Department of Health, Education and Welfare. 1974. Preparing Registered Nurses for Expanded Roles 1973-74, DHEW Publication Number (NIH) 74-31, U.S. GPO, Washington, D.C.

Other Sources

Journals:
American Journal of Nursing

Associations:
American Nurses' Association
American League for Nursing

3. Experimental Training Programs

A. Experimental Training and Manpower Utilization Programs (Primary Care)

Teach thy tongue to say "I do not know."

—*Maimonides (1135-1204)*

Health manpower training and utilization in this country has been largely directed toward specialization. The very nature of specialization, however, tends toward neglect of day-to-day health problems, and lessens access to care. Traditionally medicine has been responsible for diagnosis and treatment, nursing for care of the ill, public health for prevention, and universities for education, with ever increasing specialization and diminishing interaction. The result is chaos, with jealous guarding of the rights of professional domain to the detriment of total health care. This is particularly true of the psychiatric-mental health services. But recently there has evolved a trend toward primary health care linked with specialty services and educational centers, bringing beneficial changes in health care, in both education and service.

The primary care concept involves a return to the generalist, a middle-level worker who is a primary health care practitioner, e.g. nurse practitioner or physician assistant. This practitioner combines the basic skills of nurse, physician, and public health worker. He or she is a front-line worker who is trained by an inter-disciplinary team to assess the health status of individuals and the family and to initiate selective preventive measures; to manage health and the related social-emotional problems, using specific protocols for diagnosis and treatment for selected conditions; and to provide emergency services in the absence of the physician. Responsibilities include consultation with or referral to other members of the health team, and delegation of authority when appropriate. Scope of activity may or may not involve midwifery, pediatrics, or geriatrics.

Ideally, primary care service and training centers, should operate in the community served. In other words, training should occur where the action is, not in isolation, but linked into networks of education, consultant, and specialty services with regional (hospital and college) and state medical care and university centers. At the same time primary care centers require sufficient autonomy to re-

180

main responsive to local community needs. Patterns will vary depending on the population of the area served, manpower and other resources, and financial support. But no family in modern America should be farther than 20 minutes travel time from primary care.

One of the earliest primary care and training centers to remain in continuous operation in this country is the Frontier Nursing Service which introduced the nurse-midwife as a primary health care provider to Kentucky in 1925. Medical directives were developed and apprenticeship training in the diagnosis and management of common health problems was started when a physician was added to the staff. In 1939, the Service established a nurse mid-wifery training program and in 1970, a formal family nurse training program.

As a primary care agency the Service established an extensive network of supporting services with the State Health Department and other health agencies, hospitals, and medical clinics. The health team was expanded as the agency took on new responsibilities commensurate with 1) technological and scientific advances; 2) community needs and demands; 3) health manpower availability; and 4) financial feasibility or readiness. Duke University developed the first physician assistant program in 1965 and Colorado the first pediatric nurse practitioner program in 1966. Now several hundred such programs are operating or developing. Initially the health generalist concept was not accepted by either medicine or nursing and it is still ignored or fought by many individual practitioners. However, it has been endorsed by The American Medical Association, The American Nurses' Association, The American College of Obstetrics and Gynecology, and The American Academy of Pediatrics.

Organizations for the mid-level health practitioner have been established including the American College of Nurse Mid-wives (ACNM), the National Association of Physician Assistants, and the National Association of Pediatric Nurse Associates and Practitioners. The American Nurses' Association has approved councils for the Pediatric Nurse Practitioner and the Family Nurse Practitioner. The ACNM has established national examinations for graduates of ACNM-accredited programs. The National Board of Medical Examiners certifies training programs and has established national examinations for the assistant to the primary care physician, which may be taken by Registered Nurses who have completed selected programs in primary care.

Many states are in the process of changing legislation to accommodate the primary health care practitioner, with varying degrees of restriction. Restrictions appear to be designed more to protect the economic status and prestige of the professions and educational institutions than for the protection or care of the public. The State of Washington was first to introduce exemplary legislation.

Controversies concern the degree of independence of individual practitioners, reimbursement, licensure, accreditation of service and training as well as other issues related to legality. Fears exist about the impact these new workers will have on the quality, economics and professionalism of health care.

To date, approximately 2,000 nurses (nurse-midwives, pediatric nurse practitioners, family nurses, primexes, etc.) and 1,000 physician assistants (clinical and health associates, etc.) have received primary health care training. Training programs vary from 3 months to 2 years for registered nurses, at the certificate, baccalaureate and masters or post-masters level; and 1-2 years at the associate, baccalaureate and masters level for physician assistants. There is a wide variation in program content, e.g., with some but not all programs emphasizing the psychological and social aspects of health and disease. Graduates are employed in a wide variety of settings, ranging from the traditional to primary care models, such as neighborhood health centers and nursing clinics established in isolated areas where health care was not previously available.

Evaluations of the primary health care practitioner are highly favorable. Federally supported research in Primex and Medex programs assesses productivity, accessibility, care objectives, curriculum design, and admission requirements of the training programs as these relate to service benefits. Further exploration is needed to determine which of the mid-level practitioner programs are most feasible and acceptable to society.

The aim of this movement is to bring health care back into the mainstream of day-to-day living; to make health care more accessible; to integrate physical, mental, and social health care; to correlate specialty care with primary care; to lessen the rate and duration of hospitalization and eliminate needless institutionalization; to correlate service and training; and to improve cost-benefit ratios. The success of such program development depends largely on the ability of the various disciplines and institutions to develop trust and work together in the interest of the patient.

The primary care concept opens new avenues for providing mental health care at the local level, if training and service is based on the assumption that health care consists of three parts: physical, mental, and social, each inseparable from the others. If one part flourishes or suffers, the others are correspondingly affected. If the family is similarly viewed as an entity with many parts, family health care too becomes an essential process.

It is under stressful circumstances that the primary health care practitioner can be most helpful, and experience the greatest acceptance particularly if situated in a community and already familiar

182

with its families. Such a practitioner is in a position to 1) know when illness or disaster strikes, or stressful situations occur, and provide crisis intervention; 2) offer counseling and support in problem situations; 3) provide maintenance care to the chronically ill; 4) give guidance to families who require specialty care and make the necessary referrals; and 5) educate the public. The primary care provider is of inestimable help in providing the specialist with information regarding history, home or community conditions and in providing follow-up. A strong linkage with mental health services and educational facilities, including consultative services, is essential if the primary care practitioner is to provide optimal mental health care along with other health services.

Gertrude Issacs, D.N.Sc.

References

Sadler, Alfred M., Sadler, Blair, L., and Bliss, Anna A. 1972 The Physician's Assistant. Yale University Press.

Extending the Scope of Nursing Practice. November 1972. A Report of the Secretary's Committee to Study Extended Roles for Nurses. DHEW Publication No. (HSM) 73-2037.

Primary Care. 1974. Clinics in Office Practice. Published Quarterly by W.B. Saunders Co.

B. Policemen as Mental Health Agents

> Perhaps Solomon the Wise had specialists in mind
> when he tested the love for a child by the unwill-
> ingness to have it dismembered. Certainly the
> studies of the specialists themselves constantly are
> showing that to understand fully the kinds of trouble
> into which people fall—sickness, poverty, difficul-
> ties in home or job—we need to know all the factors
> that affect their lives.
>
> —Lillian Wald
> Survey LXIII:458, 1930

The following illustrates the mental health importance of only one profession not considered as a primary mental health resource but, like the teacher, general physician, and clergyman, a front-line caretaker. There are approximately 40,000 police departments in the U.S. employing 400,000 policemen. Because he is still the only community agent available seven days a week around-the-clock, the modern police professional is obligated to increase his behavioral science expertise and accept the legitimacy of his role as mental health agent.

In the past, the policeman was handed the emblems of author-ity, given little relevant training, and sent out into the community to handle in some pragmatic way the myriad human problems. He func-tioned alone and in relative isolation. Partly because of his personal vulnerability and partly as a result of his meager preparation and lack of professional supports, the policeman often developed resent-ment toward mental health professionals, antagonism frequently reciprocated by mental health workers. These negative attitudes need to be changed, and this can be done over time by sharing common problems, goals and everyday work in upgrading the community services system.

Approximately 80% of the average officer's total time is spent in public service functions unrelated to crime. Intervening in family disputes, handling mentally disturbed and suicidal individuals, dealing with rape and child-abuse victims and locating lost/run-away children and senile citizens are some of the mental health re-lated activities which, collectively, dominate the officer's time.

Traditionally police have engaged in primary prevention activi-ties by participating in summer camp programs, sponsoring athletic teams and events, establishing deputy auxiliary police programs for small children, teaching in public schools, and being involved in community organizations. It is clearly appropriate to augment the officer's effectiveness by teaching crisis theory and behavioral science generally.

Although police training programs have expanded considerably in recent years, the main emphasis still is on crime-related strategies and tactics. There is a need for more attention to criminal psychology, child and adolescent development, family problems and mental health principles. (Reiser, 1973) Crisis intervention should occupy a key position, and early recognition, intervention, counseling and referral techniques should be taught using role playing, simulations, video-tape feedback, clinical observation and field experiences.

Over the last five years, forward looking police departments around the country have experimented with some new approaches to human relations training. A few examples include Bard's (1970) family crisis intervention program in New York, Shev's (1968) small group consultation program with police in Sausalito, California, Reiser and Sokol's (1972) early warning mental health program for police sergeants in Los Angeles, the Houston police-community relations experiment, (Sikes & Cleveland, 1973) the Dayton crisis intervention pilot project, (Barocas, 1971) the Covina, California project to increase empathy of policemen by including an experience as a prisoner, (Johnson and Gregory, 1971) and others (Newman, & Steinberg, 1970).

Those innovative programs have been developed with the assistance of behavioral science consultants, usually working part-time and often on a voluntary basis. Others have been funded via department budgets and grants. Recently, a trend has been started with the establishment of full-time, in-house behavioral science positions as an integral part of the police department.

The Los Angeles County Department of Mental Health has established Psychiatric Emergency Mobile Teams (PET) in the 16 regional offices. These teams are on call by police, citizens and others to respond promptly to requests for emergency mental health services in the community. Interestingly, the mental health professionals have on occasion requested training from the police in handling violent, emotionally disturbed individuals.

The Los Angeles Police Department has a Mental Evaluation Detail of experienced investigators whose function it is to consult with field policemen about the criteria and arrangements for involuntary hospitalization of emotionally disturbed citizens. They maintain liaison with hospitals and other mental health resources in the community in order to facilitate referrals.

Mental health consultants both in-house and outside have already contributed in a beginning way; however, the surface has barely been scratched in providing the kinds of mental health expertise which are presently available. Routinely, police departments should have outside professional consultation in the training and human relations programming areas. Mental health experts should share the training rostrum with experienced police officers in teaching about mental health problems. Human relations programs can only be effective if attitude change on the part of officers and citizens is an outcome. Ironically, some recent research on human relations suggests that loosely structured, poorly planned training programs can have the opposite effect, resulting in hardening of negative attitudes and in polarizing individuals. In this connection, the dynamics of the human relations training process need to be studied.

In practice, the police officer has to become a social scientist (Singer, 1970). He is dealing with human problems and so to be effective must become a specialist in human relations. Mental health professionals must also recognize the realities of this role and join the policeman as a partner in the process of teaching, sharing and learning. Forward-looking police departments will be eager to have full-time behavioral science experts on the staff to assist in these endeavors. Those which are too small to afford it will nevertheless recognize its importance and acquire it in cooperation with local universities, mental health centers, and private practitioners.

Police recruits in larger departments are above average in intelligence, in emotional stability, and in their desire to serve the community (Reiser, 1972). The educational level of young people entering police work is improving, with greater numbers of applicants having had courses and/or training in the behavioral and social sciences. Currently, recruits on the Los Angeles Police Department have an average of over 90 college credits. Several police agencies now require two years of college, either before or within a specified time period after appointment, and the projection is that by 1985, a four-year degree will be a standard prerequisite (Nat. Comm., 1973). Police leadership is also being upgraded, with emphasis on graduate education in administration and on the utilization of modern management and a more open, less authoritarian system.

In the foreseeable future, the police will continue to play an important role in the front-line of the mental health system. Much like a triage team, they will be called upon to intervene, evaluate and "diagnose," provide brief crisis counseling, and refer for more intensive help. However, these extremely critical functions will need to be better coordinated in a cooperative alliance with other professionals in the mental health network.

Martin Reiser, Ed.D.

186

References

Banton, Michael. 1964. The Policeman in the Community. Basic Books.

Bard, M. 1970. Training Police as Specialists in Family Crisis Intervention. Law Enforcement Assistance Administration.

Barocas, H.A. 1971. A technique for training police in crisis intervention. Psychotheraphy, Vol. 8, pp. 342-343.

Becker, Harold & Felkenes, George. 1968. Law Enforcement—a Selected Bibliography. Scarecrow Press.

Bittner, Egon. 1970. The Functions of the Police in Modern Society. MINH, (November).

Blum, Richard. 1964. Police Selection. Charles Thomas.

Chevigny, Paul. 1969. Police Power. Pantheon Books.

Clark, Ramsey. 1970. Crime in America. Simon and Schuster.

Conrad, John. 1967. Crime and its Correction. University of California.

Cressey, Donald and Ward, David. 1969. Delinquency, Crime and Social Process. Harper.

Danish, S. and Brodsky, S. 1970. Training of policemen in emotional control and awareness. American Psychologist, pp. 368-369.

Elkins, A.M. and Papanek, G.O. 1966. Consultation with police: an example of community psychiatry. American Journal of Psychiatry, Vol. 123, pp. 531-535.

Empey, LaMar and Lubeck, Steven. 1970. Delinquency Prevention Strategies. U.S. Dept. HEW.

Geis, Gilbert (ed.). 1968. White Collar Criminal. Atherton.

Halleck, Seymour. 1967. Psychiatry and the Dilemmas of Crime. Harper.

Johnson, D. and Gregory, R.J. 1971. Police-community relations in the United States: a review of recent literature and projects. The Journal of Criminal Law, Criminology and Police Science, Vol. 62, No. 1, pp. 94-104.

Liberman, R. 1969. Police as a community mental health resource. Community Mental Health Journal, Vol. 5, pp. 111-120.

Mann, P. 1973. Psychological Consultation with a Police Department. Charles Thomas.

Menninger, Karl. 1968. The Crime of Punishment. Viking.

Mental Illness and Law Enforcement. 1970. Law Enforcement Study Center, Washington University.

Newman, L.E. and Steinberg, J.L. 1970. Consultation with police on human relations training. The American Journal of Psychiatry, Vol. 126, April, pp. 1421-1429.

New York Police Department, 1969. Police Response to Family Disputes. A Training Manual for Family Crisis Intervention.

National Commission on Criminal Justice Standards and Goals. 1973. Police Task Force Report. Law Enforcement Association Administration.

Reiser, Martin. 1973. Practical Psychology for Police Officers. Charles C. Thomas.

Reiser, Mchology for Police Officers. Charles Thomas.

Reiser, M., Sokol, R.J. and Saxe, S.J. 1972. An early warning mental health program for police sergeants. The Police Chief, (June), pp. 38-39.

Roland, L.W. and Matthews, R.A. 1960. A Manual for the Police Officer: How to Recognize and Handle Abnormal People. National Association for Mental Health.

Shev, E.E. 1968. Psychiatric techniques in the selection and training of a police officer. The Police Chief, (April). pp. 10-13.

Siegel, A. et al. 1963. Professional Police-Human Relations Training. Charles Thomas.

Sikes, M.P. and Cleveland, S.E. 1969. Human relations training for police and community. American Psychologist, Vol. 23, pp. 766-769.

Singer, H.A. 1970. The cop as social scientist. The Police Chief, (April). pp. 52-58.

Sokol, R.J. and Reiser, M. 1971. Training police sergeants in early warning signs of emotional upset. Mental Hygiene, (July). pp. 303-307.

Sterling, James W. 1972. Changes in Role Concepts of Police Officers. International Association of Chiefs of Police.

Talbott, J. A. and Talbott, S.W. 1971. Training police in community relations and urban problems. American Journal of Psychiatry, (January). pp. 894-900.

187

President's Commission on Law Enforcement and the Administration of Justice, 1967. Task Force Report: Juvenile Delinquency and Youth Crime.

President's Commission of Law Enforcement and the Administration of Justice. 1967. Task Force Report: The Police. U.S. Printing Office.

President's Commission on Law Enforcement and the Administration of Justice. 1967. The Challenge of Crime in a Free Society. U.S. Printing Office.

Final Report of the National Commission on the Causes and Prevention of Violence. 1969. To Establish Justice, to Insure Domestic Tranquility. U.S. Printing Office.

Watson, N.A. 1966. Police-Community Relations. International Association of Chiefs of Police.

Wilson, James Q. 1968. Varieties of Police Behavior. Harvard.

Wolfgang, Marvin and Ferracuti, Franco. 1967. Subculture of Violence. Tavistock.

Other Sources

Journals:
Abstracts on Criminology and Penology
American Journal of Psychiatry
Crime Control Digest
Criminology
FBI Law Enforcement Bulletin
Journal of Police Science and Administration
Mental Hygiene
Police Chief

Associations:
American Psychology-Law Society
American Society of Criminology
International Association of Chiefs of Police

4. Educational Strategies for the Future

> In teaching the medical student, the primary requisite is to keep him awake.
>
> —*Chevalier Jackson (1865-1958)*

In the final section of this chapter, we plan to examine some implications of the preceding discussion for manpower training efforts in the immediate future, say the next decade or so. It is tempting to project an idealized program of educational objectives and guidelines for some dimly perceived future system of optimal service delivery and manpower utilization; however, to do so would be to ignore the historian's dictum that those who will not learn from the past are doomed to repeating their past errors. In the present context, this means looking at how we arrived at where we are now in order to better plan future directions for mental health manpower training. The suggestions we offer are based on an analysis of (a) existing manpower problems, and (b) implications of some contemporary sociopolitical forces affecting the kinds of manpower needed and the systems within which services are likely to be delivered.

A pronouncement that effective training for mental health service roles must be closely tied to role functions may appear to be a pretentious statement of a self-evident verity, one that is already widely known and applied. Yet, to reflect even briefly on the instance of psychologists and psychiatrists, usually the most highly trained of the mental health professionals, is to recognize how completely this cardinal principle has been disregarded. With increasing frequency and vigor, psychologists and psychiatrists, most often those who have recently completed training, have complained that the bulk of their professional preparation was irrelevant to the kinds of functions they later performed and that other kinds of training experiences would have better prepared them for what they actually do (Talbott 1974). On the other hand, a positive illustration in support of the principle of function-focused training is to be found in the well known NIMH-sponsored experiment in training mature housewives as mental health counselors (Rioch, et al, 1963).

In brief, we start from the position that one of the most urgent imperatives for educating mental health manpower in the future is the need to more closely relate training efforts to actual functioning in the various kinds and levels of service roles.

The successive surges of social activism which swept the United States in recent years have altered some of the basic assumptions on which mental health practitioners operated. With minor exception, practitioners had been trained to locate the source of mental health problems as being within the individual. With the explosion of the civil rights movement, women's liberation, gay liberation, and various other minority rights programs, practitioners were forced to view some of the sources of individual pathology as being within the larger society. At the same time, many began to interact professionally with communities whose service needs were great and were largely unmet.

It is of interest that many of the professionals who became involved in the larger community soon discovered that, no matter how well trained they were to deal with individuals or even with individuals in groups, they had not been trained to fully appreciate social influences on individual mental health. Nor had they been trained to deal with the social setting as a primary object of professional attention. It was with considerable pain and dismay that many discovered that the concepts and techniques which fitted them for one treatment role did not transfer to a treatment role in which the broader society was both the patient and the locus of treatment (Morrison, et al, 1973). There were, of course, other reasons why so many professionals failed as they moved into the community. However, the lack of specialized preparation for this specific role seems to have been the single major source of difficulty. It follows, therefore, that, to the extent that individual ills are seen as rooted in social ills, and, as the object of professional attention becomes the larger community, practitioners will have to have specific preparation for expanded community roles.

It is well known that, with the possible exception of the mental hospital setting, the roles of the traditional mental health professionals are frequently more similar than they are unique (Guiora and Harrison, 1973). Further, they have begun within the last decade to more overtly share their common functions with paraprofessionals, subprofessionals, new careerists, volunteers, etc. That this overlap of roles and blurring of disciplinary boundaries is a continuing source of internecine conflict need not detain us. The important point to be noted here is that a disciplinary structure necessarily results in duplication of training effort and, hence, a considerable waste of educational resources.

At a time when federal support for professional education is being withdrawn, it would seem to make sense to combine certain of the curriculum content common to the training of the several mental health professions into a unified program of basic preparation (Bandler, 1973). Such a core program might be structured into two roughly equal parts. The first would provide the student with

190

preparatory academic background in the usual areas of human development; the family as a social system, human crises (sexuality, loss, old age, death); principles of learned behavior; coping and adaptation; etc. The other half of the program might be devoted to classroom and practical experience in understanding patterns of adaptive failure and becoming familiar with principles and techniques of intervention at the levels of primary, secondary and tertiary prevention/intervention.

The preceding comments about a curriculum core were deliberately vague as to student movement after core training. Besides economy, another major advantage of a common curriculum at the entry level into mental health careers is that it may lend itself to the recently introduced concept of a lattice structure for mental health careers. As opposed to the more familiar notion of the career ladder (Riessman, 1967),the lattice analogy implies a structure in which mental health workers have an opportunity to move laterally into other programs and types of work as well as advancing vertically in a single career sequence. How such a structure would relate to, or whether it might replace, the existing structure of parallel career development is still unclear at this time. We have introduced the topic at this point primarily because of its compatability with the suggestion for a core curriculum.

Another approach to reducing overlap in training and function of advanced professionals has been the notion of merging professions. A new third profession would evolve from a merger of selected features of the roles of psychologist and psychiatrist; a new fifth profession might be evolved by extending the merger to include selected features of the roles of psychiatric nurses and social workers.

Considering that merger suggestions have been around for many years (Kubie, 1954), it is obvious that any logic dictating such amalgamation is effectively outweighed by practitioners' commitments to existing disciplinary structure. We introduce the topic because disciplinary commitments could be dramatically affected by the host of unknowns which will affect future delivery of services: health maintenance organizations, increased insurance coverage for mental health problems, extension of insurance reimbursement to non-physician providers, reductions in federal support for mental health research and training, delivery of mental health services within a human resources structure as opposed to a health framework. In turn, any of these developments could profoundly influence educational patterns (Daniels, 1973).

Having identified a few of the major needs and developments relevant to the future education of mental health practitioners, mention must be made of perhaps the most urgent need in the area of manpower and training. Quite obviously, this has to do with

191

continued development and involvement of new classes of service providers.

This is being written at a time when the general population is afflicted by a vague but pervasive malaise, dysphoria, and distrust. The search for solutions to personal and social problems appears to have intensified, as witness the development of encounter groups, "touchy-feely" marathons, self-help groups, consciousness raising rap sessions, etc. Impending economic decline could well intensify awareness of existing mental health problems, even to the point of reversing the consistent decline in inpatient mental hospital populations (Brenner, 1973).

Given the tenor and tempo of the times, previous efforts to develop new service providers and to involve existing groups in offering mental health service (as in the case of the police program above) appear not have kept pace with need and will have to be intensified. To paraphrase an exhortation made famous by George Miller in his 1969 Presidential Address to the American Psychological Association, traditional service providers will need to surrender more of their prerogatives and exclusivity and give away mental health expertise to other providers. Such a movement is obviously under way; the point is that it must proceed at a faster pace. The tempo of developing the skills of the several variants of new careerists and mental health associates must be accelerated. It seems especially important that we involve and train those whose primary function is other than providing mental health services: the police, the clergy, teachers, primary care physicians, recreation leaders, etc.

Implicit in this all too familiar prescription is the view that mental health needs will not be met until established professionals turn away from an exclusive concern with increasing the adaptive potential of those already labeled as sick (tertiary prevention) to decreasing the sickness potential of those who are well (primary and secondary prevention). It is in this connection that we urge the development of broader networks for provision of mental health services. Just in terms of sheer numbers, there is no indication in current manpower projections that the traditional professions can meet the nation's health needs—or even demands. Nor do we see more than an occasional evidence that the existing professions are prepared to reverse their traditional concerns with individual pathology and tertiary prevention and devote a substantial part of their energies to primary and secondary prevention.

Without romanticizing them, and without overlooking many of the attendant problems of introducing new careerists, there is abundant informal evidence that the new careerists have been particularly successful in meeting just those needs not previously addressed by the traditional professionals. Although the development of new careerists and the expansion of responsibility of related providers were initially seen as partial solutions to problems of manpower shortages, their value in mental health service delivery has exceeded the initial limited objective (Durlak, 1973). In particular, it became evident that mental health services are not analogous to medical areas such as surgery, where formal education and training generally insure superior performance and where personality factors are of minor relevance to technical performance. Rather, with the expanded use of new careerists, it became evident that personality factors and life history experiences were important determinants of success in mental health service delivery (McPheeters, et al, 1972). In fact, some of these successes pointed up many areas in which a high degree of professionalization interfered with job performance.

The rather obvious implication of this discussion is that educational strategies must increasingly encompass various forms of experiential learning which will make use of existing personal assets and which will sharpen and refine personal skills appropriate for expanded efforts in primary and secondary intervention.

Lee Gurel, Ph.D.

References

Bandler, B. 1973. Interprofessional collaboration in mental health. American Journal of Orthopsychiatry, 43, 97-107.

Brenner, M.H. 1973. Mental Illness and the Economy. Cambridge, Mass.: Harvard Univ. Press.

Daniels, R.S. 1973. Changing human service delivery systems: Their influences on psychiatric training. American Journal of Psychiatry, 130, 1232-1236.

Durlak, J.A. 1973. Myths concerning the nonprofessional therapist. Professional Psychology, 4, 300-304.

Guiora, A.Z. & Harrison, S.I. 1973. What is psychiatry? A new model of service and education. American Journal of Psychiatry, 130, 1275-1277.

Kubie, L.A. 1954. The pros and cons of a new profession: A doctorate in medical psychology. Texas Reports on Biology and Medicine, 12, 692-737.

McPheeters, H.L., King, J.B., & Teare, R.J. 1972. The middle-level mental health worker: I. His role. Hospital & Community Psychiatry, 23, 329-334.

Morrison, A.P., Shore, M.F., & Grobman, J. 1973. On the stresses of community psychiatry, and helping residents to survive them. American Journal of Psyciatry, 130, 1237-1241.

Riessman, F. 1967. The new careers concept. American Child, 49, 2-8.

Rioch, M.J., et al. 1963. NIMH pilot study in training mental health counselors. American Journal of Orthopsychiatry, 33, 678-689.

Talbott, J.A. 1974. Radical Psychiatry: An examination of the issues. American Journal of Psychiatry, 131, 121-128.

VIII. | Social Issues

1. Sex, Family Planning, and Population

Where did you come from, baby dear?
Out of the everywhere into here.

—*George Macdonald (1824-1905)*

The past decade has brought health professionals and the public to a keener awareness of normal sexual development, family planning, and population growth. Courses in sexuality and demography now abound in colleges and health professional schools. Public health and mental health jointly have a stake in understanding and responding to issues in these fields.

The number of individuals on earth has more than doubled since 1900. In the last few years, the birth rate in the United States has fallen and by 1973 was below the level necessary to produce zero population growth. However, even at replacement level, i.e., two children per couple, the population will still increase for about 60 years because of the large number of persons of childbearing age.

According to classical demographic teachings, problems of population growth occur during the transition from agricultural (or preindustrial) societies to industrial societies. With the onset of improved living conditions and medical care, death rates begin to drop causing an overbalance of births compared to deaths and the population increases rapidly. When the society modernizes, the death rate continues low but the birth rate falls closer to the death rate for reasons which seem to involve personal, social and economic factors.

John Calhoun, in experiments with colonies of rats, discovered that once the rat population reached a given size within a limited space, the animal society began to deteriorate, lose motivation, and die off without reproducing (Calhoun, 1973). Similarly, in a society during demographic transition, one can see profound social, emotional, economic, and other effects on, for example, a family with ten or more surviving children, when only four or five were expected to live based on recent past experience.

Americans are now well aware of the impact of population on the environment and human ecology. Although the industrialized nations have seen their birth rates fall, their relative affluence plays a major role in multiplying the effects of their population on the environment. Each affluent child uses many times more irreplaceable resources (and produces much more waste) than a poor child.

At least in part for reasons relative to "quality of life," more American couples are choosing to delay, limit or forego parenthood than ever before.

In the 1970's, there are more socially acceptable family variations than ever before. For example, in addition to the usual two parent monogamous family, there are also many single parent families and communes. These new models of family structure are setting new roles for the children who are growing up in them. Within conventional family patterns there seem to be at least six critical interrelated factors related to childbearing, which affect the mental health of families and children.

The timing of the first child is perhaps the most important event of the family history. When a couple becomes three, the roles of family members change and new interaction patterns must be established. The way in which the first pregnancy impinges upon the couple, i.e., voluntarily or by accident, may in large measure determine the psychological readiness of the couple to respond in constructive ways to their first child. Similarly, the ways in which the couple redefines its roles, needs, and patterns of relating after birth doubtless determines the number and spacing of their children and particularly whether or not future offspring are desired.

The spacing of births may be influenced by a number of factors, e.g., by the desire for an infant in order to gratify dependency needs, or by the sex of the first child. Reluctance to use birth control is a major factor leading to poorly planned birth intervals.

The potential importance of optimum spacing for psychological development of children cannot be over-emphasized. A one-year interval is short by obstetrical criteria; two years may catch the older sibling just short of autonomy, language skills and toilet training. Three years finds the older sibling well-developed in ego capacity and yet separated by more years than may be desirable for close comradeship. In the end, the best spacing may depend more on parents' comfort with the time between children than on any other factor.

The number of children in a family is related to health and mental health. Larger families have more difficulty attending to the developmental needs of their children, particularly to those later born. The Scottish mental study of 1947 showed progressive decline in intelligence score with increasing family size, independent of social class (Scottish Council, 1953). Sometimes parental functions may be taken over by the older offspring in large families, who as a result may lose part of their experience of childhood.

Being desired as a family member would seem to be a critical factor for the healthy psychological development of a child. Forssman showed that increased delinquent behavior, increased frequency of psychiatric visits, and lower educational achievement resulted in offspring of mothers who were denied abortion as compared with a control group (Forssman and Thuwe, 1966).

Eventually, perhaps soon, parents will probably be able to influence the sex of their offspring prior to conception. This possibility would reduce the need to try "one last time" for a child of the opposite sex, and would thus result in smaller families and fewer unwanted children. Many couples probably would stop at two children if they had a girl and a boy.

Parental competence includes emotional and intellectual readiness in each individual as well as interpersonal maturity in the marriage and family relationship. Suggestions for society's assuring parental competence include requirements for training in childrearing and even licensing for parenthood. These ideas contrast markedly with the laissez-faire attitudes toward parenthood which have existed to date, although recent visibility of child abuse in our society has tended to counteract this complacency.

Major personal and social changes have occurred in such areas as sexual behavior, contraception and abortion, sex education, obscenity, homosexuality, treatment of sexual problems, and women's rights. Most of these are highly relevant to mental health and public health practitioners.

In the past 15 to 20 years, there has been a gradual lessening of sanctions against non-marital sexual intercourse, particularly premarital coitus (Hunt, 1973). Liberalization has coincided not with a total revolution in sexual behavior, but chiefly with an increase in the number of women having premarital sex.

The advent of new and more effective forms of contraception, particularly the pill, may be in part responsible for any increase in sexual activity that may be taking place. Attitudes toward contraception have become increasingly positive, even for unmarried teenagers. With the removal of most legal constraints, abortion is also a more acceptable and available form of birth control.

Sex education continues to be filled with controversy. Some feel it is a plot to brainwash the minds and lower the morals of our children; others feel that no child can be prepared to face life without it. The age at which sex education should begin in any given setting has been argued, as have the qualifications of teachers, the specific curricula, and the degree of explicitness of materials. Sex education appears to be an appropriate area for application of the preventively oriented activities, such as consultation and education, which are provided by community mental health centers.

The burgeoning of the X-rated movie business and sale of sexual materials is testimony to the increasing interest in the "obscene and pornographic." There is intense disagreement about the value, appropriateness, and legality of these explicit erotic materials. The President's Commission on Obscenity and Pornography recommended that restrictions be aimed at protecting children, and voiced the opinion that no harm has been shown to result from adults having access to explicit sexual materials.

The term sexual deviation may refer to a wide variety of different behaviors and may, in fact, be a misnomer. For example, many gay people decry the term homosexuality and prefer that it be replaced by "same-sex behavior" which they feel should be recognized as legitimate sexual expression, free of stigma or legal restraint for consenting adults in private. In 1974 the American Psychiatric Association voted to remove homosexuality from its classification as a psychiatric disorder, replacing it with "sexual orientation disturbance" to describe those who were genuinely troubled about their sexual identity or behavior.

A variety of new methods have sprung up for the treatment of specific sexual symptoms. The best known of these is the Masters and Johnson approach presented in *Human Sexual Inadequacy* (Masters & Johnson, 1970). These new therapies offer intensive short-term intervention for sexual symptoms which previously were treated less effectively or not at all. The increasing acceptance by the public of the legitimacy of sexual symptoms and of the need for discussion of sexual issues probably has contributed to the rapid expansion of this new field.

In the past decade, equal rights for women has been a major social issue. Apart from the hostile rejection of males sometimes heard in this context, support for equality is widespread as evidenced by passage of the Equal Rights Amendment by the Congress in March of 1972.

In summary, it is imperative for public health practitioners to be well-informed about and active in addressing the critical issues related to sexuality, family planning, and population increase. Each of these areas has profound potential consequences for satisfying personal intimacy, maintaining a productive society, and for the achievement of global survival.

Scott H. Nelson, M.D., M.P.H.

References

Abse, D. Wilfred, et. al. 1974. Marital and Sexual Counseling in Medical Practice, New York: Harper & Row.

Bogue, Donald J. 1969. Principles of Demography, New York: John Wiley & Sons, Inc.

Calhoun, John B. 1973. "Death Squared: The explosive growth and demise of a mouse population," Proceedings of the Royal Society of Medicine, Vol. 66.

Forssman, Hans, and Thuwe, Inga. 1966. "One hundred and twenty children born after application for therapeutic abortion refused," Acta Psychiatrica Scandinavia 42.

Group for the Advancement of Psychiatry. 1973. Humane Reproduction, Vol. VIII, Report No. 86, (August).

Hunt, Morton. 1973. "Sexual behavior in the 1970's" Playboy, Vol. 20, No. 10, (Oct.).

Kaplan, Helen Singer. 1974. The New Sex Therapy: Active Treatment of Sexual Dysfunctions, New York: Brunner/Mazel.

Lieberman, E. James and Peck, Ellen. 1973. Sex and Birth Control: A Guide for the Young, New York: Thomas Y. Crowell Co.

Masters, William H. and Johnson, Virginia E. 1970. Human Sexual Inadequacy, Boston: Little Brown Co.

Scottish Council for Research in Education. 1953. "Social Implications of the 1947 Scottish Mental Survey," London.

Taylor, Donald L. 1970. Human Sexual Development: Perspectives in Sex Education, Philadelphia: F. A. Davis Co.

Toman, Walter. 1961. Family Constellation, New York: Springer Publishing Co., Inc.

2. Poverty and Affluence

The poor is never free; he serves in every land.

—F. Voltaire (1694-1778)

One major thrust of American society in the 1960's was to uncover the so-called "poor" and to define and deal with the problems of poverty. Considerable emphasis was placed on research, programming and development of new ways to deal with the poor. Some of the resulting programs are difficult to evaluate. Who did we identify as poor in the course of trying to help them? Did those in need receive any benefit? Did the emphasis on poverty merely serve to delineate more clearly who the affluent were and then set the middle-class even farther on the road to economic security?

The poverty threshold for a non-farm family of four was $4,137 in 1971, when over 25 million Americans fell within this definition (USBC, 1971). In the same year the Census Bureau estimated the average annual income for all American families to be $11,176. More than half the people falling within the definition of poverty, some 15.1 million Americans were receiving assistance from federal, state or local resources (DHEW, 1972). Although it is popularly believed that able-bodied, employable adult males make up a large proportion of those on the welfare rolls, the fact is that only one out of every hundred poor Americans on welfare is an unemployed, able-bodied male. The rest were helped by special funds for dependent children and their mothers, the aged, or the blind and disabled (GAP, 1973).

Although blacks made up about eleven percent of the population at large in 1971, about one-third (7.9 million) of the blacks were officially "poor," and about one-third of all poor people were black (USDC, 1973). Further, about one-fourth of all men who were heads of low-income families had full time jobs the year around. Poverty as a chronic condition must therefore be viewed as a continuum without clearly defined boundaries. And since there is much more that goes into poverty than lack of money, income statistics are only a crude measure of impoverishment in its full sense.

There have been numerous explanations as to how those in poverty happen to be there and why it is that they remain. Kenneth Clark (1965) places Negro youths in a "tangle of pathology" of school and work failure, emotional disorder, and criminal activities, pathologies which Moynihan (1965) attributes primarily to the dys-

202

functions of the Negro family. Others, such as Oscar Lewis (1966) speak of the "culture of poverty," where the poor are alien in a dominant society and their culture presumably keeps them from making use of the educational or constitutional deficits, are difficult to research because of the complexity of variables involved. And the nagging question remains: even if the individual's symptoms were removed, would not the structural conditions which generate and sustain poverty remain?

It is clear that factors such as inadequate employment, housing, nutrition and physical health all play a crucial part in the plight of the poor. The Joint Commission on the Mental Health of Children (1973) cites the above concomitants of poverty as major barriers to mental health. Mental health not only depends on physical health, a stable family life, and wholesome environment, but also requires community and societal values and attitudes that encourage and support individual self-esteem, intellectual and emotional development, and equal opportunity.

Welfare, as it has been institutionalized in our society, has come to have many different meanings. For those on welfare, it is seen as demeaning and emphasizing their economic plight, thereby lowering their self-esteem. The rules and regulations of the welfare system are viewed as being designed to control the private life of the recipient. Those who have little direct contact with the welfare system tend to see it as a free financial ride for the lazy and inept. This latter view enjoys widespread support despite the fact that studies consistently show that fraud or misrepresentation occurs in less than one percent of the total welfare caseload of the nation (GAP, 1973). Questions concerning racial prejudice also arise because of the disproportionately large number of minority persons receiving aid.

The aid given in welfare programs has tended to focus on monetary relief at the subsistence level rather than helpful solutions to the problems of individuals that led to their seeking assistance in the first place. Not sufficiently emphasized in welfare programs are such needs as job training, the education of couples, or proper daycare facilities for children. Programs addressed to employment problems still receive inadequate attention. The need to project good "success" rates, as well as the criteria established for admission to these programs, have served to screen out many of those who are most in need of assistance. Almost totally forgotten in welfare programs have been the emotional needs of the recipients.

In recent years, issues such as housing, education, aging, unemployment, nutrition, crime and racism have come to be considered as problems by all classes in our society. However, these are of concern to the poor and the affluent in different ways. For the middle-class, for example, nutrition might have significance in terms of well-balanced meals; for the poor the significance may be the un-availability of resources to provide any meals at all.

Hence, the manner in which the issue of nutrition is addressed depends greatly on one's social and economic situation. The Joint Commission on Mental Health of Children pointed out that malnutrition among the poor often leads to difficulties in other areas of life; low protein diets in children, for example, are associated with low educational attainment and poor sociability. The implication is that protein deficiency prevents a child from making full use of the educational opportunities which are available to him. Furthermore, education and employment can be viewed as interlocking variables which have powerful implications for success in our society. In a technological society such as ours, education is the vehicle to a good paying job. However, for blacks and other minorities, the poor quality or complete lack of education or other formal training forces them into lower paying jobs or into unemployment.

For the middle-class, education continues to be stressed as one of the main avenues to social and economic mobility, although many middle-class persons are beginning to question the kind of educational processes to which their children are exposed. Poor people, of course, want as much for their children as affluent persons do, but most are, for the present, more immediately concerned about their children simply gaining access to a minimally decent system of formal education.

Housing continues to be a problem for the poor, and has become a concern of the middle-class as well. The recent upsurge in real estate values has made housing less available to the middle-class while the poor have been priced out of the market altogether. This makes the task of providing adequate shelter and a healthy family life even more difficult for the poor, and over-crowding continues to be a problem, especially for blacks and other minorities. In 1970, for example, twenty percent of black households lived in units with one or more persons per room compared to only 7% of white households (GAP, 1973).

Racism continues to be a social issue with which minorities continue to struggle. Discrimination has direct and profound effects on employment, housing, education, and many other areas affecting the quality of life of minority group members. These effects have been systematically explored by James Comer (1972) and others who have written about the difficulties of being black in a white society. Black and other minorities continue to struggle with the majority society's value orientation which downgrades their individual and collective worth. The recent increased acceptance of the rights of minority groups has led these groups to continuing reassessments of self-identity as they struggle for further recognition and access to opportunities. Racial prejudice and discrimination will not be easily eliminated, but the use of constructive mental health approaches across the board may help.

A crisis of poverty also exists for the elderly. Older people are faced with increasingly difficult and complex problems, many of which revolve around their limited financial resources and unavailable services. Basics such as food and housing are often inadequate. More than most other groups, the elderly find it difficult to attract attention and to organize in order to make effective claims on the society. The elderly feel used and wasted when they have much they could give and share with the rest of society.

The Social Security Administration recently estimated that there are between fifteen and twenty million elderly persons. This number will increase approximately ten percent over the next several years. With a longer life expectancy, issues of how to render more effective services and provide greater opportunities for this population become critical. Among other things, we must find ways to make use of the skills, energy and experiences the elderly have to offer society. At present, however, the structure of service delivery systems for the elderly and for welfare recipients inhibits their movement toward self-sufficiency by providing little support for meaningful alternatives to their present conditions. Social service programs with built-in mechanisms for increasing economic leverage and improved quality of life are essential if the elderly are to gain increased functional independence, a sense of self-worth, and general psychological security and well-being.

Our society seems to be in a state of confusion, apprehension, and fear. There is a feeling that we have lost our capacity for mutual trust and understanding and for dealing effectively with the broad range of problems that daily confronts us. The social order appears to be in disarray with increasing fragmentation of our social institutions such as family, school, work and community. It is not clear what steps are being taken to reverse or even halt this process. At the core of this disarray—or very near it—is the fact that a significant number of families simply do not have enough money to support themselves at a minimally decent standard of living. As a first step toward the reintegration of all groups in our society, we must develop a jobs/incomes policy that ensures, as a matter of right, a minimally decent level of income for all Americans.

A closely related problem is the destructively wide gap between rich and poor in our society. A social service program, however broad and effective, can at best only chip away at the edges of the problem. An effective approach requires that we address directly the issues of employment, education and housing in ways that, while admitting competition between different racial, class and interest groups, sets them in a legal-political framework consistent with our shared values concerning social justice, equity, and fair play.

If one accepts the almost self-evident proposition that the well-being of one segment of our society affects the mental health of our entire society, then we must look again at the attitudes and assumptions behind our system of mental health care. For example, it has repeatedly been observed that middle-class patients are preferred by mental health professionals while the lower class is seen as less treatable and is usually characterized as more maladjusted and with poorer prognosis for improvement. Our attitudes therefore have much to do with how and to whom mental health care resources are distributed. If progress is to be made in improving the self-esteem and individual effectiveness of all members of our society, then such attitudes and biases must be brought into the open and re-examined for their implications and consequences.

Finally, it is no longer appropriate to deal with the poor or welfare recipients as isolated groups who require special attention. The mental health of the whole society importantly depends on the delivery of services which are relevant, sufficient and effective for all of its parts, and on policies and programs which take into account the relationship of the parts to one another. Similarly, the prevailing attitude that we must plan *for*, rather than *with* the poor, must be changed. In this way, the poor can become directly involved in the process of their own betterment. The effort then becomes not only one of economics but of improving their total life situation.

For the welfare recipient, the elderly, and other poor people, improving their economic base is only one vital step in the direction of improving their mental health. As basic needs are more adequately met, then the other elements that effect adversely one's mental health can be confronted and dealt with. However, to continue the current inadequacy and fragmentation of services will only reinforce the belief of the affluent that the poor are shiftless and the welfare recipient is getting a free ride at their expense. The time has long been ripe for innovative constructive programs that address the real issues of the poor and encourage their participation in the process of social change.

Edward R. Turner, M.S.W.

206

References

Billingsley, Andrew. 1968. Black Families in White America. Englewood Cliffs, New Jersey: Prentice-Hall, Inc.

Billingsley, Andrew and Giovannoni, Jeanne. 1972. Children of the Storm, New York: Harcourt, Brace-Jovanovich.

Bureau of the Census. 1971. Characteristics of the Low Income Population, 1970. Series P-60. No. 81. Social and Economic Statistics Admin., U.S. Dept. of Commerce.

Clark, Kenneth. 1965. Dark Ghetto. New York: Harper and Row.

Comer, James P. 1972. Beyond Black and White, New York: Quadrangle Books.

Comer, J. P. 1970. The Black Family: An Adaptive Perspective. New Haven: Child Study Center, Yale University.

Galbriath, John Kenneth. 1958. The Affluent Society, Boston: Houghton Mifflin Company.

Glazer, Nathan and Moynihan, Daniel P. 1970. Beyond the Melting Pot, 2nd ed. Cambridge: M.I.T.

Grier, William H. and Cobbs, Price M. 1968. Black Rage, New York: Basic Books.

Group for the Advancement of Psychiatry. 1973. The Welfare System and Mental Health, Vol. VIII, Report No. 85.

Hollingshead, August and Redlick, Frederick C. 1958. Social Class and Mental Illness, New York: John Wiley and Sons.

Joint Commission on the Mental Health of Children. 1973. Social Change and the Mental Health of Children, New York: Harper and Row.

Lewis, Hylan. 1967. (Arthur Ross and Herbert Hill, eds.) Culture, Class and Family Life Among Low-Income Urban Negroes, in Employment, Race and Poverty, New York: Harcourt, Brace Jovanovich, Inc. pp. 149-172.

Lewis, Oscar. 1966. La Vida: A Puerto Rican Family in the Culture of Poverty. New York: Random House.

Moynihan, Daniel P. 1967. The Negro Family: The Case for National Action, Office of Policy Planning and Research, U. S. Department of Labor, March, 1965. In the Moynihan Report and The Politics of Controversy. (Lee Rainwater and W. L. Yancey, eds.).Cambridge, Mass: MIT Press.

Pearls, Arthur & Riessman, Frank. 1965. New Careers for the Poor, New York: The Free Press.

President's Commission on Income Maintenance Programs, Report of 1969. Poverty Amid Plenty. November 1968.

Riessman, Frank & Popper, Hermine I. 1968. Up From Poverty, New Career Ladders For Non-Professionals, New York: Harper & Row.

The Social and Economic Status of the Black Population in the United States. Current Population Reports, Series P-23, No. 42, Special Studies. U.S. Bureau of Census. 1971.

Social and Rehabilitation Service. Public Assistance Statistics, June, 1972. DHEW Publication No. SRS 73-03100. NCSS Report A-2 (672). Wash., D.C.: U.S. Dept. of Health, Education, and Welfare.

U.S. Dept. of Commerce. 1971. The Social and Economic Status of the Black Population in the U.S. Special Studies, Current Population Reports, Series P-23. No. 42. pp. 2-7.

3. Discrimination

All looks yellow to the jaundic'd eye.

—*Alexander Pope (1688-1744)*

The ordinary meaning of prejudice has to do with positive or negative feelings about a person or an object that are inappropriately generalized to the whole group or class of person or objects. Gordon W. Allport in his classic study. *The Nature of Prejudice*, says that an adequate definition of prejudice contains two essential ingredients: "There must be an *attitude* of favor or disfavor; and it must be related to an overgeneralized (and therefore erroneous) *belief*." Thus, prejudice has to do with both attitudes and belief systems. Not all persons of course, are aware of the prejudices they hold, nor are prejudices always held openly by those who have them. The individual who translates his prejudices into action may be said to be practicing discrimination. Since it refers primarily to what people actually do, "discrimination," notes Allport, "has more immediate and serious social consequences than has prejudice."

Discrimination, like so many other facets of life, has been used for both good and bad purposes and is part of both the progress and degradation of the human spirit. Today, discrimination is more prominent as a negative, destructive force. Negative discrimination on the basis of race, sex, creed, age and national origins is responsible for much of the aggression and hostility which threaten the structure of our society.

The need to reduce discrimination and to lessen the destruction which often flows from it requires an alertness to every aspect of discrimination, including the consequences for those who practice it as well as for its victims. How in the psycho-social development of individuals does the need arise to discriminate against others? What role does culture play in the transmission of patterns of discrimination from generation to generation? How can discrimination and its effects be reduced so that society can evolve humanely? These are a few of the questions that need attention if we are going to improve intergroup relations in our society and enhance individual functioning.

Prejudice and discrimination feed on one another at both the psychological and social level. They are interdependent parts of a self-justifying system in which those who are discriminated against are forced into roles that reinforce the prejudicial beliefs of the discriminators. Clearly, both the individual members and the society-at-large are damaged thereby. If one accepts prejudice as a mechanism in the personality development of individuals which limits their potential for positive growth, then prejudice is a mental health problem. If one accepts the fact that discrimination has destructive consequences for the physical and mental health for all the participants in the discriminatory social system, then discrimination is a public health problem. From this perspective, prejudice and discrimination are clearly appropriate concerns of mental health and public health practitioners. The connection can be seen most easily by examining the single most destructive force of discrimination in our society—white racism towards blacks.

White racism is supported by the prejudice that whiteness is superior to blackness. This belief encourages behavior in which whites overtly and covertly exploit, dehumanize and oppress blacks. White racism can be seen as a perceptual disorder in that in any negotiation between white and black, whites as a group tend to perceive themselves as normal and superior and blacks as abnormal and inferior. White racism is anchored in a system of mistaken beliefs and serves the same psychic function as does a delusion. Because white racism is shared by many individuals and is ingrained in institutional values, its delusional quality is often not recognized, especially by whites. This lack of awareness on the part of many whites has public health significance. For example, it is commonplace to observe the greater morbidity and mortality rates among blacks as compared to whites, but society has not yet learned to recognize the adverse effects of racism on the physical and mental health of whites, effects that undoubtedly are expressed through increased anxiety levels, psychophysiologic disorders, and other emotional problems.

Schools and television are among the major institutions that tend to present a negative view of blacks, often demeaning them—in the eyes of both black and white children—in subtle but unmistakeable ways. One result is that white children are often confused and even develop internal conflicts between the principles of fair play and the demonstration of inhuman approaches to black and other minority children. Other consequences are equally destructive: the white child who enhances his prestige by comparing himself with an image of dehumanized blacks is denied the strengthening experience of earning his self-esteem; myths of racial sexual roles and intermarriage add to the stress of adolescent psychosexual development; psychic energies are consumed and wasted in interracial tension; the strong irrational forces required to maintain prejudice limit the psychosocial flexibility and adaptability of prejudiced persons; individuals bound by their racial prejudices are often resistant to new modes of thought, intolerant of ambiguity and uncertainty, and poorly able to differentiate between the qualities of minority persons; guilt and anxiety recur frequently with the realization that one's own behavior and one's belief in democratic principles of equality are inconsistent; since the self-image of prejudiced whites includes the concept of being non-black, they deny to themselves those positive qualities (e.g., "soul") which whites have ascribed to blackness, or which blacks have successfully laid claim to for themselves. And on and on.

The 1960's were marked by a heightened awareness of black consciousness which demanded that white society change or experience even greater psychological impairment in its attempts to maintain the illusion of superiority. Civil disorder and increasing racial tension aroused white fears and a closer examination of their long-term self interest, and both of these developments may have helped to accelerate the pace of social change toward a more democratic society. The black power movement fostered black self-esteem and at the same time forced whites to examine their prejudices and modify their behaviors.

Women's involvement in the civil rights movement did much to give them further insight into their own limited lives, limitations which have been enforced by sex role traditions and exacerbated by mass media. The greater awareness of racial discrimination provided a catalyst for the new feminism. The black movement showed women that an attack against one form of discrimination can help to weaken other forms of discrimination as well.

The destructive effects of prejudice and discrimination at the level of psychological functioning have too long been ignored or denied. One result is that problems of prejudice and discrimination are conceptualized so as to provide the illusion that they are simply black social problems. The effects of racial prejudice are then seen only in terms of specific social consequences for the black community that are dealt with by remedial programs of one kind or another. These programs, many of which have been designed to deal with the social consequences of discrimination against minorities, often avoid confrontation with the nature of prejudice and racism as an irrational mental state among whites who are themselves, in a very real sense, victims of their own irrationality.

Models are needed for intervention in the processes of discrimination if the mental health of the nation is to be improved. The mother-child interaction may be one of the most important and susceptible relationships around which some models could be developed. The desire of parents to develop the full potential of their children could be utilized to increase the self-awareness of parents about their own prejudices and thereby avoid transmitting them to their children. The child would then be free to develop a healthier personality and a more productive life, since he would not have the

210

burdens of prejudiced beliefs and discrimination which keep him from learning productively in his world or from relating to those individuals with whom he shares interests and rapport.

There is also a need to develop a systems theory of institutional discrimination sufficiently comprehensive to relate the dynamics of institutions to the difficulties of individuals who are affected by them. A theory of this nature would allow for the possible establishment of more effective therapeutic relationships between the mental health professions and the various political, social, and economic institutions in our society.

Black and other minorities must also develop expertise in politics and communications so that they may make larger contributions to the individual and collective decisions which affect them if they are to redirect the racist institutions which surround them. Importantly, blacks and whites must work together if the processes of racism are to be eliminated, along with the crime, delinquency, alienation, and all the other social ills that racism sustains and nourishes.

The progress of a civilized society depends on the lessening of aggression and increasing harmony between different groups. This can be achieved at least partly through the control of negative discrimination and the elimination of its effects. Racism is one example of discrimination in America which hurts all its citizens. It plays such a significant and central role in our lives that racism may well be the keystone of the social and psychodynamic mechanisms which support all forms of harmful discrimination in our society. The struggle against this particular form of discrimination is a struggle against all forms. If racism in America were eliminated, then other forms of discrimination could not easily endure.

The most effective way for mental health workers to lead the struggle against racism is to regard it as both a public health problem, which places the problem within the purview of the largest public institutions in this country—government, health and education—and as a mental health problem, which confronts discrimination at its source—the personal and interpersonal racist beliefs and practices within the dominant culture.

Barbara S. Williams, M.D., M.P.H.

References

Allport, Gordon W. 1958. The Nature of Prejudice, Garden City, New York: Doubleday and Co., Inc.

Comer, James P. 1972. Beyond Black and White, New York: Quadrangle Books, Inc.

Cromwell, Phyllis E. ed. 1974. Woman and Mental Health, Selected Annotated References, 1970—1973. Rockville, Md.: National Institute of Mental Health.

DeBeauvoir, Simone. 1970. The Coming of Age, New York: Warner.

Glazer, Nathan and Moynihan, Daniel P. 1970. Beyond the Melting Pot, 2nd ed., Cambridge: M.I.T. Press.

Glock, Charles Y. and Siegleman, Ellen, ed. 1969. Prejudice U.S.A., New York: Praeger Publishers.

Huber, Joan, ed. 1973. Changing Women in a Changing Society, Chicago: Univ. of Chicago Press.

Kovel, Joel. 1970. White Racism: A Psychohistory, New York: Vintage Books (Random House).

Poussaint, Alvin F. 1972. Why Blacks Kill Blacks, New York: Emerson Hall Publ.

Cruz, H. S. 1971. Racial Discrimination, New York: United Nations.

Wortis, Helen and Rabinwitz, Clara. 1972. The Women's Movement, New York: John Wiley and Sons, Inc.

Pierce, C. M. 1969. Violence and counterviolence: the need for a children's domestic exchange, Amer. J. Orthopsychiat. 30:553-568.

Pierce, C. M. 1969. Our most crucial domestic issue, Amer. J. Psychiat. 125:1583-1584.

Pierce, C. M. 1966. A psychiatric approach to present day racial problems, J. Nat. Med. Assn. 51:207-210.

U.S. Commission on Civil Rights. 1970. Racism in America. Clearinghouse Publication, Urban Series No. 1.

U. S. Government Printing Office. 1968. Report of the National Advisory Commission on Civil Disorders. Wash., D.C.

Willie, Charles V., Kramer, Bernard M., Brown, Bertram S. (eds.). 1973. Racism and Mental Health. Pittsburgh: Univ. of Pittsburgh Press.

212

4. Violence

> ... we must face once more how far civilized man
> may have sunk in some respects below the animal
> and probably also below his early human ancestors:
> for it is civilized man, morality and all, who is, or has
> become, in Loren Eiseley's terrible phrase, the lethal
> element in the universe.
>
> —*Erik H. Erikson*
> *Gandhi's Truth (1969)*

Violence both repels and attracts us. Its political use among
nations is widely condemned, yet the front pages of our newspapers
are repetitively filled with reports regarding it. We eschew its use in
ordinary daily activities, yet our spectator sports and art forms frequently involve violence or the threat of it. Such apparent contradictions seem beyond comprehension. However, neurophysiologists,
ethologists, psychoanalysts, and other students of human behavior
agree that violence—or the urge to do it—is closely tied to sexuality,
self assertion, and indeed, to survival itself.

For our purposes here, violence is defined as the use of force to
harm people or to damage property. One person may be involved, as
in self-mutilation, self-induced accidents, or suicide. Or violence
may involve two or more people, as with homicide, child abuse, or
rape. Ethnic or national groups engage in mass violence such as riot,
civil disorder, and war. Damage to property is referred to as van-
dalism; it may involve arson. (Though germane to mental health matters, property damage does not ordinarily concern public health and
will not be addressed here.)

From a psychodynamic perspective violence has its origins in
aggression, a hypothetical psychological attribute that helps individuals and groups to survive by initiating pursuit of vital sustenance
and by prompting action taken in self-defense. Aggression thus can
be viewed as the source of achievement and self-confidence, and of
murder and mayhem. Violence and aggression have long been of interest to health workers, who have sought to understand aggression
and to prevent or reduce certain kinds of violence (Ilfeld, 1969).

Violent death from accidents, suicide, and homicide occurs considerably more often among males than among females. Such death
is often associated with depression, acute alcohol or drug intoxication, and the problems of chronic chemical dependency (Porterfield,

213

1960; Walker, 1971). Beyond these few consistent observations, other demographic findings vary markedly with ethnicity and socio-economic class.

For example, vital statistics data throughout the United States show suicide rates which far exceed homicide rates for white Americans, and the reverse for black Americans and American Indians. Age specific rates also demonstrate differences, though with some overlapping: American Indians and black Americans reach peak violent death rates in late adolescence and early adulthood, while white Americans attain high violent death rates in middle and old age (Ogden, et al, 1970; Pettigrew & Spier, 1962).

Other variables can be noted to occur consistently with each kind of violent death. These include geographic setting, month of year, day of week, time of day, and specific instruments or means of death. For example, the vehicular death rate is greatest from the early evening to early morning hours, from Friday evening to early Sunday, during national holidays, at certain locations, and in specific vehicular types. While psychological factors have not proven to be very predictive, inordinate risk-taking and impaired masculine image have been adduced for certain types of accidents (Graham, 1969; Richman, 1972).

Violence may wax and wane in an epidemic fashion within a given community. For example, homicide death in core cities of some metropolitan areas has been increasing over recent years. Often associated with alcohol or drug usage, these homicides occur mostly during arguments among relatives and friends. The availability of inexpensive handguns has been implicated as one major reason for this increase (Hirsch, et al, 1973).

Suicide prevention programs, consisting of emergency telephone and clinic services, have not clearly demonstrated their effectiveness in reducing suicide rates over the last decade (Lester, 1974). Clinical services in out-patient clinics and emergency rooms for violence-prone and homicidal people have also been established in the last few years. Such clinics have taught us much regarding such people (such as their high rate of organic brain dysfunction). (Roth, 1972). The impact of these services on homicide rates, if any, has not yet been reported.

Depression is often found not only with suicide, but also among accident and homicide victims and perpetrators; indeed certain accidents and homicides are regarded as "suicide equivalents" (Lion, 1972). Early diagnosis and treatment for depression may decrease these tragedies. Violent behaviors of all kinds are associated with both acute and chronic use of intoxicants (Amir, 1967; Rushing, 1969). Industry-based counseling and court-affiliated educational programs, in-patient and out-patient services, half-way houses and therapeutic communes now provide secondary and tertiary services

214

for chemically dependent persons. Counseling services for families undergoing crisis and social activities for the alienated and lonely probably aid in alleviating violent death. Technological, legislative, and educational advances can also be effective: seat belts, divided highways, lower speeds, vehicular standards, and driver education have resulted in lower vehicular accident death rates in recent years.

Sexual assault, injurious assault, and child abuse are—like homicide—most often perpetrated by men. While all groups and ages are represented, most of these men belong to lower socioeconomic classes and are older adolescents and young adults. These acts are often associated with acute alcohol or drug intoxication. They tend to occur in a context of frustration, powerlessness, and unemployment. Case reports indicate that persons prone to assaultiveness were often physically abused by their parents during childhood. Anecdotal data also suggest that depression may be a frequent concomitant (Barclay, 1971; Edgcumbe, 1971; Steinmetz & Straus, 1973).

Early detection and intervention in child abuse has recently become a major focus of physicians, social workers, and public health nurses working with families. Many state and city welfare departments have Child Abuse divisions that assist identified families. The number of child abuse cases appears to be rising, since previously undetected cases are now reported. It will therefore be several years before the efficacy of secondary prevention programs can be assessed.

Treatment of certain sexual offenders now includes behavior modification as well as more traditional therapies. Experimental drugs and psychosurgery have also been proposed and opposed for certain cases of assaultive individuals. Since the techniques could possibly be employed to control or intimidate minority peoples, or political dissenters, their use is subject to moral, ethical, legal, and political discussion and debate. Services for the victims of rape are now evolving in many metropolitan areas; they seek to ameliorate the emotional and social sequelae which often afflict the victim.

Most behavioral scientists and many mental health workers argue that power, work, and goods must be distributed more equitably in society in order to reduce the frustration, unemployment, and powerlessness that accompany widespread violence. More limited social strategies, such as public safety methods and mental health services might then prove useful with residual "hard core" cases. However, health and public safety resources in many areas cannot presently begin to address this extensive problem. Collaboration among legislators, government agencies, social scientists, and mental health workers might initiate more effective social problem solving than now exists.

215

When other means of conflict resolution fail, recourse to violence has been frequent in all societies at one time or another. Only recently have social scientists begun to study those factors which make societies prone to inter-group violence (Sipes, 1973).

No proven methods presently exist for preventing or ameliorating societal violence. However, a number of reasonable suggestions to avoid war have been voiced: (1) a supra-national government that could settle disputes among nations; (2) fostering mutual dependence among nations by trade agreements and inter-dependent industries; (3) nonviolent competition, such as sports contests and cultural exchanges; (4) more open communication and greater travel among nations; (5) cooperative scientific endeavors.

Civil disorder may potentially be reduced by: (1) a more equitable distribution of power, wealth, and work; (2) a greater role for government in resolving conflict among groups of citizens, as in class action law suits; (3) use of nonviolent methods to effect social change (e.g. strikes, boycotts, public demonstrations); (4) avoiding the demonstration or use of force where feasible, since force tends to polarize opposing groups; (5) early deployment of well trained law enforcement personnel in adequate numbers when violence appears likely to occur.

Joseph Westermeyer, M.D., M.P.H., Ph.D.

References

Alinsky, S. D. 1971. Rules for Radicals. New York: Random House.

Amir, M. 1967. Alcohol and forcible rape. Brit. Journal of Addict. 62:219-232.

Barclay, A. M. 1971. Linking sexual and aggressive motives: contributions of "irrelevant" arousals. J. Pers. 39:481-492.

Daniels, D. N., Gilula, M. F., Ochberg, F. M. (eds.). 1970. Violence and the struggle for existence. Boston: Little, Brown and Co.

Edgcumbe, R. M. 1971. A consideration of the meaning of certain types of aggressive behavior. Br. J. Med. Psychol. 44:373-378.

Fawcett, J. (ed.). 1971. Dynamics of Violence. Chicago: American Medical Association.

Graham, H. S., Gurr, T. R. (eds.). 1969. The History of Violence in America. New York: Bantam Books.

Graham, J. W. 1969. Fatal motorcycle accidents. Journal of Forensic Sci. 14:79-86.

Hedlin, H. 1969. Black Suicide. New York: Basic Books.

Hirsch, C. S., Rushford, N. B., Ford, A. B., Adelson, L. 1973. Homicide and suicide in a metropolitan county, 1. Long term trends, J. Amer. Med. Assn. 223:900-905.

Ilfeld, F. W. 1969. Overview of the causes and prevention of violence. Arch. Gen. Psychiat. 20:675-689.

Lester, D. 1974. Effect of suicide prevention centers on suicide rates in United States. Health Serv. Rep. 89:37-39.

Lion, J. R. 1972. The role of depression in the treatment of aggressive personality disorders. Am. J. Psychiat. 129:347-349.

Lorencz, K. 1966. On aggression. New York: Bantam Books.

Ogden, M., Spector, M. I., Hill, C. A. 1970. Suicides and homicides among Indians. Public Health Reports. 85:75-80.

Pettigrew, T.F., Spier, R.B. 1962. Ecological pattern of Negro homicide. Am. Journal of Sociology. 67:621-629.

Porterfield, A. L. 1960. Traffic fatalities, suicide, and homicide. Amer. Sociol. Review. 25:897-901.

Pouissaint, A. 1973. Why Blacks kill Blacks. New York: Emerson Hall.

Richman, J. 1972. The motor car and the territorial aggression thesis—some aspects of the sociology of the street. Sociol. Rev. 20:5-27.

Roth, M. R. 1972. Human violence as viewed from the psychiatric clinic. Am. Journal of Psychiatry. 128:1043-1056.

Rushing, W. A. 1969. Suicide and the interaction of alcoholism (liver cirrhosis) with the social situation. Quarterly Journal Stud. Alcohol. 30:93-103.

Short, J.F., Wolfgang, M.E. 1972. Collective Violence. Chicago: Aldine-Atherton, Inc.

Sipes, R. G. 1973. War, sports and aggression: an empirical test of two rival theories. Amer. Anthropologist. 75:64-86.

Steinmetz, S. K. and Straus, M. A. 1973. The family as a cradle of violence. Society. 10:50-56.

Toch, H. 1969. Violent Men: An Inquiry into the Psychology of Violence. Chicago: Aldine-Atherton, Inc.

Walker, J. A. 1971. Drugs and highway crashes: can we separate fact from fantasy? Journal of the American Medical Assn. 215:1477-1482.

Weinberg, A. and Weinberg, A. (eds.). 1963. Instead of Violence. Boston: Beacon Press.

Other Sources

National Institute of Mental Health, 1974. Lystad, Mary (Editor). Violence at Home. U.S. Government Printing Office, Washington, D.C.

5. Catastrophe: Natural Disasters

> The general alarm and the individual suffering; the
> silence of the grass-grown streets; the thousands of
> human bodies, carried in heaps, many of them un-
> ceremoniously to a common grave, without any of
> the decent rites of sepulture; the despair of some,
> the religious prostration of others, the depravity of
> many on the very verge of eternity; the benevolence
> and fortitude of the few; the mutual charities of kin-
> dred broken sometimes by unnatural fears, even be-
> fore the final separation; the dread of death and sus-
> picion of danger at the sight of every friend; the inef-
> ficacy of art; the more than doubtful cruelty of some
> of the police regulations; the universal horror and
> the uncontrollable devastation; all these and many
> more such occurrences at the height of the calamity,
> afford ample room for reflections.
>
> —*Thomas Hancock, M.D.*
> *Observations on the Laws and*
> *Phenomena of Pestilence (1821)*

As with most writers in the field of disaster, I became interested in this area both because of some personal involvement, and
by chance. In 1943, I passed the scene of the Coconut Grove fire in
Boston just as the victims were being evacuated, and I joined with
other college students in helping with the rescue.

Most of the significant publications in this field occurred in the
period between the end of World War II and the early 1960s, with a
marked dropping off of interest and productivity since that time. The
individual or family is not ordinarily taken as the unit for research,
and consequently the literature is much richer in investigation of
community responses, of group interaction.

There is a lack of studies of long-term outcomes with a few
major exceptions, notably, studies of the survivors of Hiroshima and
of concentration camps. In those cases the anger of the victims could
realistically be focused on the perpetrators, rather than on the
whims of nature.

In anticipation of the possibility of nuclear attack in the late
1940s and 1950s, much of the early research is centered around
military events which have actually occurred or which might be expected. In 1952, the National Academy of Sciences-National Re-

218

search Council appointed a Committee on Disaster Studies. In 1957, this became the Disaster Research Group, and utilized both federal resources and foundation funds. Baker and Chapman review the studies of this group: a wide variety of disasters and emergencies, incompassing over 21,000 interviews.

After this research group was discontinued, there appears to have been little organized work in the field until the recent development of the Disaster Research Center at Ohio State University. A series of publications is in progress; "Organized Behavior in Disaster" serves as a bridge between the 1962 review by Baker and Chapman and present studies.

For purposes of analysis, disaster can be placed in a time frame of reference. This phase description provides a convenient basis for discussion of both (social) global and (individual) personal events and thus has special value for multi-disciplinary studies. J.W. Powell and J.F. Rayner (Baker and Chapman, 1962) propose a division of disaster into seven time periods: Warning, Threat, Impact, Inventory, Rescue, Remedy and Recovery.

Data concerning the warning phase, threat, and the impact, are largely gathered retrospectively, and rely upon the recollections, and sometimes the fantasies, of the disaster victims. Wolfenstein observed marked repression of anxiety on the part of some victims with over-reactivity on the part of others. She, among others, points out that anxiety is handled well by the majority of victims. Despite the popular impression that panic usually seizes individuals during the first three or four phases of disaster, repeated observations find panic is usually absent; it is newsworthy when it occurs and receives disportionate publicity. The same is true for episodes of heroism. One may infer that most disaster victims remain remarkably cool and goal directed.

"Tornado," by Taylor, Zurcher, and Key (1970), describes leadership after a Kansas disaster: the differences in response between formally organized support structures (e.g. the Red Cross) and informal spontaneous neighborhood groups which organize quickly for a short period of time and then tend to disintegrate. This and Wallace's observations (1954) indicate that existing formally organized structures react rather slowly in case of disaster, perhaps because of bureaucratic inertia. The communities struck by disaster evolve new, effective, and transitory organizations, which operate well for a few days and then yield to the previously organized structures.

Prior to 1962, Janis attempted to determine what information about an impending disaster can instigate effective preparatory action. As a corollary to this, he became interested in under- and over-reactions to such stresses. Outcomes vary from the appropriate compromise formation to indiscriminate vigilance and blanket reassurance. The nature of the threat will be, in his view, a major factor in determining how well the individual copes with the given disaster.

Other studies have pointed out the possible relationship between being the victim of a disaster and developing subsequent physical illness. Bennet, studying floods in Bristol, England (1968) found a 50 percent increase in the number of deaths among those whose homes had been flooded, as compared to the control group. He found a rise in deaths from cancer in the study group and their attendance at doctors' offices and hospitals rose dramatically. He noted that men appear less able to cope with the experience of a disaster than women.

Leopold and Dillon examined 27 survivors of a marine disaster when two ships collided, killing nine immediately. There were substantial disturbances of mood and affect. Many had somatic reactions, particularly gastrointestinal and sleep disturbances. Six men reported no psychological disturbances whatever just after the accident. Psychiatric evaluation revealed that most patients were functioning at a fairly efficient level, although some few were overwhelmed by the experience. Of five patients hospitalized during the first few days, only one was admitted for purely physical reasons.

Most striking was the amount of psychological deterioration which occurred in the roughly four years between immediate evaluation and the follow-up interviews. Out of a total of 34 patients seen either immediately after the explosion or at some time thereafter (including nine from the freighter), at least 26 had received some psychiatric care in the intervening four years. At least twelve of these were hospitalized. There had also been an increase in somatic symptoms, particularly in musculoskeletal reactions.

Only twelve of thirty-four men were able to resume their usual (and lucrative) work. Of the eighteen men who continued to work at sea, all reported being greatly disturbed emotionally. Among a number of factors studied, it was found that increasing age was most nearly correlated with psychological difficulty. It appears that the *nature of an accident* is a more significant determinant of the post-traumatic accident state than is the pre-accident personality. We believe that when psychological damage is incurred in life-threatening situations, it tends to grow worse with time if untreated.

Cohen and Poulshock, of the Department of Community Medicine, University of Pennsylvania, are studying the impact of Hurricane Agnes in northeastern Pennsylvania over a three-year period. Their data will include considerable information on short- and long-term individual methods of coping with disaster. C. M. Parkes and others are studying a landslide disaster in Wales which took the lives of over 100, mostly children at school.

Grauer finds in his study of concentration camp survivors evidence that with extreme environmental stress, a condition similar to psychosis may develop. Lifton's major work on post World War II Japan deals with adaptation of atomic bomb victims.

Luchterhand reviews current sociological thinking in approaches to massive stress in natural and man-made disasters, while Kettner reviews the effect of combat strain on subsequent mental health in an elaborate follow-up study of Swedish soldiers serving in the United Nations forces in Africa in the years 1961 and 1962.

Recent advances in the field, as summarized by Dynes, stress the organizational and community response to disaster, and give little emphasis to the individual response.

Robert L. Leopold, M.D.

References

Baker, George W. and Chapman, Dwight W., Eds. 1962. Man and Society in Disaster. New York: Basic Books.

Bennet, Glin, M. F., F.R.C.S., D.P.M. 1970. Bristol Floods 1968, controlled survey of effects on health of local community disaster. Brit. Med. J., 3, pp. 454-458, Aug. 22.

Dynes, Russell R. 1970. Organized Behavior in Disaster. Heath Lexington Books, p. 78.

Grauer, H., M.D. 1969. Psychodynamics of the survivor syndrome. Canadian Psychiatric Assn. J. 14, pp. 617-622.

Hammerschlag, Carl A. and Astrachan, Boris M. 1971. The Kennedy Airport snow-in: an inquiry into intergroup phenomena. Psychiatry, 34, pp. 301-308, Aug.

Hocking, Frederick, M.D. 1970. Psychiatric aspects of extreme environmental stress. Dis. Nerv. System 31, pp. 542-545, Aug.

Kettner, Berth. 1972. Combat strain and subsequent mental health. Acta Psychiatria Scandinavica, Supplementum 230, Munksgaard, Copenhagen.

Lacey, Gaynor N. 1972 Observations on Aberfan, Journal of Psychosomatic Research, Vol. 16, pp. 257-260. Elmsford, New York: Pergamon Press.

Leopold, R. L. and Dillon, H. 1963. Psycho-anatomy of a disaster: a long-term study of post-traumatic neuroses in survivors of a marine explosion. American Journal of Psychiatry, 119, pp. 913-921.

Lifton, Robert Jay. 1967. Death in Life (Survivors of Hiroshima). New York: Random House.

Lifton, Robert Jay. History and Human Survival. Vintage Book V-690.

Luchterhand, Elmer. 1971. Sociological approaches to massive stress in natural and man-made disasters. Int. Psychiat. Clin. 8, pp. 29-53.

Powell, J.W. and Rayner, J.F. 1962. "A brief introduction to contemporary disaster research," Chapter by D.W. Chapman in Man and Society in Disaster. Baker, George W. and Chapman, Dwight W. Eds. New York: Basic Books.

Schulberg, Herbert C., Ph.D., and Sheldon, Alan, M.D. 1968. The probability of crisis and strategies for preventive intervention. Arch. Gen. Psychiat., 18, pp. 553-558, May.

Sims, John H. and Baumann, Duane D. 1972. The tornado threat: coping styles of the north and south. Science, Vol. 176, pp. 1386-1392. June 30.

Taylor, James B., Zurcher, Louis A., Key, William H. 1970. Tornado. Univ. of Washington Press.

Wolfenstein, M. 1957. Disaster: A Psychological Essay. Glencoe: The Free Press.

IX. | Policy Making

1. Quality of Life: Time and Caring

Sow an act, and you reap a habit.
Sow a habit, and you reap a character.
Sow a character, and you reap a destiny.

—*Charles Reade (1814-1884)*

In the past decade there has been an increase of attention to the quality of life as a measurable complex statistic. Some legislators and social scientists have urged that the annual "State of the Union" assessment should include indices of the quality of individual, family and group relationships. Perhaps by knowing more about the day-to-day status of personal relationships that are based on some depth, will we know what is good or bad about local community life.

The effectiveness of a treatment or a program is always a controversial topic. It could be helpful and economical to learn, for example, that a certain program reduced the commuting time of single parents, and increased their time with their children. Or, that the frequency of joint meals went down in a certain industrial community when an additional workshift was introduced. Looking to the past experience of blacks and Indians, their plight could have been signalled earlier if intimacy variables had been examined. They may have shown that hunting and informal training time between fathers and sons was going down; that the white man was increasingly becoming a parent-surrogate to minority adults; that private conversations were dropping in frequency; that participation in public ritual was going down in the younger age group. Just as price and consumer issues are now publicized and discussed, so could the public grow aware of, and discuss the issues posed by reported changes in the type and frequency of intimate transactions.

Concurrently, there has been a less worshipful attitude toward "hard" statistics such as divorce rates, employment rates and psychiatric hospital admissions. The press and the public, as well as policy-makers, today increasingly consider that a divorce may be a positive act, and so can a job change, or temporary unemployment. Thus, there has appeared a growing concern about the impact of new laws and programs upon individual human lives and upon communities. If impact upon the natural environment can be quantified and reported, can we attempt the same for the human interpersonal environment?

This may be feasible if we can arrive at norms for the allocation

225

of time per calendar unit (such as a week or a year) to the satisfaction of intimate transactions. There are 72 hours a week usually left after work and sleep. How are they spent? For each sub-culture and age group the norms would differ. So would the work and play values. But if one could examine how each individual in a sub-group fared, in terms of "intimacy time" compared to his peers, some conclusions about the quality of that person's life could be made. A husband who holds two jobs and spends three hours daily commuting will usually have less than optimal time with his family. A senior citizen with a lot of leisure time but little company will usually be a less than happy person. A brother and sister who seldom have a meal in their parents' company may reflect the erosion of that family. *Quality as a part function of time* is something we already largely accept. We measure education in semesters or years; the strength of a friendship in years; the satisfaction of a vacation in weeks, etc. The second assumption in this proposal is less widely accepted: It is that *mental health is primarily an expression of appropriate and sufficient intimate transactions.*

The achievement of desired vocational and educational goals is important to most people. So is the availability of sufficient participation in recreation, public ritual, religious observance and political life. But, under this proposal, these are considered *secondary* to the maintenance of appropriate intimate bonds at each stage of an individual's life.

Intimacy would gradually have to be defined for each social group involved. For the general population of the United States in a national census, it would probably include, but not be limited to, the basic time/function allocations in the parent-child relationship; the marital relationship or its equivalent; the very close friend relationship; the play group relationship, and others. The functions involved would probably include, but not be limited to, the physical care and feeding of a person; conversation; sexual relations; organized play and games; exposure to role-example and training; meals taken together; parties and social gatherings; discussion groups, and others.

The policy-maker, the citizen and the public health professional could then possibly have an interesting index to the quality of life in a given community; a tangible measure of the end-product of a given intervention, program or law. Instead of simply voting for increases in social and professional services, it may be possible to spot and alter those social conditions which create the need for more funds and personnel.

To start using psycho-social indicators as an aid to public policy would at first require much use of skilled interviewers and the trial of a diversity of approaches and concepts. Mass survey techniques would develop later. Problems would be posed by considerations of

226

privacy and cultural differences. However, these are not insurmountable and are within the scope of techniques we already possess in survey and census work. The greatest barrier would probably be temporary public and professional resistance to the assumption that *intimate relationships are the major expression of mental and community health.*

In a world and a society where the time necessary for economic sustenance is decreasing, and where, paradoxically, overpopulation and resource scarcity threaten, it is crucial that we find a way of measuring the effects various policies have upon the individual and the family, to know how each program or invention alters the delicate relationship network that surrounds and sustains each human being.

Isaiah M. Zimmerman, Ph.D., M.S.W.

2. The Role of the Federal Government in Promoting General Welfare

> Unfortunately, in the heat of political crisis, govern-
> ment and the men that wield its power become
> frightened by opinions they dislike. Their reaction is
> to combat those views by any power they have at
> hand—except the power of better ideas and better
> government.
>
> —Senator Sam J. Ervin, Jr.
> in The Washington Post, Feb. 2, 1975

The United States ranks fourteenth in the world in infant mortality; eleventh in maternal mortality; twenty-second and seventh in
life expectancy for men and women, respectively; sixteenth in the
death rate for middle-aged men; and, eighth in doctors per population (DHEW, 1971). We are encouraged to believe that our nation is
on the brink of tackling these issues, e.g., with national health insurance, and yet, there are still some who would question the efficacy
and appropriateness of national government involvement in medical
and psychological health care delivery. A brief review of our history
is very revealing of the national government's longtime interest in
our general welfare.

The Secretary of the Interior, Ray L. Wilbur, in 1932, recognized the pressing need to provide satisfactory medical service, in
quality and quantity, to all American citizens at equitable costs. His
report put forth five recommendations: strengthen public health services; coordinate all health services, manpower, education, and
training; provide comprehensive medical care through regionally organized groups of practitioners; and, establish group payment of
medical costs whether by insurance or taxation or both (CCMC,
1932).

The group practice-group payment recommendations did not
gain consensus within the CCMC. However, many of its proponents
were very active and influential during the Depression years when
the federal government made emergency interventions because
local and state governments were unable to provide funds for medical care, job development, work relief, and, in general, to support
needy citizens.

Despite or because of the unfortunate exclusion of medical care
benefits from the Social Security Act of 1935, compromise congres-

sional enactments established maternal and child health and crippled children's programs; and other significant health legislation. Public health, including medical care, thus became a federal concern; and the responsibility for medical care, long the province of medically dominated institutions now involved lay citizens. This federal involvement was a long time delayed in view of the Constitution, Article I, Section 8: "The Congress shall have the power to . . . provide for the common defense and general welfare . . ." which subsumes public health as well as psychological well-being.

In 1948 President Harry Truman received a report from his Federal Security Administrator Oscar Ewing recommending national health insurance as the only possible way to provide the funds required to deliver adequate medical services to large numbers of low-income citizens having limited access to health care. Ewing saw local and state level planning as the only foundation upon which communities and individuals could promote better health standards and believed that federal assistance would be insufficient without planning by the local people. Ewing's recommendations, defined a role for the federal government, describing nine health goals of which mental health was given fourth priority.

Since then two major programs have come into being: Medicaid which provides benefits for the poor who are blind, disabled, and aged; and Medicare to provide health care for the elderly (1965).

The 1932 and 1948 reports can be considered benchmarks in the review and assessment of the role of the federal government in providing for our general welfare. Recommendations from these two reports are reflected in many current legislative efforts to upgrade health status and care in the United States.

For the first time in this nation's history, in 1963, mental illness and retardation, our youth and elderly were singled out as subjects of special Presidential messages (DHEW, 1963). The Kennedy program to fight mental illness and retardation included concepts of prevention, treatment, rehabilitation, research, and manpower development.

Seven years later, 1970, DHEW Secretary Elliot Richardson's White Paper reminded U.S. citizens that our "health care crisis" is still with us (DHEW, 1971). His strategy was to modify the entire health care system since it was clear that our most fundamental problems were systemic. The report recommended against continuation of piecemeal and categorical efforts (in 1972, DHEW administered more than 200 categorical health, educational and social service programs) since these would increase, not ameliorate, our health care problems.

Health maintenance organizations (HMO's) were extolled as emphasizing prevention and early care; providing incentives for holding down costs while increasing the productivity of resources;

229

offering the opportunity to improve care quality and geographic distribution; and, reducing the need for federal funds and direct controls by mobilizing private capital and managerial talent (Roy, 1972).

Emerging from the many proposals and health care plans, both publicly and privately initiated, seems to be one clear and basic belief: there has to be established some form of corporate organization with the necessary and sufficient authority, capability, responsibility, and foresight to ensure comprehensive care delivery to our entire population. Current ideas about this corporate form seem to converge around a non-governmental organization which will be subjected to federal government regulation and scrutiny (Res. Comm. 1973).

The proposals for bringing health care to our entire population raise, mostly by their omission, two issues that are particularly relevant to the themes of this book. First, a review of the various proposals reveals that outpatient psychiatric care, prescription drugs and dental care for children are conspicuously absent and apparently are viewed as additional and feasible benefits for the future. Second, while there have been improvements over the years, grave problems remain, for example: job discrimination and poor schooling which together limit employment opportunities, and low income levels which, combined with racial discrimination, diminish the opportunity to attain good health education and care.

While our focus has been comprehensive health care, which includes mental health, it is clear that no single phenomenon such as health can be studied in isolation from other related issues such as education and job development, or poverty and ethnic group discriminatory practices. Also, it is because an individual's conception of his personal welfare, at any moment in time, involves the fusion of multiple life experiences, that investigations of and programming around single issues are bound to retard our understanding and produce unworkable remedies. We have revealed in this historical review, that the federal government has had a long-standing commitment to a role in providing for the general welfare of all its people, but the truth is that the people cannot wait for the national government to conceptualize or foresee the problems and resolutions at their individual and community levels. Also, the federal government cannot possibly respond effectively without proper stimulation from its citizens and their expressions of needs.

Programs which ensure good medical and psychological wellbeing cost money, but the federal government has the resources, and has been committed to assume accountability and leadership in overseeing that these guaranteed rights are implemented properly and well. The experience of preparing this brief survey has left the authors with an undisturbed feeling that our hopes for better health welfare are more likely to be realized when we begin to tackle issues which are clearly at hand, as opposed to looking grimly at the future.

This presentation has been designed to be more informative than critical in reviewing the role of the federal government in promoting the general welfare. Documentation has been necessarily selective, but the additional references provided will allow the reader to obtain a more complete and current view.

Nolan E. Penn, Ph.D.
Barbara P. Penn, M.A.

References

Committee on the Costs of Medical Care. 1932. Medical care for the American people. Committee Publication No. 28, adopted Oct. 31. Chicago: Univ. of Chicago Press, 213 pp. (Reprinted (1970) by the Community Health Service, HSMHA, Public Health Service, DHEW, Wash., D.C.)

DHEW Publication. 1972. The allied services act of 1972. Office of the White House Press Secretary, Wash., D.C. (May 18).

DHEW Publication. 1971. Towards a comprehensive health policy for the 1970's: A white paper. Wash., D.C. (May)

DHEW Publication. 1963. New directions in health education and welfare. Wash., D.C.

Ewing, O. 1948. The nation's health: a 10-year program. Federal Security Administration Publication. Wash., D.C.

Falk, I.S. 1973. Medical care in the USA: 1932-1972. Problems, proposals and programs from the committee on the costs of medical care to the committee for national insurance. The Milbank Memorial Fund Quarterly, Health and Society 51:1-39.

Kissick, W. and Martin, S. 1972. Issues of the future in health. The Annals (January) pp. 151-159.

Medicare Program. U.S. statutes at large for 1965. U.S. Government Printing Office, pp. 290-422.

Research and Policy Committee for Economic Development. 1973. Building a national health care-system. New York (April)

Roy, W.R. 1972. The proposed health maintenance organization act of 1972. Science and Health Communications Group. Wash., D.C. 285 pp.

Somers, A. 1972. The nation's health: issues for the future. The Annals (January) pp. 160-174

Strickland, S. 1972. U.S. health care: what's wrong and what's right. New York: Universe Books.

Berki, S. and Heston, A. (Special Eds.) 1972. The nation's health: some issues. Philadelphia.

Somers, A. (Editor) 1971. The Kaiser—Permanente Medical Program. New York: Commonwealth Fund.

Other Sources

Journals:
  Mental Health Digest (NIMH/HEW)
  Social Policy (White Plains, N.Y.)
  Social Problems (Worcester, Ma.)
  Monthly Catalog of U.S. Government Publications (USGPO)

3. Law, Accountability, Consumer Participation

> It has been considered from the point of view of the hygienist, the physician, the architect, the taxpayer, the superintendents, and the nurse, but of the several hundred books, pamphlets, and articles on the subject with which I am acquainted, I do not remember to have seen one from the point of view of the patient.
>
> —*John Shaw Billings (1874)*

No one knows precisely what "mental illness" means or what causes it. Some argue that "mental illness" is a theoretical construct which "explains" behavior we do not otherwise understand. It is widely assumed that mental illness produces aberrations in thought and/or feeling which then appear in deviant behavior to the consternation of "normal" society. One can think all the "crazy" thoughts one pleases, no matter how extreme, if he never makes these known to other people either verbally or by acting out in some peculiar or deviant way. It is observable behavior which produces the diagnoses and which brings the law to bear.

The law proceeds on the assumption that a person's activities are rationally motivated and that one should be held accountable, in most instances, for the consequences of one's behavior. The major issue underlying the approach of the community to the "mentally ill" is whether such persons can exercise judgment and thus be held responsible for their actions. Establishing clear and coherent policies on this has proven quite difficult.

Society has the dual and sometimes conflicting interest of protecting the human and constitutional rights of the individual.

As society changes, limits placed on deviant behavior fluctuate with the change in values within the society. Society defines when a person is to be regraded as mentally incompetent or when a person accused of a crime should be excused from responsibility because of mental illness. Society also defines the point at which it is reasonable to involuntarily treat a patient for a psychiatric condition on the assumption that he is unable to appreciate his need for treatment. However, there is no coherence within our society on the point in mental illness at which a person may not be responsible for his behavior, is unable to exercise reasonable judgment, or is incapable of making decisions relevant to his own welfare.

A major source of confusion in the law has been the use of vague and nebulous descriptive terms, illustrated by the variety of statutory definitions of "mentally ill," "mentally deficient," "epileptic," "alcoholic," "drug addict," "incompetent," and "psychopath." Often the same term is used in different parts of a statute to define a different class and to accomplish a different result. The same term is often applied to different mental conditions. For example, a person may be "mentally ill" for the purpose of involuntary hospitalization, but competent to execute a will, to marry or to refuse a certain type of treatment.

Over the years several varying standards of criminal responsibility have evolved. It is debatable whether there will ever be a test of criminal responsibility which will enable the judicial process to discriminate between those cases where a punitive correctional disposition is appropriate and those in which a medical-custodial disposition is believed to be proper.

In dealing with mental disability, the law has twin objectives: preservation of the maximum rights and liberties of the mentally disabled, and maintenance of the physical and mental welfare of the patient and the community.

Current advances in psychiatric knowledge, including the more accurate use of medical terms, have not appreciably eased the difficulty of relating that knowledge to the law. Before psychiatry existed, the lawyer had to take charge of the psychotic homicidal maniac or criminally insane disturber of the peace and see to his property being taken care of in some legitimate way. Until recently it has been mainly this concern with property rights and community welfare that has preoccupied the law and lawyers. In common law England, the laws that were promulgated continued to reflect concern for the property of the disabled, with little attention given to his person.

In colonial America the family was the primary social unit, and each family was expected to care for its own. In America, early instances of community action seem to have been motivated by a desire to aid the impoverished family in caring for its charge rather than by any desire to aid directly the victim of a mental disability.

In the last decade a new expression of community concern for the mentally ill has occurred in the United States. Many states are moving to improve treatment and services for the mentally ill and retarded within and outside of large public institutions, partly in response to legal actions taken on behalf of patients.

Certain court decisions have the effect of stimulating treatment and care in a community setting rather than in an institutional environment. In 1969 the United States Court of Appeals for the District of Columbia decided the case of *Rouse* v. *Cameron*, 373 F.2d 451 (1966). In an opinion by Chief Judge Bazelon, the Court reasoned that since the only rationale for the increased confinement of persons involuntarily committed, after being found not guilty by reason of insanity, is the *need for treatment*; it follows that the failure to provide such treatment presented constitutional questions of due process, equal protection and cruel and unusual punishment. The court did not reach the constitutional grounds in this case but decided on the basis of statutory law for the District of Columbia.

In 1968 (*Nason* v. *Bridgewater*), the Massachusetts Supreme Court upheld a Commissioner's finding that Bridgewater State Hospital was not providing adequate treatment and ordered that a program for adequate treatment be determined and followed. Two years later a federal judge in Alabama in *Wyatt* v. *Stickney* (now *Wyatt* v. *Aderholt*), held that there is a constitutional right to treatment, stating: "To deprive any citizen of his or her liberty upon the altruistic theory that the confinement is for humane therapeutic reasons and then fail to provide adequate treatment violates the very fundamentals of due process." The Court went one step further and set up minimun standards for constitutionally and medically adequate treatment. In a similar case, *Burnham* v. *State of Georgia*, a federal judge held that there is no constitutional right to treatment. Both cases are now consolidated and on appeal in the Fifth Circuit. If the lower court's decision is ultimately upheld, state mental institutions can then be held judicially accountable for the minimum adequate treatment.

A recent Michigan state court decision promises to have far reaching effects on the right of mental patients. That case, *Kaimowitz* v. *Department of Mental Health*, held that a state cannot obtain legally adequate consent from an involuntarily confined mental patient for the purpose of performing experimental psychosurgery. So it seems that two theories are separately and simultaneously developing in the law: the duty of the state to provide adequate treatment and the right of the patient not to be mistreated.

Professionals and consumers do not necessarily share the same ideals and values. For example, when the poor are given a voice in the management and design of programs operated for their benefit, they become advocates of their own, and may be in conflict with service providers.

Participation may include any form of involvement in community, government and health affairs such as being a consumer representative, a patient advocate, or a member of community advisory councils and other decision-making bodies, and grievance committes; it also includes writing letters, routine non-medical visiting of agencies, public discussions, and voting in election campaigns and other electioneering procedures.

234

More important than the fact that community boards exist is the question of who serves and what amount of control is vested in the board to govern. The present trend is that these boards are more often appointive rather than elective; they are self-perpetuating and reflect middle-class attitudes to citizen involvement, and do not have representatives typical of their communities.

The legal-mental health movement, has accelerated the evolution of consumer participation in providing an "open window" on institutional conditions which were once considered privy to only institutional employees. As Alfred Freedman, President of The American Psychiatric Association said, "The public no longer views the lack of adequate mental health care as a misfortune, but as an intolerable injustice." This change in public attitude has evolved in large part as a result of the current legal activism to articulate and vindicate certain rights of the mentally handicapped. Litigation, as a tool for effecting social change, has brought many issues to the forefront of public attention which historically had been ignored; it has provided a forum for articulating the needs and rights of mentally handicapped persons and has acted regarding inadequate programs for treatment and prevention.

Alix H. Sanders, J.D.

References

Ash, Sidney H. 1973. Mental Disability in Civil Practice, The Lawyers Cooperative Publishing Co.

Brakel, S. and Rock, R.S. 1971. (Rev. Ed.). The Mentally Disabled and the Law, American Bar Foundation.

Cahn, E.S. and Barry, A.P. 1969. Citizen Participation, New Jersey Community Action Training Institute.

Ennis, B. and Siegel, L. 1973. The Rights of Mental Patients, an ACLU handbook.

Kramer, R.M. 1969. Participation of the Poor. Englewood Cliffs, N.J.: Prentice-Hall, Inc.

Marshall, D.R. 1971. The Politics of Participation in Poverty. Berkely: Univ. of California Press.

Mental Health Law Project. 1973. Basic Rights of the Mentally Handicapped.

Thompson, T. 1973. Community Involvement in Health: A Conceptual Approach to Evaluating the Consumer Participation Process in Neighborhood Health Centers, Howard University.

Department of Health, Education and Welfare. 1970. Report of the Task Force on Medicaid and Related Programs.

Other Sources

Journals:
American Journal of Public Health
American Journal of Orthopsychiatry
Journal of Rehabilitation
International Journal of Group Psychotherapy
Journal of the National Medical Association

Associations
National Council of Community Mental Health Centers
National Clearinghouse for Mental Health Information
National Association for Neighborhood Mental Health Centers
Mental Health Law Project
Office for Health Affairs Planning and Evaluation (OEO)

4. Institutional Change and Resistance to Change

Opinions do find, after certain Revolutions, men and minds like those that first begat them.

—Sir Thomas Browne
Religlo Medici (1642)

The study of organizational structure and function is a relatively new enterprise. Although the study of natural human groups and group behavior began early in the twentieth century, it was not until the late 1930's that serious attention was given to formal organizational structure. These early studies focused on the small work group, and only after World War II was serious attention given to large scale organizational structure. To date we have accumulated substantial knowledge on the formation, structure, and operation of organizations. But despite a quarter-century of effort, we still lack effective methods of organizational change, or even reliable models for experimental trial.

Interest in mental health organizations began around 1950 with studies on mental hospitals. These investigations revealed the dysfunctional and even destructive social organization of mental hospital structure, but led to little institutional change. Then in 1963 the community mental health movement was born through congressional legislative fiat. Money was provided for the development of new mental health organizations and the accompanying change in the old hospital institutions. In addition, the move into community life brought to light the importance of other human service organizations, such as the welfare, probation, and health departments. Other institutional systems were soon found to impinge upon the new community mental health organizations. These include religious organizations; special public interest organizations such as those particularly interested in drugs, alcoholism, or retarded children; taxpayer's associations concerned about public programs; police and law enforcement agencies; as well as various governmental regulatory bodies. In addition, the main line mental health organizations soon discovered other professional organizations in the public domain having their own mental health or human service programs, including Big Brother and Big Sister agencies, Family Service programs and various academic institutions.

In sum, we have been forced to look not only at the nature of mental health institutions, but the relationship between mental health programs and a wide array of community organizations. The history of the community mental health movement over the past fifteen years is one of many experiments in the creation of new organizational structure.

No one system of classification is entirely satisfactory, nor do organizations usually fall into one pure type of structure. Briefly, we may consider the following types of organizations. The total institution organizes and controls the life of the membership, while providing all the basic life-sustaining necessities, e.g. prisons, reformatories, boarding schools, and the traditional mental hospital. Bureaucratic institutions are typically governmental structures that have regulatory and supervisory functions over the governed, based on legal sanction, e.g. census bureau, public health department.

Business institutions are organized to deliver a product or service at a profit, e.g. a cannery, an auto plant, a personnel consulting firm, a private hospital, or a psychotherapy clinic. A service institution is generally organized to meet a necessary public need, often not at a profit and requiring public subsidy, e.g. a municipal transit system, a garbage collection agency, a welfare program, or a community mental health center. Volunteer institutions meet public service needs that are not met through more formal organizations. At times this may become quasi-institutionalized as in United Fund/Red Feather community agency programs. Self-help groups serve those who cannot or will not avail themselves of more socially acceptable service programs.

Finally, evanescent institutions may be considered under any of the above. However they may represent a temporary need, such as the drug-rap centers. Or they may represent social experiments that fail to maintain political viability such as the many anti-poverty and ethnic assistance programs the federal government sponsored in the 1960's. A single community mental health program system is currently likely to contain organizational structures of almost all the above types in some form or another.

We may look at the life history of organizations as the reflection of interacting forces. Analysis of the life stage of an organization may be a critical element in any attempt at change.

The creation of institutions may be seen as a response to felt need. It may be typically American to make the first step in problem solving one of, "Let's get organized." Institutions may begin as informal groups that meet direct personal goals or needs, such as a missionary establishing an informal ministry in a ghetto; or an organization may be legally created immediately by legislation. Whether an organization actually meets the needs it was created to meet will vary with many circumstances. And the continued exis-

238

tence of an organization may not necessarily depend on organizational utility. The development and elaboration of institutions after their creation is a typical next step. "Bigger is better" is a dominant motif that influences most organizational growth. Thus far, little attention has been given to optimal organizational size in relation to function. With growth in size and complexity, there is usually a need for structural change in the organization. However, structure may not necessarily relate to function. A formal structure may exist, while an informal and covert structure which follows functional lines begins to develop, producing strain between the formal and informal structure. Also, the original need may pass, in which case the organization may explicitly shift its goals, or may again develop a new covert structure in relation to new goals.

Organizations bear a relationship to the culture at large. Some, like a Mafia or a rural Amish community maintain themselves in the face of societal opposition. Others have marginal social sanction, like free clinics or anti-war protest organizations. Some gradually gain social acceptance, and become firmly incorporated, as in the case of the labor unions. Mental health organizations vary in their degree of social enculturation. Avant-garde sexual treatment and counseling clinics face social opposition, methadone clinics for drug addicts are marginal, while mental hospitals have long-standing cultural acceptance and sanction.

Although organizations may justify themselves in relation to external goals, bureaucratic and service organizations in particular tend to lose sight of these and focus on internal goals. The maintenance and growth of the organization per se become overriding values, often at the expense of the stated goals. For example, a community mental health center may devote its activities to services rewarding to the professional staff, which bear little relation to the mental health needs of the surrounding community.

The demise and death of institutions occurs through technological obsolescence, changing demands for services or products, economic instability, inadequate structure to maintain function, and loss of social mandate. Death of an organization can be gradual, as in the decay of a resort hotel as the area becomes industrialized, or very rapid, as when a state suddenly decides to close its mental hospitals, or the government closes down its poverty programs. Even strong, well-structured, and enculturated organizations are vulnerable, but less so when an organizational function is central to the primary needs of society.

In sum, organizations change over time, but the variables that influence change are so numerous and complex that it is difficult to anticipate and plan organizational change. Often an organization experiences mounting stresses that demand change, resulting in accommodation to these stresses, rather than planned and rational organizational movement. On the other hand, there is such enormous inertia in most organizations, that usually it is only in times of organizational stress and crises that attempts at change are successful.

Every institution has several levels of social organization. The *manifest* function of a mental hospital may be to treat the emotionally ill, yet the *latent* function may be to protect society from persons perceived as dangerous, or vice versa. Similarly, the *overt* function of an institution may differ from the *covert* function. Thus a mental health clinic may overtly function under direct medical supervision, although the covert function may totally evade medical control. As noted above, the *formal* organizational structure may vary from the *informal* structure. Finally, the organization cannot be comprehended solely by a social analysis, but must include the personality, style, and relationships between the actual people who fill the various organizational role slots.

No organization exists in isolation. The structure and function of an organization exists in reciprocal relation to other organizations in the community. An organization that has a monopoly will differ from an organization in a highly competitive social field. Just as in human interpersonal relations, the behavior of an organization covaries with those who exist in the same social field. Thus we can observe organizational bargaining, scrambles for prestige, status, and power, concern for boundaries and territories, and self-aggrandizement rather than collaboration or cooperation. Organizations with altruistic goals and values are no less immune from these problems of mutual relations. In fact, mental health professionals often assume that such "political" behavior between organizations is unnecessary and irrational, and might be solved if all the people in other organizations were as mentally healthy as the mental health professionals. Yet this chauvinistic view precludes awareness of the very same behavior by the mental health organization. The discomfort and unwillingness of mental health professionals in the arena of inter-organizational behavior often leads to ineffective mental health leadership both with their own organization and in relations with other organizations.

Much of the early work on organizational behavior focused on the formal sociological structures described thus far. This view took organizations to be impersonal. Hence change of an organization could be accomplished without regard to the individuals involved. At the extreme, this view is Marxian social theory, holding that the organization, or society, takes precedent over the individual.

More to the point, this sociological view of organizations assumes that if one changes the social structure of the organization, the organization will change. The human behavioral movement in business management, popularized by the National Training

Laboratories, and exemplified notably in the work of Chris Argyris has asserted that this social change is not enough. Change in an organization requires a change in the people in the organization. The human relations movement of the past 25 years has been devoted to this emphasis, under the general rubric of applied behavioral science.

Both points of view have merit, and can be seen as complementary. Organizational dysfunction can develop on both counts. There may be *social role strain*. Here the social structure is dysfunctional, as when a worker has three bosses of equal power. Or there may be *personal role strain*. Here the person may be emotionally disturbed, as in the case of the paranoid president, or more likely is unsuited by temperament or skill to the tasks required in his job slot.

Therefore, an analysis of organizational behavior must take into account both the social and the personal. Likewise, change in organizational behavior must deal with both social structural change and personal attitudinal and behavior change.

Consideration of organizational change as an area of mental health action must include a capacity for social analysis and personal analysis. Further, a social system may be seen as a state of calibrated equilibrium. Any change in one part of the system will upset the equilibrium of the entire system, requiring accommodation, resistance, or change. Therefore, change of any part of the system requires an analysis of the ensuing effects on the total system.

Change-agents may be professional consultants, internal personnel charged with development and change, or partisan agents such as special interest lobbies, militant laymen, or governmental regulatory agents. In the mental health arena, we are concerned particularly with institutional change based on concerns for human welfare. In brief, the most critical issues at this experimental state of organization intervention, are questions of gaining access, sanction, and power.

Intervention in organizations to effect change can be defined at three levels of human organization. *Macrosystems* are large, complex social systems, and intervention is aimed at effects on large, geographically scattered populations. An example would be intervention to change federal prison policy or federal poverty policy. *Mezzosystems* are institutions and their subunits that directly work with individuals, families, and groups. Intervention here would influence the well-being of people locally. An example would be a change in local probation procedures, or health department services to transients. *Microsystems* are individuals, families, and small groups. Intervention here might include creating or assisting self-help groups, or block organizations. Access, sanction, power, and strategies will vary with each level of intervention.

241

Changes in organizational program ultimately relate to change in personal behavior. Each person exists in an equilibrium in his role, just as the entire social system of the organization exists in an equilibrium. Thus any change will likely benefit some groups in the organization, and cost other groups (or a mix of each). Those that mainly profit will support the change; those that lose will oppose change.

Six dimensions of personal concern may be considered as potential sources of resistance. (1) Power. How will my status and influence change? (2) Beliefs, Values, Norms. Will they be supported or undermined by change? (3) Competence. Will change allow me to demonstrate my ability, or challenge my ability? (4) Legal and administrative considerations. How will change be related to mandates or restrictions given me? (5) Information (participation). How will I participate in change, or be helpless to officially resist? (6) Energy. What is the money, time, and amount of work that will be involved in change?

Resistance to change need not be considered abnormal, unhealthy, undesirable, or unnatural. Failure to identify resistances and to deal appropriately with them is to fail at a critical part of a total system analysis.

There is an old saying in medical practice, that every new drug is effective during the first six months it is on the market! The same is true for organizational intervention. Research of effectiveness is embryonic. We can only study living systems that move and change while we are in the process of introducing an intervention, and that keeps on moving while we try to measure the effects. Despite the sometimes staggering technical problems, the best position to take is to support research on intervention strategies, and remain benevolently skeptical of all methods.

Organizations have often been seen as immutable structures, built for eternity. Change is then seen as disruptive and unwanted. This is a static view of organizations. The challenge is to construct and maintain organizations that are *process-oriented*. Thus change is expected, anticipated, and desired. To change organizations, we must change our view of organizations.

E. Mansell Pattison, MD

5. The Irrational as Illness, the Irrational as Policy

> Political commotions, by arousing to greater activity all the intellectual faculties, by rendering more intense the depressing and vindictive passions, fomenting the spirit of ambition and revenge, overturning public and private fortunes, and changing the circumstances of all men, produce a vast amount of insanity.
>
> —J. E. Esquirol (1772 - 1840)

A system of mental health must never be thought of as an independent entity. It does not exist outside the framework and social fabric of the larger culture, but rather is a fixed and integral part of it. The moment we forget its interrelationships, we run the risk of thinking that our ideas are absolutely right, when in reality they may only be right within the limited purview of our own culture and worldview. When our concepts of mental health become reified, they may also become deified. Human ideas and agencies change little enough, without adding divine resistance.

One of the best ways to see our mental health concepts in proper perspective is to see them cross-culturally. Some study of anthropology, or living in another culture for a period of time, can contribute immeasurably to a mental health professional's outlook. Chronic assumptions may be questioned acutely for the first time. We see our system of care, with all of its component parts and antecedents, in relief against other systems. (H. Miner 1958; F. Torrey 1972)

In particular, our system of mental health interacts and intersects with our system of religion and ethics, our economic system, and our political system. The interaction of these systems, and not our mental health system alone, determines how we view human behavior, what is considered to be normal and abnormal, what constitutes psychopathology, and at least to some extent behavior itself.

One of the mainsprings of the American system of morality and religion is what has been called the Protestant ethic (although it is almost equally evident among Catholics and Jews). This principle states that work is better than play. Implicit in it is a suspicion of pleasure and a sanctification of goal-oriented, preferably hard-to–do, and often, but not always, productive work.

243

As long ago as 1938 Kingsley Davis showed how profoundly the Protestant ethic had influenced the ideals of the then mental hygiene movement, which was dominated by proper Bostonians. Not surprisingly, the mental hygiene movement espoused individualism, self-reliance, self-sacrifice, enhancement of wealth and social status, rationalism, and hard work.

More recently a similar study confirmed the association of ideals advocated by the mental health movement with the ethical ideals of the American middle-class. Examination of the content of mental health literature showed that ninety percent of a series of pamphlets on mental health almost perfectly reflected middle-class ethics and values. The authors concluded "... that the mental health movement is unwittingly propagating a middle-class ethic under the guise of science" (Gursslin et al, 1964).

Practically, the Protestant ethic has had and continues to have an important effect on our ideas of mental health and illness. We often measure cures by the patient's ability to return to work, or justify psychoanalysis by saying that the person will become more productive. One wonders also to what extent opposition to pornography or marijuana, which often invokes a concern for mental health, is in reality a protest against the pleasure principle. In extreme terms the Protestant ethic would make pleasure a criminal offense, and if that could be justified as in the interest of mental health, so much the better.

Similarly our system of economics impinges on our system of mental health at several points. As with our ethics and religion, however, we grow up taking economic assumptions as givens, unaware of how profoundly they influence our thinking in mental health. We advocate free enterprise and profit but we don't specify if and when these cease to be laudable American economic goals and become instead cheating and avariciousness. What is the dividing line between the successful entrepreneur and the sociopath or psychopath? His level of income? Whether or not he gets caught? When does making a profit, which by definition must be at the expense of other people, begin to cause guilt and remorse in an individual who also holds a Judeo-Christian ethical system emphasizing sharing and equality? What should the mental health professional diagnose when asked to evaluate a slumlord who paints his apartments with less expensive, leaded paint? A corporation executive who conspires with other corporations to fix prices? A ghetto youth who steals only expensive cars for resale? A vice president who takes bribes? Which of these is sociopath and which is just a good American?

Our economic system confronts us with problems in more practical ways as well. Mental health professionals in private practice must distinguish the needs of their patients, both inpatients and outpatients, from the professional's own economic needs. If business is slow, what harm will it do to keep Mrs. X or Mr. Y in therapy (or in the hospital) for a little while longer than would usually be necessary? Another facet of this is the recent purchase of private psychiatric hospitals by large, profit-oriented corporations. How can the needs of the patient and those of the economic system be equitably served, when the patient has so little power; the organization, so much? Still another point where economics conflicts with mental health needs is in the sphere of personal relationships. Each extra hour which a man or woman spends on the job is an hour less with their family. And as people become greater economic "successes," as defined by our culture, we often see those close to them suffering because of it. But we rarely address this conflict of interest directly.

Finally, it can be shown that our political system may impinge on our mental health system in important ways. Most recently (and dramatically) this has become evident in the accusations which have been directed at psychiatrists in the Soviet Union. Normal citizens, simply expressing their displeasure at actions of their government or restrictions of their liberty, have been said to have been labeled as schizophrenics (or occasionally as psychopathic personalities) and incarcerated in mental hospitals. A Soviet textbook of psychiatry (Morozov and Kalashrik, 1970) makes it clear that these doctors are not just facile tools of the Soviet secret police; they really *believe* in what they are doing and that it is part of psychiatry. After all, a person who writes tracts against the Soviet State, or hands out leaflets in Red Square, clearly *must* be crazy. He has a delusion defined as "a rational judgment that does not conform to reality." And since Marxist-Leninism is reality there, the man is "sick," schizophrenic. A further symptom is argumentativeness, "a tendency toward unnecessary disputation and vacuous, fruitless casuistry," in other words, the behavior of a person who disagrees with the party line and continues to verbalize his disagreements.

Now since psychiatrists hold the needs of the patient uppermost, the least they can do is to remove him from danger to himself and others until he gets well. Since he is "sick," he is not responsible. And once labeled as schizophrenic, he may need care for a long time—even after he has gone into remission.

It would appear, then, that the psychiatric incarceration of dissidents in the Soviet Union can be rationalized as in the patients' best interest. That it is also in the best interests of the State is evident. That it is more likely to happen in a political system in which the State is thought to be as important (or more important) than the individual seems also likely, and in this way the political system has influenced the mental health care system. It can also happen in our democratic system of government during lapses as the cases of Ezra Pound or General Edwin Walker attest (Szasz, 1963).

These are of course not the only ways in which the system of religion and ethics, the economic system, and the political system interact and influence the system of mental health care. Nor are they the only parts of our culture to do so. The point is that the mental health system influences, and is influenced by, other systems. To try to isolate mental health considerations and to view them as independent of the wider culture is to see them very dimly. By putting on cultural glasses and looking at ourselves from another world-view, we can see more clearly the irrational as illness and the irrational as policy.

In practical terms, is there anything which we can do to become more aware of how our system of mental health interacts with our systems of politics, economics, and religion and ethics? Is there anything which will decrease the irrational aspects of our policy making? One general rule is to keep an in-house critic in every mental health program—one who constantly doubts, questions, and acts as a cerebral irritant. We lapse into irrational habits so quickly that we need someone around to jar us with questions. Why do we do it this way or that way? Why don't we try it another way? Even if such a critic is off-target much of the time, he/she has at least kept us from simply accepting our habits as Truths. Experience shows that programs which have the least tolerance for in-house critics are the ones which are least effective; old habits and ways of doing things have, like the minds of the people working there, become embedded in concrete.

Another important step to minimize irrational policy making is to ensure that the policy decision-making process is spread among as wide a spectrum of ethnic and socio-economic strata as exists in the community being served.

Finally, a well-structured mental health program should support occasional staff travel to see how things are done elsewhere, in other socio-economic areas, other subcultures, and other cultures. Conversely, visitors from other programs and other countries should be encouraged and they should be asked to describe alternative ways of doing things. A good program for obtaining a short- or long-term overseas (primarily European) person to help do this is The Council of International Programs, 1817 Superior Building, Cleveland, Ohio, 44114.

E. Fuller Torrey, M.D.

246

References

Body ritual of the Nacirema. 1958. American Anthropologist 58, pp. 503-507

Davis, K., 1938. Mental Hygiene and Class Structure, Psychiatry 1, 55-65.

Gursslin, O.R., Hunt, R.C., and Roach, J.L., 1964. Social Class and the Mental Health Movement in F. Riessman, J. Cohen, and A. Pearl (eds.) Mental Health of the Poor, New York: Free Press.

Morozov, G. V., and Kalashnik, I. M., eds., 1970. Forensic Psychiatry, White Plains: International Arts and Sciences Press.

Szasz, T. S., 1963. Law, Liberty and Psychiatry, New York: The Macmillan Co.

Torrey, E. F., 1972. The Mind Game: Witchdoctors and Psychiatrists. (Chapter 6). New York: Emerson Hall

6. Future Prediction

I am going to seek a great Perhaps

Francois Rabelais (1494-1553)
(Spoken shortly before his death)

Future transitions may possibly be extrapolated from recent trends in mental health care and from speculations about emerging political, economic, and cultural environments.

The past decade witnessed an extensive public policy reorientation towards care of the mentally ill, i.e., a shift from almost complete reliance on state hospital care towards outpatient short-term crisis intervention and preventive efforts. Along with broadened requirements for mental health services has come public concern both for the effectiveness of these services and for patient rights. Agencies find that their funding sources impose more conditions and constraints on programs. In addition, the referent for mental health services has shifted from the welfare of selected individuals to that of the community-at-large. An agency must attend not just to those persons presenting themselves for treatment but also to those whose needs have not been expressed in visits to the agency. Early case finding, support of other human service agencies, and aftercare have become integral parts of mental health care.

In short, the conditions under which mental health care is provided, as well as the techniques of doing so, are not only changing but are changing rapidly. An agency's operating decisions are more frequently being scrutinized by representatives of the community; these decisions involve more than professional judgment regarding therapeutic practice, they concern effective resource utilization. The agency must obtain funds from multiple sources and allocate them to diverse services for which the agency must gauge the public demand, as well as their effectiveness.

While current trends may not extend to the limits indicated, the following possibilities warrant consideration. The hiatus of a major economic depression could retard or accelerate movement in these directions.

The goals, policies, and practices of economic and political institutions will be significantly influenced by shifts from nationalism to internationalism, from centralized to decentralized govern-

248

ment, and in economic power among nations. Technological innovations and restraints on population and economic growth will also impact on institutions. Access to food, shelter, health care, and education will be regarded as a right rather than a privilege for all. Changing political and economic environments will, in turn, interact with modified life styles revolving around changes in nuclear family and redefinitions of the quality of life. (Trend Report, 1974).

Institutional changes, education from birth to death, employment in multiple careers over a wider age span, and serial family arrangements over the life cycle will combine to make personal dependency upon traditional rolls an even less viable style of life. By facilitating and by providing the basic opportunities guaranteed to all people, human service agencies will play a vital part in helping society avoid disintegration while accommodating to radical change.

Along with increasing demands for innovative human services of all kinds, current requirements for program accountability, efficiency, and responsiveness will be continued and strengthened. The autonomy of professional specialties with their attendant arbitrary boundaries and credentialism will be challenged.

An immediate mandate is for intensified program evaluation. Topical questions arising from recent trends include: Have we substituted one form of therapeutic nihilism (responding only to crises) for another (custodial care)? Have we benefited the patient while reducing costs by moving the "elite" professional one step away from the patient to the position of supervisor and trainer of therapists? Have we improved cost-effectiveness by replacing centralized, large volume service at low cost with local, small volume service in the community? Has the reorientation of public attitudes towards mental illness resulted in greater tolerance for a pluralism of values and for aberrant behavior?

Beyond creative therapeutic interventions and their evaluation lies the larger issue of appropriate resource allocation and the imperative for management skills and technologies in mental health administration. Accountability demands that agency personnel know how resources are spent in pursuing specific objectives and that this be communicated to the community and funding sources.

Pressures for openness and shared responsibility may force changes in operating style. The traditional diagnosis and triage function may be replaced by a cafeteria of services among which clients could shop for those that meet their needs. Such an arrangement would be practical if effectiveness depends less on particular treatment techniques than upon the client's acceptance of technique and therapist style. An agency would have to make visible the alternatives it has available and facilitate the client's movement throughout the network of services until he found a satisfactory relationship (Pattison, et al., 1938).

249

More effective treatment of the temporarily infirm and support of the disadvantaged might be achieved by further reduction of boundaries among human services by combining them into multi-faceted departments or truly integrated agencies. The repertoire of skills to be applied would include not only those of mental health workers but also those of welfare, law enforcement, medical, probation, and education. A wider range of resources would permit a comprehensive approach to cope with all dissocial behaviors (such as dependency, mental and physical illness, crime and delinquency, and antisocial behavior) and to improve the quality of life of the community.

Survival of private human service institutions might require comparable integration of services as foreshadowed by the health maintenance organization approach. This operating concept, in theory, mandates emphasis on preventive efforts as a means for keeping costs within contracted limits. A further step might involve incorporating financial, legal, and career counseling, as well as physical and mental health care, in one provider organization for total human services support to a client throughout his lifetime. Such a step would require public and private agency cooperation for which there are no administrative structures at present. Such service integration might imply developing broadly-based, quasi-public-non-profit corporations.

Traditional roles both for individuals and for institutions have eroded and are likely to continue to do so. Professional specialists no longer have the freedom to establish either the goals or policies of their agencies as they see fit. Accountability, legal rights of clients, and responsiveness to community needs are all imperative terms of the contract between human service agencies and the public. What purposes these agencies are to serve, and the amount of support accord them, is determined by the public, and that public is becoming impatient with professional guild distinctions that plague service and increase cost.

The mandate for mental health professionals extends beyond increased effectiveness in alleviating the symptoms of mental illness. The more challenging problem by far is that of seeking, in combination with other disciplines, diagnosis and treatment of society's ills that derive from radical and inevitable environmental change.

Transitioning mental health care to meet future needs requires dealing with man in the context of the institutions he forms and which form him, as he strives for quality of life in a changing and shrinking world.

Robert L. Chapman, Ph.D.
J. Richard Elpers, M.D.

References

Pattison, E. Mansell, Coe, Ronald, Doerr, Hans O. 1973. "Population variation among alcoholism treatment facilities," The International Journal of the Addictions, Vol. 8, No. 2, pp. 199-229.

Platt, John R. 1972. The world transformation and what must be done. Pages 161-192 in George V. Coelho and Eli A Rubinstein (eds.), Social Change and Human Behavior: Mental Health Challenges of the Seventies. DHEW Publication No. (HSM) 72-9122.

Trend Analysis Program. 1974 (February). The Life Cycle, Trends in Life Stages and Living Patterns. Trend Report No. 8. New York: Institute-of-Life-Insurance, 277 Park Avenue, New York, New York 10017

Other Sources

World Future Society

X. | Information Sources

1. Consumer's Guide to Mental Health Services

> It's strange how many phases go into the making of a good physician. Some have hands, just good surgeon's hands, and if by luck they have a head and heart to go with them, they can reach the heights. Others are a menace to the community they inhabit. How are you going to tell them apart? Most of their fellows know them. But the human animal is an untrustworthy self-seeker, and the worst doctors know how to make themselves attractive. They are usually popular.
>
> —*William Carlos Williams, M.D. (1883-1963)*
> *Autobiography*

Who needs mental health care? Don't some people drift into therapy out of boredom or as a fad, while others who may be quite disturbed can't or won't admit they need help? Are there any guidelines for choosing and judging good mental health care? The purpose of this section is to suggest how accountability is possible in a mental health system, and to help lay people decide whether an individual practitioner or a service organization is satisfactory.

The interventions used to treat disorders and promote mental health are diverse, numerous, and not precisely measurable because they involve complex human interactions, and intangibles such as feelings, fantasies, and wishes. Unlike some other aspects of health, where there are precise diagnostic procedures and where the range of normal and abnormal is definable, mental health offers vague definitions, and the most important elements are people: unique, complex, always changing.

Patients of surgeons and internists often share information concerning their doctors in casual conversation. Mental patients are less likely to do so because stigma still exists about the subject. Also the therapist may advise them not to discuss therapy outside the office, lest they dilute or subvert the experience. Therefore, users of mental health services—except, perhaps, patients in group therapy—tend to be isolated. On the other hand, this branch of the healing arts has been widely discussed in the popular press and in serious books for the general reader. But the subject is as broad as humanity itself, so the plethora of materials does not constitute a

255

clear guide to consumer protection or professional excellence.

Social status and education play a major role in self referral for mental health service. Psychoanalysis, especially (4 or 5 hours a week on the couch for several years) and psychotherapy (once or twice a week, face-to-face) are sought most by educated individuals whose functioning may be adequate or nearly so. At the other extreme, mental health service is avoided by many people until psychosis, alcoholism, drug addiction, or attempted suicide occurs. They may not recognize impending trouble; they insist on trying to work it through alone; or they are frightened by tales, true or false, of men-in-white-coats and the "nut house." Between these extremes are most people who, feeling rather severe stress, are referred to a professional (psychiatrist, clinical psychologist, psychiatric social worker, nurse, counselor) by the clergyman, physician, or friend to whom they first turned. Such clients commonly receive short- (10-20 visits) to moderately long-term (1-2 years) therapy—once or twice weekly. Medications are often used. Group therapy, family therapy, and behavior modification are common adjuncts or alternatives to the commonest form, individual psychotherapy. Electric convulsive therapy (ECT) or shock treatment is sometimes prescribed; it is generally accepted as best used mainly for severe late-life (involutional) depression.

Referrals for professional help are often made by other professionals, many of whom do some counseling; in the case of non-psychiatric physicians, tranquilizers and anti-depressants are widely prescribed in addition to—or, alas, instead of, counseling. In sum, the decision to seek help is highly personal, mediated through others who may encourage or discourage the move toward therapy at any particular stage.

People who are very uncomfortable, who notice a major change for the worse, or who suddenly or finally become dissatisfied with life, are those who seek out a therapist. Others with the same feelings may continue to function smoothly in restricted areas, resisting any suggestion that therapy might help. Those who are flagrantly abnormal—the expansive manic, the psychotically depressed, the acute paranoid—may be impervious to the need for help although it is evident (painfully so) to everyone else around.

Two major indicators of need for therapy include anxiety to the point of distraction and depression to the point of marked slowdown or withdrawal. Both anxiety and depression are exaggerations of normal; indeed people who are completely free of such feelings are abnormal in that their defenses against strong but normal feelings operate to cover up emotions which are healthy, albeit stressful. The "workaholic" is an example; the obsessive compulsive and the ulcer patient are types who adapt well in a restricted environment and may be quite productive. Or the problem may be focused on a parti-

256

cular symptom which, like elevator phobia, is disabling in one context but leaves the person relatively symptom-free otherwise.

Apart from the symptoms that give a clue to mental illness, there are larger constellations that deserve mention. Freud cited the ability to love and to work as the indicators of maturity or mental health; others have produced long or short lists as a guide. We might add the ability to reflect and to argue: a healthy person can view life with perspective, use imagination and fantasy for pleasure and profit, and be assertive in support of ideas, feelings and values to which he or she is committed. To be depressed when your home is swept away by a tornado is normal; to be a patsy or a doormat in marriage is not. Trouble in important relationships is a key issue; close relatives and friends often have the difficult task of translating concern, annoyance or puzzlement into a recommendation for help.

There is no generally accepted logic of choice in assigning patients to a particular kind of therapist or therapy. The psychiatrist, being first an M.D., enjoys the top spot on the professional totem pole, and can prescribe medications; legally can, but usually does not, perform physical examinations. Psychiatrists will sometimes claim that they are less likely to miss organic illness (e.g., brain tumor) than other mental health workers are, but essentially all psychotherapists depend on outside medical examinations for their patients. The medical background is a bone of contention in discussions about the licensing of psychologists and other psychotherapists, whether they need to be medically supervised, and whether health insurance covers their services (when it does, at present, these therapists usually are supervised, or at least endorsed, by physicians). The irony here, and an irritant to non—medical mental health workers, is that *any* M.D. technically may receive payments for psychiatric service even though that physician never had any psychiatric training beyond medical school and internship.

Training in psychiatry is, for the M.D. graduate, an additional three years of specialty training. Child psychiatry adds another year. Even so, there is no guarantee that the "fully-trained" psychiatrist will be competent and comfortable doing family therapy, prescribing drugs, or using behavior modification—three modalities which are widely regarded as helpful in many cases. Clinical psychologists, social workers, nurses, and marriage counselors increasingly have clinical training akin to that of psychiatrists. Certification, licensing, professional society listing, honors such as fellowships, and accomplishments such as publications, teaching appointments, etc. may be an indicator of competence or at least professional respectability. But most clients do not take the trouble to ask about credentials, much less shop around for a therapist, even though entering treatment may be a major life decision. In some states, the terms psychologist, psychotherapist, or marriage counselor may be used by anyone who wants to gouge the unsuspecting public. Unfortunately, the professions have been preoccupied with protecting guild interests or "domains" and the public gets little guidance from them—except the assurance that all abhor quackery and put the patient's welfare first.

What can the professions offer lay people as a guide to evaluation of service? The seriousness of this question is supported by the fact that in 1973 the American Psychiatric Association had a committee study "What is mental illness?" and "What is a psychiatrist?" Those are important issues within the profession, but even before they are answered, if indeed they can be, professionals should provide some guidelines for patient satisfaction, and for public education. The latter could and should result in greater participation on clinic, hospital, and licensing boards by lay people. While it can be understood that professionals are reluctant to be constantly scrutinized, especially by "outsiders" who cannot fully appreciate the problems of the professional, it is also incumbent upon professionals to offer criteria for evaluating services for which they are paid. Without such criteria, there is no hope that quackery or incompetence can be dealt with effectively.

The following is a distillation of advice from professionals, an example of guidelines to patients, not intended to be definitive:

1. A mental health professional should make sense to the client. Even if a patient is disturbed or a family upset, the therapist has to have their confidence, and this must be based on personal contact, not merely on a recommendation from outside. Of course, there will be times when patients are mistrusting or dissatisfied in the course of therapy; we do not recommend changing therapists at whim. But at the outset, in the first few visits, the therapist must establish himself/herself as someone with whom the patient can work.

2. Although the work of therapy can be painful and difficult, in general a sense of progress, improvement, comfort, etc. should prevail over distress and pain. In other words, the patient who complains of lack of progress but continues with the therapist anyway is partly responsible for the dilemma. In cases where the therapist makes recommendations in a direction counter to the inclination of the patient, and a stand-off results, a consultant should be brought into the case.

3. Therapists should respond to questions about their training, professional background, and philosophy of treatment. They should also give an indication of what results would be considered good in the present case, and approximately how long it may take. He should meet with important family members occasionally, with the patient present in most instances.

For patients who have doubts or grievances about a therapist,

258

the pertinent professional organization or the local Mental Health Association should be contacted. They generally have committees on ethics and public relations, and increasingly on peer review. Professionals are exercising a public trust in being licensed and practicing their professions. Obviously, if a therapist is not a member of a licensed group adhering to professional and ethical standards, the patient has less protection; then, the organizations, such as those listed in Section 3 of this Chapter, can help in uncovering fraudulent or unfair practices.

In regard to children, a recent report by Nicholas Hobbs (1974) includes some relevant guidelines for professionals who work with handicapped children and their parents:

- Have the parent(s) involved every step of the way.
- Make a realistic management plan part and parcel of the assessment outcome. Give the parents suggestions for how to live with the problem on a day-to-day basis.
- Write your reports in clear, understandable, jargon-free language. Professional terminology is a useful shortcut for your own note-taking, but in situations involving the parent it operates as an obstacle to understanding. Keep in mind that it is the parent who must live with the child, shop for services to meet his needs, support his ego, give guidance. The parent *must* be as well informed as you can make him.
- Be sure he understands his child's abilities and assets as well as his disabilities and deficiencies. What the child *can* do is far more important than what the child cannot do.
- Warn the parent about service insufficiencies. Equip him with advice on how to make his way through the system of "helping" services. Warn him that they are not always helpful. Tell him that his child has a *right* to services. Tell him to insist on being a part of any decision-making about his child.

It is unfortunate but true that these guidelines are needed, and that many parents have to be told to insist on clear and sensible explanations and management help.

There are two goals for good public information on mental health and illness. First, to reduce the stigma of seeking help, and second, to make help available and of high quality. Only an informed public can determine whether its needs as individuals and as a community are being met in an effective and economical way.

E. James Lieberman, M.D., M.P.H.
Carol A. Pewanick

References

Channing L. Bete Co., Inc., Revised Ed. 1974. What everyone should know about mental health. A Scriptographic Booklet. Greenfield, Mass: Channing L. Bete Co., Inc. 15 pp.

Consumer Reports, Revised Ed. 1974. The medicine show. Mt. Vernon, NY: Consumers Union

Freedman, A.M. and Kaplan, H.I. eds. 1972. Treating mental illness. New York: Atheneum Publishers.

Kadushin, Charles, 1969. Why People Go to Psychiatrists, Atherton Press, Inc., 373 pp.

Heck, E.T., Gomez, A.G., and Adams, G.L. 1973. A Guide to Mental Health Services. Pittsburgh: University of Pittsburgh Press, 139 pp.

Hobbs, Nicholas, 1974. The Futures of Children. San Francisco: Jossey-Bass, Inc.

Hunt, Gerard J. 1973. Citizen Participation in Health and Mental Health Programs: A Review of the Literature and State Mental Health Acts. Arlington, Va.: National Association for Mental Health, Inc.

Kiernan, Thomas. 1974. Shrinks, Etc. A Consumer's Guide to Psychotherapies. New York: 264 pp.

Mental Health Materials Center. (Rev. Ed.) 1973. A Selective Guide to Materials for Mental Health and Family Life Education. Northfield, Ill.: Perennial Education, Inc. 842 pp.

Shapiro, Evelyn. Editor. 1973. Psycho Sources: A Psychology Resource Catalog. New York: Bantam Books, Inc./published by arrangement with Communications Research Machines, Inc. 215 pp.

Shulman, Dr. Lee M. and Joan Kennedy Taylor, 1969. When to See a Psychologist, Award Books (Paperback), 298 pp.

Stern, Edith M., Mental Illness: A Guide for the Family, NAMH publication, 1800 W. Kent St. Rosslyn, Arlington, Va. 22090, 124 pp.

260

2. Information Sources

> There is a dead medical literature, and there is a
> live one. The dead is not all ancient, the live is not all
> modern. There is none, modern or ancient, which, if
> it has no living value for the student, will not teach
> him something by its autopsy.
>
> —*Oliver Wendell Holmes, M.D.*
> *Medical Libraries (1878)*

Resource material has been selected on the basis of a broad approach to mental health and the most comprehensive coverage in the field. Publications cover the five-year period from 1968 to 1973.

Many government agencies are responsive to various aspects of mental health. Several agencies of the Department of Health, Education, and Welfare are important sources of information, especially the National Institute of Mental Health, the Social and Rehabilitation Service, and the Social Security Administration.

Public libraries, medical and special psychiatric libraries, mental health associations, and health departments are important facilities to contact in obtaining information. A list of eleven Regional Medical Libraries is appended. These libraries coordinate the automated MEDLINE (computerized bibliographic storage and on-line retrieval system of the National Library of Medicine) service in a particular region, but may also provide other information in the medical field. A few special psychiatric libraries are also listed in the appendix. Three reference sources listing libraries and librarians are the (1) Directory of the Medical Library Association, 1972; (2) Directory of Special Libraries and Information Centers, edited by Anthony T. Kruzas, 1968; and (3) Directory of Health Sciences Libraries in the United States, edited by Frank L. Schick and Susan Crawford, 1970

Automated Information Systems. Bibliographic services provided by several computerized retrieval systems selected on the basis of relevance of subject matter and type of service offered are listed.

Institute for Scientific Information (ISI), 325 Chestnut St., Philadelphia, Pa. 19106. Provides retrospective searches on a specific topic at a cost of $25 per hour with a 2-hour minimum. The data base includes citations to 2,300 multidisciplinary journals.

261

National Clearinghouse for Mental Health Information (NCMHI), National Institute of Mental Health, 5600 Fishers Lane, Rockville, Md. 20852. Abstracts with Bibliographic reference information are available upon request. There is no charge for service. An on-line system, "Bert", is also available for searching in institutions utilizing the program.

National Library of Medicine, Bibliographic citations are retrieved on-line or off-line from the MEDLINE and related data bases consisting of citations from about 2,900 indexed journals published over about 3 years. There is no charge at the Library, but other institutions in the MEDLINE network may charge. For access to this service, and for current information about new data bases, contact your Regional Medical Library.

American Psychological Association, 1200 17th St., N.W., Washington D.C. Abstracts with bibliographic citations are available for a 5-year period on written request to the American Psychological Association (PASAR service) or through PADAT, (direct access terminal) at the researcher's institution. The charges vary according to computer time.

Other automated bibliographic services which include psychosocial aspects relevant to their particular subject coverage are (1) the Educational Resources Information Center (ERIC), Office of Education, Department of Health, Education, and Welfare, Washington, D.C. 20202, and (2) Science Information Exchange (SIE), 300 Madison National Bank Building, 1730 M Street, N.W., Washington, D.C. 20036.

Directories and Guides. Directories of facilities providing specialized types of service have been selected on a nationwide basis. More specific questions relating to services or regional facilities may be obtained either through the identifying information in the sources or by contacting local mental health associations, medical societies, or health departments. Guides to reference material are available in public or medical libraries. The government publications are available from the Superintendent of Documents, U.S. Government Printing Office (USGPO), Washington, D.C. 20402.

Directory for Exceptional Children: A Listing of Educational and Training Facilities, 6th ed., edited by D.R. Young, 1969. Descriptive listing of facilities providing special services and classified according to the specific requirements, e.g., Psychiatric and Guidance Clinics. Published by Porter Sargent Publishers, 11 Beacon St., Boston, Mass. 02108.

Directory of Facilities for the Learning-Disabled and Handicapped, compiled by Careth Ellinson and James Cass, 1972. Directory, arranged by state and city, of facilities providing diagnostic, remedial, and therapeutic services, with descriptions. Published by Harper & Row, 10 E. 53rd St., New York, N.Y. 10022.

Directory of Medicare Providers and Suppliers of Service, 1969 (DHEW, Social Security Administration). Names and addresses of medical care facilities, including extended care facilities, as well as independent laboratories. These facilities and services meet the requirements under the Health Insurance for the Aged Act. Available from USGPO.

Mental Health Directory, 1971, (National Clearinghouse for Mental Health Information). Comprehensive reference book containing information about federal, state, and local mental health facilities. Available from USGPO.

Public Welfare Directory, edited by David Karrabee, 1972. Federal, state, and local welfare programs and their administrative structure in the United States and Canada. American Public Welfare Assoc., 1313 E. 60th St., Chicago, Ill. 60637.

Mental Health Reference Guides. Guide to Literature in Psychiatry, compiled by Bernice Ennis, M.D., 1971. An extensive guide to reference resources available in psychiatry. Among topics covered are journals, books, abstracts, indexes, and libraries. Partridge Press, Los Angeles, Calif.

A Guide to Psychiatric Books in English, by Karl A. Menninger, 3rd ed. 1972. Classified arrangement of about 3,600 books in psychiatry and related fields, with a list of publishers and their addresses. Grune and Stratton, New York, N.Y.

The Sociology and Anthropology of Mental Illness, compiled by Edwin D. Driver, 1972. A comprehensive bibliographic reference guide to articles and books published between 1956 and 1968 focusing on the social and cultural aspects of mental illness. The University of Massachusetts Press, Amherst, Mass.

A Selective Guide to Materials for Mental Health and Family Life Education, 1972. Comprehensive compilation of articles, pamphlets, plays, and films related to the whole spectrum of mental health, and arranged by subject area. For information: Mental Health Materials Center, 419 Park Avenue South, New York, N.Y. 10016.

Selected Sources of Inexpensive Mental Health Materials (DHEW Pub. No. (HSM) 72-9084). Annotated list of mental health materials for use by the non-professional. Includes pamphlets, play scripts with discussion guides, and films. Lists state and territorial organizations providing educational materials. Available from USGPO.

Audiovisual Guides and Catalogs.
NAMH Film Catalog. Synopses of films for general mental health

263

educational programs with rental and purchase information. Available from local mental health associations.

National Medical Audiovisual Center Catalog. Section I: Annotated listing of 16 mm films arranged by subject. Section II: Annotated listing of videotapes available for duplication. Information available from the National Medical Audiovisual Center, Station K, Atlanta, Ga. 30324.

Selected Mental Health Films: A Film Guide, National Clearinghouse for Mental Health Information. National Institute of Mental Health, Office of Communications, 5454 Wisconsin Ave., Chevy Chase, Md. 20015.

General Reference Guides.

DHEW Catalog of Publications, HEW-72-4. Publications listed by agency or subagency of the Department of Health, Education, and Welfare. References listed by subject, title, and publication number. Available from USGPO.

Forthcoming Books. Authors and titles of books published in the U.S. with an update of information about books to be published within 5 months. R.R. Bowker Co., 1180 Avenue of the Americas, New York, N.Y. 10036.

Subject Guide to Books in Print, 1971 book list classified according to Library of Congress subject headings. Published annually with a midyear supplement. R.R. Bowker Co.

Ulrich's International Periodical Directory, 14th ed., 2 vols., 1971-1972. A subject classified directory of current periodicals in science, medicine and technology. Minimum bibliographic and purchasing information is given. R.R. Bowker Co.

Reader's Guide to Periodical Literature. A cumulative subject-author index to periodicals of general interest. 22 issues per year. H.W. Wilson Co., 950 University Avenue, Bronx, N.Y. 10452.

Bibliographies. There are many index and abstract publications in the mental health field. *Index Medicus* (citations) and *Excerpta Medica* (abstracts) are comprehensive medical information sources; both services provide special bibliographies on specific subjects. Information is available in the monthly *Index Medicus* and from the *Excerpta Medica* Foundation for those derived from their data base. *Excerpta Medica* abstracts pertinent to Public Health and Psychiatry are in Sections 17 and 32, respectively, and are classified by subject headings. They are published at irregular intervals. *Index Medicus* lists citations to articles in 2,300 international health-related journals, using subject headings and subheadings for specificity. Each monthly issue also contains a bibliography of review articles. There is a *Cumulated Index Medicus* at the end of each year.

Selected Bibliographies. The Conceptual Index to Psychoanalytic Technique and Training, edited by Henry H. Hart, M.D., is an extremely comprehensive subject-classified index to books and articles which display the development or modification of a concept.

A few bibliographies pertinent to psychiatry, special-interest areas in the field of mental health, and allied areas are presented.

Cumulative Index to Nursing Literature. Index to nursing literature since 1956. Bimonthly issues include book reviews, pamphlets, and audiovisual materials. Published by Glendale Adventist Hospital Publications Services, P.O. Box 871, Glendale, CA, 91209.

International Nursing Index. Bibliographic citations pertinent to nursing from international journals. Includes a nursing thesaurus and listings of nursing books, doctoral dissertations, and publications of organizations and agencies. Published quarterly in cooperation with the National Library of Medicine by the American Journal of Nursing Company, 10 Columbus Circle, New York, N.Y. 10019.

Digest of Neurology and Psychiatry, edited by John Donnelly, M.D. "Abstracts and reviews of selected literature in Psychiatry, Neurology and their Allied Fields"; includes journals and books. Published monthly by The Institute of Living, Hartford, Conn.

Mental Health Digest, National Clearinghouse for Mental Health Information. Condensations of current literature reflecting the "whole spectrum of mental health." Published monthly. Available from USGPO.

Current Contents: Behavioral, Social and Educational Sciences. Tables of contents of more than 1,100 journals published weekly, often in advance of journal publication. Author index and address directory, as well as an index to the journals cited, printed in each issue. Institute for Scientific Information, 325 Chestnut Street, Philadelphia, Pa. 19106.

Social Science Citation Index. Index to articles cited by authors in their bibliographies and covering more than 1,000 journals; includes a "permuterm" subject index and a source index. Published quarterly, with an annual cumulation as a part of the third-quarter issue. Institute for Scientific Information, 325 Chestnut St., Philadelphia, Pa. 19106.

Psychiatry Digest, edited by W. Walter Menninger, M.D. Original articles selected on the basis of their broad interest to practicing psychiatrists. Published monthly by Psychiatry Digest, Inc., 445 Central Ave., Northfield, Ill. 60093.

Psychological Abstracts. Summaries of articles from international journals in psychology and related areas, as well as citations of current books, arranged alphabetically by author and classified under

17 primary categories. Each issue has an author and subject index. Published monthly with cumulative subject and author indexes. American Psychological Association, 1200 17th St., N.W., Washington, D.C.

Sociological Abstracts. Primarily a sociological publication, with sections on mental health. Unpublished material, books, and journal articles are abstracted. Abstracts available on tape, hard copy, or microfilm. Published bimonthly by Sociological Abstracts, Inc., 73 8th Ave., Brooklyn, N.Y. 11215.

Abstracts for Social Workers, National Association for Social Workers. Journal articles pertaining to social work and related fields abstracted and classified into major categories, with subject and author index. Published quarterly. Publication office: 49 Sheridan Ave., Albany, N.Y. 12210.

Noteworthy bibliographies reflecting special interest areas are:

Child Development Abstracts and Bibliography, Society for Research in Child Development, Inc. Abstracts of articles pertinent to child development from biomedical and behavioral science journals. Concise book reviews also included. Published quarterly by the University of Chicago Press, 5801 Ellis Ave., Chicago, Ill. 60637.

Exceptional Child Education Abstracts. Abstracts from over 100 journals, many in the behavioral sciences, concerned with the handicapped or gifted child. Published quarterly by the Council for Exceptional Children, 1411 S. Jefferson Davis Hwy., Arlington, Va. 22202.

DSH Abstracts, Deafness, Speech and Hearing Publications, Inc. Special bibliography containing summaries of journal articles on psychosocial aspects of hearing and speech disorders. Published quarterly by American Speech and Hearing Association, 9030 Old Georgetown Road, Washington, D.C. 20014.

The following are irregular or non-recurring special bibliographies.

Behavior Therapy Bibliography, 1950-1969; 1971, William R. Murrow, et al. Annotated bibliography on the broad aspects of behavior modification with a list of journals and books on the topic. University of Missouri Press, Columbia, Missouri.

Family Therapy and Research: An Annotated Bibliography of Articles and Books Published 1950-1970, compiled by Ira D. Glick and Jay Haley; 1971. Comprehensive reference on research studies concerning the family, as well as family therapy. Grune and Stratton, New York, N.Y.

Health and Crime Abstracts, 1960-1971, prepared by Robert L. Harris, 1972. Over 500 abstracts of journal articles, books, government documents, reports, papers and editorials arranged under 11 broad categories providing an interdisciplinary approach to the

266

relationship between health and crime. Available from: Project for the Early Prevention of Individual Violence, University of Texas, School of Public Health, P.O. Box 20186, Houston, Texas 77025.

Normal Child Development: An Annotated Bibliography of Articles and Books Published 1950-1969, Janice B. Schulman and Robert C. Prall, 1971. Summaries of 733 references over the 20-year period focused on the research-determined norms of behavior and attitudes characteristic of children at various ages. Grune and Stratton, New York, N.Y.

Interaction of Alcohol and Other Drugs, edited by E. Polacek, et al, 2nd edit., 1972. Bibliographic citations with abstracts focusing especially on the problems related to the use of combinations of drugs. Published by the Addiction Research Foundation, Toronto, Ontario, Canada.

Mental Retardation Abstracts, DHEW, Social and Rehabilitation Service. Comprehensive abstract information concerning all aspects of mental retardation. Published quarterly and available from U.S. Government Printing Office.

Dictionaries and Encyclopedias — These reference books are available in most libraries; therefore, only a few basic ones are listed.

Psychiatric Dictionary, Leland E. Hinsie, M.D. and Robert J. Campbell, M.D., 4th ed., 1970. Oxford University Press, London and Toronto.

Psychiatric Glossary, American Psychiatric Association, 3rd ed., 1969. Available from the A.P.A. Publications Services Division, 1700 18th St., Washington, D.C. 20009.

Encyclopedia of Social Work, Robert Morris, Editor-in-chief, 1971. National Association of Social Workers, Inc., 2 Park Avenue, New York, N.Y.

The Encyclopedia of Human Behavior Psychology, Psychiatry and Mental Health, Robert M. Goldenson, Ph.D., 2 vols., 1970, Doubleday & Co., Inc., Garden City, N.Y.

Journal Selection. Three independent studies 1, 2, 3 evaluating behavioral science journals important to mental health professionals were rated excluding peripheral ones. Of the remaining journals, 16 occurred on all three lists, 25 on two lists and 73 on one list. Ten of the authors of this book rated these journals on a 5 point scale

---

1. Behavioral Sciences Indexing for the National Library of Medicine, A Task Force Report. National Academy of Sciences, May 1967.
2. Matheson, Nina W., User Reaction to Current Contents: Behavioral, Social and Management Sciences, Bull. of the Med. Lib. Assoc. 59:(2), 304-321, April 1971.
3. Rockwell, Don A., Psychiatrists' Evaluation of Fifty Journals. Presented at the A.P.A. Meeting, Honolulu, May 1973.

from the most pertinent to the least pertinent with a score of 5 and 1 respectively. The sums of these ratings were slightly weighted to increase the scores of journals occurring on two or three lists.

The nine highest ranked journals are: American Journal of Orthopsychiatry; MH (formerly Mental Hygiene); Community Mental Health Journal; Transaction; Group for the Advancement of Psychiatry: Reports/Symposia; Archives of General Psychiatry; American Journal of Psychiatry; Psychology Today; and Journal of Consulting and Clinical Psychology.

The next ten journals are: Journal of Health and Social Behavior; Hospital and Community Psychiatry; Medical Aspects of Human Sexuality; Journal of Behavior Therapy and Experimental Psychiatry; Family Process; Developmental Psychology; Psychiatry; American Sociological Review; Social Problems; and Child Development.

There are also an increasing number of anthologies or reference works in the category of "annual reviews."

APPENDIX

Regional Medical Libraries

New England Region (Conn., Me., Mass., N.H., R.I., Vt.)
Francis A. Countway Library of Medicine
10 Shattuck Street
Boston, Massachusetts 02115

New York and Northern New Jersey Region (New York and the 11 northern counties of New Jersey)
New York Academy of Medicine Library
2 East 103 Street
New York, N.Y. 10029

Mid-Eastern Region (Pa., Del., and the 10 southern counties of New Jersey)
Library of the College of Physicians
19 South 22 Street
Philadelphia, Pennsylvania 19103

Mid-Atlantic Region (Va., W.Va., Md., D.C., N.C.)
National Library of Medicine
8600 Rockville Pike
Bethesda, Maryland 20014

East Central Region (Ky., Mich., Ohio)
Wayne State University Medical Library
4325 Brush Street
Detroit, Michigan 48201

Southeastern Region (Ala., Fla., Ga., Miss., S.C., Tenn., Puerto Rico)
A.W. Calhoun Medical Library
Emory University
Atlanta, Georgia 30322

Midwest Region (Ill., Ind., Iowa, Minn., N.D., Wis.)
John Crerar Library
35 West 33 Street
Chicago, Illinois 60616

Midcontinental Region (Colo., Kans., Mo., Neb., S.D., Utah, Wyo.)
University of Nebraska Medical Center
42nd Street & Dewey Avenue
Omaha, Nebraska 68105

South Central Region (Ark., La., N.M., Okla., Tex.)
University of Texas Southwestern Medical School at Dallas
5323 Harry Hines Blvd.
Dallas, Texas 75235

Pacific Northwest Region (Alaska, Idaho, Mont., Oregon, Wash.)
University of Washington
Health Sciences Library
Seattle, Washington 98105

Pacific Southwest Region (Ariz., Calif., Hawaii, Nev.)
Center for the Health Sciences
University of California
Los Angeles, California 90024

Partial Listing of Psychiatric Libraries

St. Elizabeth's Hospital
Health Sciences Library
Washington, D.C. 20032

Eastern Pennsylvania Psychiatric Institute
Henry Avenue & Abbotsford Road
Philadelphia, Pennsylvania 19129

Western Psychiatric Institute
University of Pittsburgh
3811 O'Hara Street
Pittsburgh, Pennsylvania 15201

New York State Psychiatric Institute
722 W. 168th Street
New York, New York 10032

Langley Porter Neuropsychiatric Institute
401 Parnassus Avenue
San Francisco, California 94122

Menninger Foundation
P.O. Box 829
Topeka, Kansas 66601

The Group for the Advancement of Psychiatry (GAP) issues periodic reports on topics of current interest in the mental health field, number of which have been cited in references in this monograph.

Edith G. Calhoun

3. Organizations in the Mental Health Field

Listed below are a number of mental health organizations that may help you find either mental health information or services. They are divided into three general categories: professional; non-professional, or voluntary; and self-help groups.

In many cases, these organizations have local or state affiliates that can provide information on services and programs. The location of the affiliate may be obtained by contacting the national office of the organization. Although this list is limited to organizations that focus primarily on mental health, other organizations, such as welfare and social service agencies, can be useful in helping people work through problems that may contribute to emotional disturbances. As such, they should not be overlooked.

The professional organizations limit their membership to persons of a particular profession. Since they have set standards for membership, it is possible to use the organizations to locate competent professionals in the community. While membership in professional organizations does not automatically ensure competence, it does ensure that the professional has completed the recommended education and training and met the standards for membership. Many professional organizations have local affiliates or district branches that can be consulted for names of members.

The Joint Commission on Accreditation of Hospitals accredits those psychiatric facilities meeting its standards. The standards for accreditation are available from the Joint Commission on Accreditation of Hospitals (645 North Michigan Avenue, Chicago, Illinois 60611). This Joint Commission also has developed standards for children's facilities, Community Mental Health Centers, alcoholism programs, etc. and will play a major role in quality assurance and professional standards.

Voluntary organizations are non-profit, made up of community members who share a common concern for the mentally ill. Lay people make up a substantial part of the membership. Membership may be mostly parents, as in the National Society for Autistic Children and the National Association for Retarded Citizens. The National Association for Mental Health is the only national voluntary agency at the present time concerned with all aspects of mental health and mental illness, including children and patients' rights; community mental health centers; public education; aftercare and mental hospital care. Voluntary agencies provide information regarding mental health and illness and treatment, and

270

assist with information and referral services, public education programs, and seminars. They may provide volunteers to work as teacher or patient aides, social club aides, after care workers, "community friends," etc. These voluntary mental health organizations represent the users of mental health services who are often unable to speak for themselves. Several of them are moving away from direct volunteer services, such as aides in mental hospitals, toward social action (e.g. lawsuits) to obtain adequate services for the mentally ill.

Self-help organizations are made up of people who meet regularly to help each other work through their problems. A mental health professional may, or may not, be included in the group. The members of a local group also maintain telephone contact with each other to help with crisis situations. Groups meet informally for discussion, give support to each other, and are useful to people having emotional difficulties, as well as to those who have recently been released from hospitals. However, the self-help groups are only as good as the local leaders and organizers. It may be difficult to know how useful a group is before joining it, for situations that are useful to some people will not be useful to others. To locate self-help organizations, contact the national organizations listed here or the local voluntary mental health organization.

PROFESSIONAL ORGANIZATIONS

●Academy of Religion & Mental Health
16 East 34th Street
New York, New York 10016
212—685-6711
Members: 3,500—clergymen, psychiatrists, psychologists, cultural anthropologists, sociologists, social workers, behavioral scientists and laymen interested in research and education in all relations between religion and mental health
Structure: 24 branches
Purpose: Promotion of research and education in all relations between religion and mental health
Publications: Academy Reporter, Journal of Religion and Health, literature

●American Academy of Child Psychiatry
1800 R Street, N.W., Suite 904
Washington, D.C. 20009
202—462-3754

Members: 246—members of American Psychiatric Association who specialize in child psychiatry

Structure: National organization only

Purpose: To stimulate and advance medical contributions to knowledge and treatment of psychiatric problems of children

Publications: Journal of American Academy of Child Psychiatry, Membership Directory

271

●American Association of
Homes for the Aging (AAHA)
374 National Press Building,
14th & F Streets, N.W.
Washington, D.C. 20004
202—347-2000

Members: 1,200 member homes/
facilities
Structure: Non-profit, voluntary
and governmental institutions
caring for the aging which
meet licensure standards or
operate under community
sanction where licensure does
not exist; Associate Mem-
bers: individuals; state associations of non-profit homes
for the aging; national organizations; state and local
organizations or agencies;
business firms; suppliers;
attorneys.
Purpose: Created to meet the
needs of residents and management of non-profit facilities for the elderly by presenting position papers on
proposed legislation to federal officials on non-profit
facilities for the aging; interpreting government regulations which affect facilities
and their residents, and conducting accredited courses
which cover new develop-
ments in the long term care
and housing field.
Publications: Washington Report,
AAHA News Scene, AAHA
Journal

●American Association of
Marriage & Family
Counselors
225 Yale Avenue
Claremont, California 91711
714—621-4749
Members: 2,000 (includes Canada)
—professional family and
marriage counselors

Structure: 15 regional divisions
Purpose: Professional trade association which serves family
life and marriage counselors.
Sets standards, has a code of
ethics. Referral service for
people interested in securing
marriage counselors in their
local area
Publications: Membership Directory, Newsletter, can refer to
literature

●American Association on
Mental Deficiency
5201 Connecticut Avenue, N.W.
Washington, D.C. 20015
202—244-8143

Members: 10,000—physicians,
educators, administrators,
social workers, psychologists,
psychiatrists
Structure: National organization
only
Purpose: To promote interest in
the general welfare of mentally subnormal and deficient
persons and study of causes,
treatment and prevention of
mental retardation
Publications: American Journal of
Mental Deficiency, Mental
Retardation, Manual on Terminology and Classification,
Membership Directory, literature

●American Association of
Psychiatric Services for
Children
1701 18th Street, N.W.
Washington, D.C. 20009
202—332-7071

Members: Staff of training clinics
providing psychiatric services
for children
Structure: Regional representatives for 11 regions of the
country, local and state affiliates

272

Purpose: To utilize and coordinate services of psychiatrists, psychologists and psychiatric social workers

Publications: Newsletter, (quarterly) Newsletter, (monthly), Membership Directory

●American Hospital Association Psychiatric Services Section
840 N. Lake Shore Drive
Chicago, Illinois 60611
312—645-9485

Members: 6,900—general hospitals with psychiatric services and psychiatric hospitals

Structure: National organization only

Purpose: To develop partnership models and linkages of service for the improvement of care of the mentally ill and to influence the entire health provider field by increasing the awareness of the psychosocial aspects of health care and of the essentiality of integrated psychiatric services into the health delivery system as a necessary component in good patient care

Publications: bulletins

●American Nurses' Association
2420 Pershing Road
Kansas City, MO 64108
816-474-5720

Members: 200,000 –Professional organization of registered nurses. Sponsors National Student Nurses' Association and American Nurses' Foundation (research in nursing).

Structure: 53 State groups—862 Local groups
Divisions: Psychiatric and Mental Helath Nursing, Community Health Nursing, Geriatric Nursing, Medical Surgical Nursing and Maternal and Child Health Nursing.

●American Orthopsychiatric Association
1790 Broadway
New York, New York 10019
212—586-5690

Members: Psychiatrists, psychologists, psychiatric social workers, and related fields, such as anthropology, sociology, education

Structure: National organization only

Purpose: To unite and provide a common meeting ground for those engaged in study and treatment of human problems —to foster research and spread information regarding scientific work in the field of abnormal behavior

Publications: American Journal of Orthopsychiatry, Monographs, Membership Directory

●American Psychiatric Association
1700 18th Street, N.W.
Washington, D.C. 20009
202—232-7878

Members: Psychiatrists

Structure: State organizations referred to as "Psychiatric Society" or "District Branch"

Purpose: To provide a forum for information exchange and to stimulate activity in field of psychiatry

Publications: American Journal of Psychiatry, Psychiatric News, Annual Membership Directory, Hospital & Community Psychiatry, literature

●American Psychoanalytic
Association
One East 57th Street
New York, New York 10022
212—752-0450

Members: 1,800 — professional
society of M.D.'s in psychiatry
specializing in psychoanalysis
Structure: 31 local affiliate societies
Purpose: To establish and maintain standards for the training of psychoanalysts and the
practice of psychoanalysis
Publications: Journal of the Psychoanalytic   Association,
Standards for Training in Psychoanalysis Glossary of Psychoanalytic Terms and Concepts

●American Psychological
Association
1200 17th Street, N.W.
Washington, D.C. 20036
202—833-7600

Members: 35,000—psychologists
Structure: 31 divisions and 50
state associations
Purpose: To advance psychology
as a science and as a means
of promoting human welfare.
To promote research in psychology and the improvement
of research methods and conditions.   To   improve   the
quality and usefulness of psychologists through high standards of professional ethics,
conduct,   education   and
achievement. To increase psychologists knowledge through
meetings   and   professional
contact,   reports,   papers,
discussions and publications.

Publications: American Psychologist, Membership Directory,
other journals, literature

●American Society for
Adolescent Psychiatry
24 Green Valley Road
Wallingford, Pennsylvania
19084
215—566-1054
Members: 1,200—psychiatrists
interested in adolescent psychiatry
Structure: 11 local societies
Purpose: Forum for exchange,
encourages and supports research
Publications: Annals of Adolescent Psychiatry, Newsletter,
Membership Directory

●Family Service Association
of America
44 East 23rd Street
New York, New York 10010
212—674-6100
Members: 322—family and children's   services   agencies
staffed by 4,500 social work
practitioners
Structure: Member agencies
Purpose: To strengthen family
life and alleviate family stress
by professional counseling,
specialized   help   and
advocacy to improve social
conditions that effect family
life. To set standards for more
than 330 non-profit voluntary
family   service   agencies
throughout North America
Publications: Social Casework,
Membership   Directory,   literature

●National Association of Social
Workers
1425 H Street, N.W., Suite 600
Washington, D.C. 20005
202—628-6800
Members: 60,000 social workers
(some   with   bachelors   degrees). 1/3 of membership is
in the health field

Structure: 172 chapters

Purpose: To promote the quality and effectiveness of social work practice in the U.S. through service to the individual, groups and the community. To promote activities appropriate to strengthening and unifying the social work profession. To promote the sound and continuous development of various areas of social work practice. To promote efforts in behalf of human well-being by methods of social action

Publications: Social Work Abstracts, Social Work, Encyclopedia of Social Work, Directory of Social Workers (membership directory), NASW News, literature

●National Association of State Mental Health Program Directors
15 E Street, N.W.
Bellview Hotel, Suite 432
Washington, D.C. 20001
202—638-2383

Members: State mental health program directors (including Puerto Rico, Guam, and the Virgin Islands)

Structure: National organization only

Purpose: To promote cooperation and information exchange between states in areas of mental health, mental health administration, hospital and community care. Represents the interest of the states and their mental health programs to Congress.

Publications: Federal Grants News, MH/MR Report, Newsletters, Membership Directory, Various studies

●National Association of Private Psychiatric Hospitals
One Farragut Square South, N.W.
Washington, D.C.
202—628-1028

Members: 140—private psychiatric hospitals

Structure: National organization only

Purpose: Forum for exchange of ideas in administration, care, and treatment of mentally ill patients, relations with physicians and public. Offers consultation in preparation for accreditation. Sponsors referral information bureau for families of patients, physicians and agencies

Publications: National Association of Private Psychiatric Hospitals Journal Newsletter, National Association of Private Psychiatric Hospitals Directory of Hospitals, Membership Roster, literature for mental health facilities

●National Council of Community Mental Health Centers
2233 Wisconsin Ave., N.W., Suite 322
Washington, D.C. 20007
202-337-0991

Members: 318 Community Mental Health Centers

Structure: 318 Community Mental Health Centers; 116 associate members (CMHC aspiring to comp. model; state depts. of MH or other organizations with similar interests to NCCMHC); 53 supporter members (individuals interested in program)

Purpose: Provides coordination and cooperation in the efforts of community mental health centers and other mental health agencies throughout the country to raise their level of effectiveness.
Publications: Community Mental Health Centers News, Federal Funding File (Jonas Morris Associates)

●National League for Nursing
10 Columbus Circle
New York, NY 10019
212—582-1022
Members: 17,800—Individual professional nurses, practical nurses, nursing aides, doctors, hospital and health service administrators, educators, and others interested in community planning for health services.
Structure: 44 State groups—90 Local groups
Purpose: Works to assess nursing needs, improve organized nursing services and nursing education, and foster collaboration between nursing and other health and community services.
Publications: Nursing Outlook, NLN News, Nursing Research (with American Nurses' Association)

●National Rehabilitation Association
1522 K Street, N.W.
Washington, D.C. 20005
202—659-2430
Members: 40,000—physicians, counselors, therapists and other interested in the rehabilitation of the physically and mentally handicapped
Structure: 82 chapters and 6 divisions in the U.S.

Purpose: To promote interest and activity for the rehabilitation of the physically and mentally handicapped
Publications: Journal of Rehabilitation, Newsletter, literature

●National Therapeutic Recreation Society
National Recreation and Park Association
1601 North Kent Street
Arlington, Virginia 22209
703—525-0606
Members: 1,200—master therapeutic recreation specialists, therapeutic recreation specialists, therapeutic recreation workers, therapeutic recreation technicians, therapeutic recreation assistants (I and II), people with equivalent background
Structure: 40 state therapeutic recreation sections which belong to State Recreation and Park Association
Purpose: To provide leisure services for the ill, handicapped, disabled, and other special populations in hospitals, institutions, and correction institutions (mentally ill, mentally retarded, physically handicapped, blind, etc.) To promote professional standards and ethics and administer registration program. To monitor and encourage and testify on federal and state legislation of importance to therapeutic recreation services. To work with colleges and universities to develop curriculum. Consulting with communities and agencies in government in expanding the services in these areas in nursing home, facilities, etc., where needed.

Encourage and cooperate in studies on research

Publications: Therapeutic Recreation Journal, NTRS Yearbook (registration directory), Therapeutic Recreation Annual (current status and expansion of therapeutic recreation services,) Impact (section of a monthly newsletter, Communique put out by the National Recreation and Park Association)

VOLUNTARY ORGANIZATIONS

●National Association For Mental Health
1800 North Kent Street
Arlington, Virginia 22209
703—528-6405

Members: 1 million members
Structure: 45 state mental health associations and 1,000 local mental health associations
Purpose: To stimulate citizen interest and activity on behalf of the mentally ill and to promote mental health. To obtain mental health services for those who need them. Most local mental health associations operate information and referral services
Publications: MH, literature

●National Committee Against Mental Illness
1101 17th Street, N.W., Suite 812
Washington, D.C. 20036
201—296-4435
Members: Non-membership
Structure: National organization only

Purpose: Public education and information in the field of mental health, including testimony on appropriate legislation when requested
Publications: literature

●National Society for Autistic Children, Inc.
169 Tampa Avenue
Albany, New York 12208
518—489-7375
Members: 4,000—anyone interested in autism
Structure: 90 local and 10 state affiliates
Purpose: Dedicated to the education, welfare and cure of all children with severe disorders of communication and behavior such as infantile autism, childhood schizophrenia, and other child psychoses. Maintains an information and referral service.
Publications: Proceedings, Directory of Facilities and Services, literature

●National Association for Retarded Citizens
2709 Avenue "E" East
Arlington, Texas 76011
817—261-4691
Members: 245,600—anyone interested in mental retardation
Structure: 1,500 local chapters and state offices
Purpose: To promote the general welfare of the mentally retarded everywhere. All offices operate information and referral services.
Publications: Mental Retardation News, Membership Directory (not released to the public), literature

SELF-HELP ORGANIZATIONS

●Al-Anon Family Group
  Headquarters and Alateen
P.O. Box 182
Madison Square Station
New York, New York 10010
212—475-6110
Members: Families of alcoholics
  or anyone effected by someone's drinking problem
Structure: 8,000+   groups
  (worldwide)
Purpose: To help families of alcoholics by informing them
  about the disease of alcoholism, giving them do's and
  don'ts helping them recover
  from the impact of alcoholism
  on their lives
Publications: Forum, Membership Directory (not released
  to public), literature

●Alcoholics Anonymous
P.O. Box 459
Grand Central Station
New York, New York 10017
212—686-1100
Members: 650,000 recovered al-
  coholics
Structure: 20,000 groups (foreign
  and domestic)
Purpose: To help the sick alcholic
  to recover from his illness
Publications: AA Grapevine, Box
  459, About AA, Membership
  Directories (not released to
  public), literature

●Neurotics Anonymous
  International Liaison, Inc.
Colorado Building, Room 426
1341 G Street, N.W.
Washington, D.C. 20005
202—628-4379
Members: 5,500 — neurotics,
  their families, and anyone
  whose emotions effect their

functioning in any way as recognized by them
Structure: 275 groups (foreign
  and domestic)
Purpose: To offer help and hope
  to the mentally and emotionally ill. Does not offer professional consultation
Publications: Journal of Mental
  Health, Newsletter (Washington, D.C. area only). Sheet
  listing   weekly   meetings,
  literature

●Recovery, Inc.
116 South Michigan Avenue
Chicago, Illinois 60603
312—263-2292
Members: 50,000—former mental
  patients and others with psychiatric disorders
Structure: Organized locally for
  purpose of group meetings
Purpose: Local groups meet frequently to provide support to
  each other through discussions of problems and fears
Publications: Directory of Group
  Meeting Places, literature

●Schizophrenics Anonymous
  American Schizophrenia
  Association
56 West 45th Street
New York, New York 10036
212—972-0705
Members: 7,000—schizophrenics
  and their families
Structure: 30+ chapters
Purpose: To help the schizophrenic and his family cope
  with his problems. To help
  people with mental problems
  (handled   through   me-
  gavitamin/psychotherapy approach to treatment)
Publications: Schizophrenia,
  Newsletter, literature

M. Frances Bradley

278

4. World Perspective

The Mental Hygiene Movement, then, bears the same relation to psychiatry that the public-health movement, of which it forms a part, bears to medicine in general. It is an organized community response to a recognized community need; and it lays its prime emphasis on the detection and the control of those incipient maladjustments with which the physician *qua* physician never comes into contact, unless specific community machinery and far-flung educational facilities are provided for the purpose.

—C.-E.A. Winslow, M.D. 1934

Social and political changes, technology and research are affecting national cultures, traditions and history. The impact is also influencing changes in public health, medical care and mental health and illness.

Every country has a system or provision for health care. While the availability of trained manpower and public and private funds influences the development and capability of the health care system, national, social, economic and political policies are equally important since they control funds and manpower resources.

With few exceptions, every country has a national level health office or ministry which deals with public health and medical care functions and has responsibility for program planning, budgeting, standard setting and the development of health resources. Other national ministries or offices are also involved with health care including Social Security, Social Welfare and Child Care, Labor, Internal Affairs, Education and Justice. Effective coordinating mechanisms between these agencies is essential.

Most countries are divided into political subdivisions as states and provinces and may be further subdivided into districts, counties and cities. The organizational structure for health in states and provinces usually replicates the national structure while the structure at the lowest level is designed to provide direct services to the citizenry through hospitals, clinics and other public health facilities. Some countries as Great Britain, France, USSR and many of the developing nations have centralized health care system with policy control at the national level. In other countries as West Germany, Austria, U.S.A., Yugoslavia and Canada, direct policy control is at the state or provincial level although the national office may set broad health policies and provide funds.

For centuries, health and illness have been the private concerns of individuals and families. During the past century public health has developed into an organized political entity supported by public revenues to deal with community health and environmental problems and eventually in many countries to provide curative as well as preventive care for physical and mental health and illness. The provisions for disease prevention and curative health services vary greatly among nations depending on the level of their industrial development. Most industrialized nations have evolved social security or insurance schemes which provide health care to individuals with the cost shared by contributions from both government and the consumer. Physicians may provide service in their private offices with negotiated fees or they may be governmental salaried employees working in public facilities or salaried employees of insurance schemes. Specialist services usually hospital based are available on referral from primary physicians. Hospitals are almost universally public facilities (prominent exceptions are the Netherlands and U.S.A. although government provides funds in various ways).

Developing nations have usually based their medical care facilities in public hospitals and clinics with care provided by salaried physicians and other personnel either free or on a sliding fee scale. Some of these countries have social security schemes with enrollment limited to certain groups of workers. Scattered populations living in remote areas may have no medical care available except that provided by native practitioners or by intermittent visits from itinerant medical workers.

Medical care is provided by physicians and nursing personnel augmented by laboratory and other technical personnel. Training schools are found in all developed countries and their establishment is of high priority in all nations. Social workers are found in more developed countries. Their functions elsewhere are usually performed by nurses.

Mental health care all over the world has traditionally been provided in religious, private or public institutions. Since World War II mental health care has begun to move out of institutions into the community. Traditionally, psychiatrists and nurses have cared for the mentally ill. As new knowledge emerged and was put into practice, new kinds of personnel developed including social workers, psychologists, psychiatric nurse clinicians, occupational, recreational and industrial therapists and vocational counselors. Each discipline became highly professionalized and more recently a new category of personnel has emerged whose training ranges from on-the-job to college level. Professional personnel usually work in institutional settings as public employees but in a few countries as the U.S., individual private practice is common with a growing pattern toward formation of small interdisciplinary groups.

The principles of the emerging community programs hold that people should be treated as close to their homes as possible, in contact with their families who also become involved in the treatment process, that care should be readily accessible and available and with continuity. Care should be provided by that worker whose skills are most appropriate for a patient's specific need at a given time and in the interest of economy by the least trained worker who can answer the need. Group methods have been found to be therapeutic as well as economic. To ensure coordination and integration of the efforts of multiple therapists, the psychiatric team must devise effective techniques of communication and decision making. There has also been a trend toward sectorization or catchmenting which places responsibility for mental health care upon a team assigned to that sector or geographic subdivision.

Mental health care has shown most change from institutional to community services in the highly developed countries since financing and personnel are more readily available. Services in developing countries range from a few mental hospitals or clinics to no services at all. Countries now seeking to develop or improve mental health services can profit by the experience of the developed countries. These include the development of locally based community services, ambulatory rather than residential, therapeutic rather than custodial, the development of new categories of personnel in the interest of patients' needs and economy, and building on existing resources. Ingenuity has been demonstrated as in Nigeria where patients and families live together in a village for the period of treatment; or elsewhere in the use of local practitioners as the curanderos and medicine men who serve as first line therapists and sources of referral. Many countries have trained nonprofessional workers as health aides or feldshers.

The experimental use of satellite communication in the delivery of health care in remote areas of Alaska is being evaluated by the Lister Hill Center of the National Library of Medicine. The Network is composed of a satellite in contact with 20 ground stations operated by health aides using VHF radio which permits voice communication at these stations and with a physician. The system if proven feasible is applicable for use in other remote areas worldwide. A satellite communications system is also being explored by a consortium of U.S. government organizations for use with the addition of video (TV) for health education.

Changes in society have also led to changes of perception about what constitutes mental health and illness. Emerging social and health related problems have mental health connotations. These include the problems of population control, aggression and violence, alcohol and drug abuse and dependence, risk taking behaviors as accidents and smoking.

Mental health in world perspective is reflected in the functions and mental health programs of the World Health Organization. WHO belongs to the United Nations related group of organizations but has its own membership and sources of financing. Established in 1948, WHO includes over 130 member states and associate members. Its program is financed by assessments and contributions from member states, the United Nations Development Fund (UNDF), voluntary contributions and through cooperative undertakings with other international and national bodies. The WHO acts as a directing and coordinating authority in international health work and among other functions, provides technical assistance on request from governments, fosters activities to promote health and well being, promotes teaching and training in health and related professions, promotes health research, proposes agreements and regulations in regard to international health matters, establishes and revises international nomenclature of disease, assists in developing an informed public opinion on matters of health and fosters mental health activities especially those affecting the harmony of human relations.

WHO headquarters are located in Geneva, Switzerland and six regional offices have been established worldwide. A mental health unit is included in both the headquarters and regional office organization. Emphasis is placed on the incorporation of mental health principles into public health and physical health programs, in training specialized mental health workers, in providing mental health orientation for physicians and other health and public health workers, and public health orientation for mental health workers.

The program of WHO is developed through a variety of mechanisms many of which are related to production and dissemination of information. Expert consultants and staff members carry out fact finding studies which result in state-of-the-art reports made available for distribution. Expert committees of consultants are convened to survey and analyze available knowledge and make program recommendations which are published.

The work of WHO in mental health is documented in the long list of meetings held and publications and reports made available during the past 25 years. They cover the fields of mental health services; psychogenetics; mental retardation; psychosocial influences and mental disorders; suicide; forensic psychiatry; psychiatry of childhood; adolescence and family, dependence on alcohol and other drugs, education and training, psychiatric epidemiology and research in psychiatric diagnosis, classification and statistics; biological aspects of psychiatry and neurology.

Lucy D. Ozarin, M.D., M.P.H.

282

Resources

Lists of publications and reports may be found in World Health Organization Publications Catalogue, 1947-1971, WHO Geneva, 1971 and in the publication Mental Health Programme of the WHO, 1949-1972, MH/72.4. Address: World Health Organization, Distribution and Sales Service, 1211 Geneva 27, Switzerland.

5. International Information Sources

> The incessant concentration of thought upon one
> subject, however interesting, teithers a man's mind
> in a narrow field.
>
> —*William Osler, M.D. (1849-1919)*

The world Health Organization issues a number of publications which contain mental health related information.

The Bulletin of the World Health Organization is a monthly periodical that contains original articles in English, French (with a summary in the other language), and Russian that report the results of laboratory, clinical or field investigations of international significance. Mental health examples: the classification of mental disorders, comparative pharmacology of psychotropic drugs, collection and utilization of statistical data from psychiatric facilities.

The WHO Chronicle provides a monthly record of the principal health activities undertaken in various countries with WHO assistance, and contains summaries or related accounts of other publications issued by the organization. It is published in separate editions in Chinese, English, French, Russian and Spanish. Mental health example: The WHO and Mental Health 1949-1961.

The International Digest of Health Legislation, published quarterly, is the only periodical in the world devoted solely to the publication of health legislation, reproduced either in full or in part, summarized, or mentioned by title. Comparative studies of legislation on special subjects are also published occasionally. Separate editions in English and French. Mental health examples: surveys of legislation concerning hospitalization and mental patients, treatment of drug addicts, abortion laws, rights of mentally disordered.

The World Health Statistics Annual, published in three volumes, contains statistical information collected by WHO on vital events and notifiable diseases in a large number of countries and territories. It also contains statistics concerning certain categories of medical and paramedical personnel in most countries.

The World Health Organization Technical Report Series contains the reports of WHO expert committees, subcommittees, joint committees with other specialized agencies, and other study and advisory groups. These reports contain the views and recommendations of international groups of experts on scientific questions or

284

public health problems. Mental health examples: community mental hospital, legislation affecting psychiatric treatment, social psychiatry, services for mentally retarded, epidemiology of mental disorders, psychosomatic disorders, neurophysiological and behavioral research in psychiatry, biochemistry of mental disorders, research on genetics in psychiatry, alcohol and alcoholism, drug dependence, psychogeriatrics. Separate editions in English, French, Russian and Spanish.

The United Nations Educational, Scientific and Cultural Organization (UNESCO) in conjunction with the Internattonal Council of Scientific Unions is exploring the establishment of a World Science Information System. Currently (1973), a UNISIST Newsletter is being issued irregularly four to six times a year to provide information on objectives, activities and plans for UNISIST. The Newsletter will also supply information concerning conferences, training courses and workshops in relation to UNISIST.

Organizations in Official Relations with WHO. Several non-governmental organizations are in official relations with WHO. The following are those most closely associated with mental health. (Each NGO was contacted and reviewed and approved its description. The information is current as of October 1973.)

International Association for Child Psychiatry and Allied Professions, The Secretary-General (Dr. A.J. Solnit), Yale Child Study Center, 333 Cedar Street, New Haven, Connecticut 06510, USA. Founded in 1948 in London to promote practice and scientific research in the field of child psychiatry by effective collaboration with allied professions, such as psychology, social welfare, pediatrics, public health. The IACP & AF holds a Congress every four years and Pre-Congress Editions are published. These can be obtained by writing to Dr. Reginald Lourie, 2125 Thirteenth Street, N.W., Washington, D.C. 20009, USA.

International Brain Research Organization, The Secretary-General (Dr. Derek Richter), IBRO Secretariat, 41 Queens Gate, London, SW 7 5HU, United Kingdom. Founded in 1960 to foster throughout the world fundamental scientific research contributing to an understanding of the brain, including both normal and abnormal aspects; and to develop, support, coordinate, promote and undertake scientific research and education in all fields concerning the brain.

International Council on Alcohol and Addictions, The Executive Director (Mr. Archer Tongue), Case Postale 140, 1001 Lausanne, Switzerland. Founded in 1907 in Stockholm to develop international cooperation in the field of prevention and treatment of alcoholism and drug dependence; to assemble documentation and disseminate information on all aspects of the problem; to organize international institutes and congresses. Maintains international reference library on alcohol and drug problems. Publishes reports, booklets, monographs, quarterly Newsletter.

International Council of Nurses Executive Director, 37, rue de Vermont, Geneva 20, Switzerland. Founded in 1899, a federation of 74 national nurses associations. Provides a medium through which national nurses associations may share their common interests, act as a spokesman for nursing internationally, help improve nursing education, legislation, social and economic welfare, and collect and disseminate information concerning all aspects of nursing. Conducts international conferences, regional conferences, and seminars. Provides counsel to national member associations and publishes books, journals, reports and monographs.

International Council on Social Welfare, The Secretary-General (Mrs. Kate Katzki), 345 East 46th Street, New York, New York 10017, USA. A permanent world organization for agencies, government representatives and individuals concerned with social welfare needs. Conducts biennial international conferences and regional conferences and seminars, national affiliates in 71 countries.

International Sociological Association, The Executive Secretary (Prof. Guido Martinotti), General Secretariat, Via Daverio 7, 20122 Milan, Italy. Founded in 1949 in Oslo under UNESCO auspices, its objectives are to secure and develop personal contacts between sociologists throughout the world; to encourage the international dissemination and exchange of information on significant developments in sociological knowledge; to facilitate and promote international sociological research.

International Union for Child Welfare, Monsieur le Secretaire General (M. Pierre Zumbach), 1 Rue de Varemble, 1211 Geneva 20, Switzerland. Founded in 1920 in Geneva to make known throughout the world the principles of the Declaration of the Rights of the Child (also known as Declaration of Geneva); relieve children in case of distress; raise the standards of child welfare; contribute to the physical and moral development of the child. Promotes and organizes relief for benefit of child victims of major international and national upheavals and disasters; encourages and assists establishment of better standards and practices of child welfare through international cooperation; exchanges and supplies information; promotes advisory committees and conferences of experts, and training seminars. Publishes International Child Welfare Review (quarterly).

Joint Commission on International Aspects of Mental Retardation, Madame la Secretaire generale de la Ligue international des Associations d' Aide aux Handicapes mentaux (Madame le Docteur Renee Portray), Commissionmixte sur les Aspects internationaux de l'Arrieration mentale, 12 Rue Forestiere, B-1050 Bruxelles, Belgique. Formed by the International League of Societies for the Mentally Handicapped (ILSMH) and the International Association for the Scientific Study of Mental Deficiency (IASSMD). ILSMH: Founded in 1960 to promote the interests of the mentally handicapped, regardless of nationality, race or religion; organize collaboration between national societies by the exchange of information and specialists, by comparative studies on legislation affecting the mentally retarded, by organizing international congresses and symposia, encourage the formation of national associations. Publishes Newsletter (periodical), proceedings of Congresses, conclusions or recommendations of symposia, and other brochures in several languages. IASSMD: Founded in 1964 to promote the scientific study of mental deficiency, through a multidisciplinary approach, throughout the world. Organizes international congresses and publishes the proceedings.

World Federation for Mental Health, The President (Professor M. Beaubrun), c/o Department of Psychiatry, University of West Indies, Kingston 7, Jamaica. Founded in 1948 in London to promote among all peoples and nations the highest possible standards on mental health, in its broadest biological, medical education, and social aspects; help and encourage member associations in the improvement of mental health services in their own countries; promote communications and understanding through meetings and international congresses. Acts as clearinghouse for information on mental health. Publishes World Federation for Mental Health Bulletin (quarterly), Annual Reports, Proceedings of Congresses and meetings, and other single publications.

World Psychiatric Association, The Secretary-General (Dr. D. Leigh), The Maudsley Hospital, Denmark Hill, London SE5 8AZ, United Kingdom. The World Psychiatric Association grew out of the Society for the Holding of World Congresses of Psychiatry. It was founded in 1961 and its aim was to form an Association of National Societies of Psychiatry. Now ten years later, the World Psychiatric Association has seventy-four Member Societies, representing over 60,000 psychiatrists in seventy-six countries. The purpose of the Association is to coordinate on a world-wide scale the activities of its Member Societies, and to advance inquiry into the aetiology, pathology and treatment of mental illness.

Ferninand R. Hassler, M.D., M.P.H.

INDEX